Bits of Ivory

Bits
of
Ivory

NARRATIVE TECHNIQUES IN JANE AUSTEN'S FICTION

LLOYD W. BROWN

Louisiana State University Press

BATON ROUGE

ISBN 0–8071–0224–5
Library of Congress Catalog Card Number 72–89112
Copyright © 1973 by Louisiana State University Press
All rights reserved
Manufactured in the United States of America
Printed by Heritage Printers, Inc., Charlotte, North Carolina
Designed by Dwight Agner

Some of the material in this volume was previously
published as "The Comic Conclusion in Jane Austen's Novels"
in *PMLA*, LXXXIV (October, 1969); and "Jane Austen and
the Sublime: A Note on *Mansfield Park*" in *Studies in Burke
and His Time*, X (Fall, 1968).

Contents

I   Introduction
3

II   Verbal Disputes
15

III   Imagery
52

IV   Symbolism
75

V   Conversation
108

VI   The True Art of Letter Writing
137

VII   Dialogue
168

VIII   Parody
199

Index
237

Bits of Ivory

CHAPTER I

Introduction

THE INCREASING TEMPO of Jane Austen criticism has produced numerous full-length critiques over the past decade, not to mention the reprinting of older works and a flood of scholarly articles. On the surface, then, another new book seems to require the time-honored convention of a prefatory apology. But the specialized approach to Jane Austen is a relatively new development among book-length studies of her novels. Most of the previous critics have preferred general surveys, and while they have contributed many invaluable insights, this kind of approach is, of necessity, unable to do full justice to any one of the manifold complexities of the novelist's art. Moreover, the inclusive coverage has occasionally suffered from attempts to subject the protean materials of Jane Austen's art to one exclusive thesis or another. On the other hand, the more recent emphasis has been on the detailed examination of specific areas, and this has had the total effect of enlarging, rather than circumscribing, our insights into the full scope of Jane Austen's techniques and moral philosophy.

B. C. Southam, for example, has produced a fairly illuminating study of the juvenilia in his *Jane Austen's Literary Manuscripts* (1964). And in *Jane Austen and Her Predecessors* (1966) Frank W. Bradbrook provides a ground-breaking but inconclusive outline of the novelist's literary and philosophical heritage. More recently, Joseph Wiesenfarth addresses his *Errand of Form* (1967) to specific interpretive problems that have accumulated over the years. Moreover, he attributes most of these controversies to "the conventional limits" of the exclusive theses which have operated "like a steam roller, leveling what was meant to be anything but flat."[1] On an even more specialized plane, Avrom Fleishman has tried to resolve the continuing *Mansfield Park* controversy by applying a "fusion of critical approaches" (historical, psychological, and mythic) to the novel. Significantly, he justifies this kind of analysis on the basis of a general need that has an obvious bearing on Jane Austen scholarship: "The pressing need—and the golden opportunity—in the criticism of fiction is for extended studies of individual works about which enough is known to permit an approximation to a total reading."[2] In fact both Wiesenfarth and Fleishman have provided useful examples of the manner in which detailed coverage of individual topics may broaden our understanding of Jane Austen's discrete art, especially when the critic combines selectivity in materials with eclectic analysis. For in so doing he transforms his chosen subject matter into a kind of prism that defines not just the area of immediate interest but also a wider range of related themes or structures. Hence when Southam's book and Q. D. Leavis's well-known *Scrutiny* papers explore Jane Austen's achievement in the juvenilia, their findings impinge directly upon the general evolution of moral insight and satiric techniques throughout the major novels. Similarly, the "critical pluralism" that Avrom Fleishman applies to the socioeconomic background of a single work succeeds in at least opening or reemphasizing hitherto neglected possibilities for students of Jane Austen's fiction as a whole. And the kind of "pressing need" that Fleishman attempts to fill with an exhaustive analysis of an individual novel is also pertinent to specific topics which are capable, when thoroughly scrutinized, of illuminating Jane Austen's multiple levels of meaning.

1. Joseph Wiesenfarth, *The Errand of Form: An Assay of Jane Austen's Art* (New York, 1967), vii–viii.

2. Avrom Fleishman, *A Reading of "Mansfield Park": An Essay in Critical Synthesis* (Minneapolis, 1967), 4.

Jane Austen's style is one such topic. And by "style" I mean not merely the details of verbal patterns and sentence structure—though these are included—but a wide range of narrative forms through which Jane Austen communicates her fictive insights. The rich texture of her prose has long been the subject of general encomiums, and such critics as Mary Lascelles and Andrew Wright have enumerated some patterns. But it is still necessary to examine her style as communication or meaning, to explore the actual *functions* of individual techniques within the narrative form and total significance of the novels. On this basis it will be possible to shed some needed light on problems that have arisen in, say, *Sense and Sensibility* and *Mansfield Park*. And generally, our insights into the broad complex of Jane Austen's art will benefit from a study of the thematic and structural roles of ironic diction, imagery, or dialogue. Conversely, we would be unduly restrictive if we overlooked the degree to which each mode of expression is imbedded in the themes of the Jane Austen novel, or if we minimized the integration of individual patterns with the total fabric of each work. In other words, we need to move beyond the familiar categorization of various components of the novelist's style. The full significance of each unit can only be grasped when it is analyzed in relation to the themes and form of each novel. In effect, the shortcomings of Jane Austen criticism exemplify a longstanding weakness in most studies of the novel—that is, the tendency to regard technique and content as inherently independent of each other. Mark Schorer, who voiced such a complaint several years ago, suggests an alternate approach which treats technique as the discovery of meaning, as "thematic definition." More recently, David Lodge and Karl Kroeber have described this issue in terms which have an immediate bearing on the traditional limitations and current needs of Jane Austen criticism. As Lodge remarks, "too often one feels that the listing of images has not been controlled by an active engagement with the text and the wider critical challenges it presents." Satisfactory studies of the novel should "define the meaning and value of literary artifacts by relating subjective response to objective text." Or, according to Kroeber, the "aesthetic function of vocabulary in fiction must be defined in terms of its relation to the design of the novel as a whole, how, in other words, even individual words in a novel are less units of language than they are units of form in fiction."[3]

Among full-length studies of Jane Austen this concept of novel criticism has been approximated, to date, by Howard S. Babb's *Jane Austen's Novels: The Fabric of Dialogue* (1962). Babb examines the emotional depth of her characters by analyzing patterns of dialogue in the novels. Moreover, he has linked certain forms of authorial commentary (conceptualization, generalizations, and figurative language) with her presentation of characters; and he has also examined the emotional and moral significance of some characters' styles. On the whole, Babb's study elucidates the psychological import and the contextual significance of his chosen patterns of style. But in addition to the immediate context, of characterization or situation, the various components of Jane Austen's narrative techniques are integrated with the total structure and prevailing thematic form of each novel. Consequently, although it is important to describe the distinctive features of, say, Henry Tilney's style in *Northanger Abbey* insofar as those features reveal his character, nonetheless, the kind of aesthetic function that Lodge and Kroeber quite justly attribute to language in fiction can only be fully elucidated when the critic demonstrates the connections between Henry Tilney's individual style and the fictive form of *Northanger Abbey* as a whole, or, to take another work, between Miss Bates's apparently chaotic effusions and the tightly organized form and vision of *Emma*.

Jane Austen herself has been quite explicit in stressing the broadly formal scope and thematic functions of narrative style. Contemporary criticism has long since dispelled the Jamesian

---

3. Mark Schorer, "Technique as Discovery," *Hudson Review*, I (1948), 68–69; David Lodge, *Language of Fiction: Essays in Criticism and Verbal Analysis of the English Novel* (London, 1966), 6, 65; Karl Kroeber, *Styles in Fictional Structure: The Art of Jane Austen, Charlotte Brontë, George Eliot* (Princeton, 1971), 18.

notion of Jane Austen as the "instinctive" novelist whose art is wholly "unconscious" and untutored.[4] But however thoroughly discredited this old viewpoint may have been, its corollary has died hard. We still hear that Jane Austen is little concerned with "critical premises," and that whatever comments she makes on the novel as a genre "seem as a rule deliberately trivial."[5] But her comments in the novels as well as in the correspondence demonstrate her imaginative self-consciousness as a writer. This is obviously true of the more famous remarks on comedy as her chosen field, or on the tone and structure of *Pride and Prejudice*. What is of paramount interest here, however, are her rather decided views on composition and style. "What should I do with your strong, manly, spirited Sketches, full of Variety and Glow?" she writes her brother Edward. "How could I possibly join them to the little bit (two Inches wide) of Ivory on which I work with so fine a Brush, as produces little effect after much labour?"[6] Comic self-depreciation aside, the painting metaphor is quite apt because it demonstrates the extent to which Jane Austen's intelligent self-awareness is centered on the mechanics of her art as a whole. And whenever she reflects on the process of composition she tends to envisage her style as communication and meaning.

Indeed, a specific pattern of style, or communication generally, is not simply that relationship with the reader which Wayne C. Booth, for one, has defined as the rhetoric of fiction, as "the art of communicating with readers—the rhetorical sources available to the writer of epic, novel, or short story as he tries, consciously or unconsciously, to impose his fictional world upon the reader."[7] It

4. Henry James, "The Lesson of Balzac," in *The Question of Our Speech* (Cambridge, Mass., 1905), 63.

5. Harrison R. Steeves, *Before Jane Austen: The Shaping of the English Novel in the Eighteenth Century* (New York, 1965), 367.

6. Jane Austen, *Jane Austen's Letters to her Sister Cassandra and Others*, ed. R. W. Chapman (2nd ed.; London, 1952), 468–69. Quotations from her fiction are based on *The Novels of Jane Austen*, ed. R. W. Chapman (3rd ed., 5 vols.; London, 1932–34), and on *Minor Works*, ed. R. W. Chapman (Rev. ed.; London, 1963).

7. Wayne C. Booth, *The Rhetoric of Fiction* (Chicago, 1961), preface.

is also an internal process within the novelist's fictive world. To return to Karl Kroeber, the matter of communication, or "point of view," is a complex issue in the art of fiction, and it embraces simultaneously "'point of action' (the character or characters whose activities are being narrated), 'the point of reaction' (the character or characters who are primarily affected by, and who often make evaluations of, the action), and so forth. The various 'points' sometimes coincide and sometimes move apart, and a truly meaningful description of point of view should define its part in these patterns of conjunction and separation."[8] Thus when such critics as Mary Lascelles and Howard Babb demonstrate the moral psychology of the Jane Austen character on the basis of style, this demonstration has implications that go beyond the immediate context of the character's self-revelations. In short, language and its usages, by both the characters and the novelist, are intrinsic to the definition of moral and intellectual values. Consequently each individual's point of view and style are integrated with, or counterbalanced by, others in order to form a pattern of viewpoints and styles which define the basic themes and shape the general structure of each novel. The importance which Jane Austen attaches to style as communication, or as "thematic definition," explains why the fastidious Marianne Dashwood is at such pains to link language with intelligence and feeling. She finds that the general deterioration in moral and intellectual standards has made a mockery of communication. Hence she has often been obliged to keep her feelings to herself "because I could find no language to describe them in but what was worn and hackneyed out of all sense and meaning" (*Sense and Sensibility*, p. 97). In spite of Marianne's usual dogmatic excesses, she appears in this instance to reflect Jane Austen's interest in the ethical and intellectual implications of linguistic usages, on personal and artistic levels.

Of course there is nothing essentially new in Jane Austen's concept of communication as a moral and psychological experience.

8. Kroeber, *Styles in Fictional Structure*, 43.

The styles of "flat" or "humour" characters in comedy are simply an exaggerated form of the artist's traditional treatment of personality as style. Similarly, it has been recognized that the comic techniques of Henry Fielding, to name but one of Jane Austen's predecessors, are partly based on the dichotomy between ideals like prudence, honor, and love, on the one hand, and on the other, rhetorical disguises or verbal equivalents that reflect social actuality rather than moral absolutes.[9] But what makes this issue of communication in Jane Austen's fiction so noteworthy is the degree to which her writing is pervaded by the conscious formulation of style and structure as parts of the moral or psychological process, and by her ability to integrate completely any one mode of communication, any single "bit of ivory," within the total framework of each novel. Hence, to analyze her patterns of style and narrative form is to investigate some of the most crucial aspects of her meaning.

This is particularly true of Jane Austen's ironic diction, the first of seven major categories that are my immediate concern. For the ambiguous connotations of terms like "friendship" or "sensibility" originate with the double-standards created by the flux of moral and social change. We must, then, examine the philosophical assumptions that are reflected in the ambiguous usages on which Jane Austen bases her structural and thematic tensions. While her ironic diction provides an approach to the neglected subject of the novelist's philosophical heritage, several insights into characterization and themes can be derived from two of the least explored patterns in her style—imagery and symbolism. This neglect has been unfortunate, for contrary to the usual allegations about Jane Austen's "unmetaphorical" style, her figurative patterns comprise some of her most significant networks of ironic implication and emotional suggestiveness. And although some of the symbolic structures have been fairly obvious, what has been less apparent is

9. See, for example, Eleanor Hutchens, " 'Prudence' in *Tom Jones*: A Study of Connotative Irony," *Philological Quarterly*, XXXIX (1960), 496–507. Compare Maurice Johnson, *Fielding's Art of Fiction: Eleven Essays on "Shamela," "Joseph Andrews," "Tom Jones," and "Amelia"* (Philadelphia, 1961), 115.

the degree to which Jane Austen repeatedly internalizes the symbolic process by integrating it within the consciousness of her characters. That is, the moral and intellectual standards of Catherine Morland or Fanny Price are demonstrated by the manner in which she uses symbols to define and express her ideas. This brings us to our next three categories, "conversation" or individual style, letter writing, and dialogue. For in these areas Jane Austen presents characters on the basis of their communication (or non-communication) with others. And this ensures that personal "conversation," even of "flat" or minor characters, is integral to the dramatic unfolding of theme and plot. Finally, Jane Austen's life-long interest in parody is consistent with her interpretation of style as moral experience. In this area she is indebted to the usual concept of parody as a rhetorical relationship with the reader. But, simultaneously, she uses these parodic patterns to explore the internal problems of communication between a Catherine Morland, or an Emma Woodhouse, and the real world.

Now obviously few, if any, of these seven topics have been completely ignored by critics in the continuous flood of Jane Austen studies. But without denying the contributions of this earlier scholarship, it still remains true that (1) most studies have not been as extensive in scope as the present one, and (2) although one specific technique or another may have been analyzed as the microcosm of Jane Austen's theme or structure, such a pioneering effort has not been followed up by broader analysis. Donald D. Stone, for example, investigates that discrimination between word usages which is often the basis of Jane Austen's themes, but which is discussed more fully here in relation to her eighteenth-century philosophical heritage as well.[10] On the other hand, some of the more notorious treatments of Jane Austen's irony, especially Marvin Mudrick's, have been soundly and repeatedly discredited on the basis of their assumption that Jane Austen's ironic structures

10. Donald D. Stone, "Sense and Semantics in Jane Austen," *Nineteenth Century Fiction*, XXV (June, 1970), 31–50.

are really a species of "subversive," defense mechanism rather than a form of committed moral judgment on her society.[11] My study also rejects this assumption, because, as I attempt to demonstrate, Jane Austen's ironic diction and insights are rooted in a strong commitment to traditional moral ideals which are represented in the philosophical conventions that shape such diction, and which are always realistically counterbalanced in her novels with behavioral traditions that subvert ideals. As for the vexed subject of her imagery, Mark Schorer's analysis of metaphoric structures in *Persuasion* has always been a fine example of the manner in which language structures may define the "body of meaning" in a work of fiction as a whole.[12] And it is one of the curious perversities of literary criticism that the possibilities which Schorer's study opened for a fuller exploration of imagery and meaning in Jane Austen's fiction have been ignored in favor of the old shibboleths about her "unmetaphorical" style. Moreover, Schorer's work is especially valuable to this study in that his handling of "dead" or "buried" metaphors and the manner in which he includes so-called unobtrusive metaphors, avoid the still prevalent but implicit assumption, in some circles, that a style without the highly *visible* nineteenth-century metaphorical flourish is, *ipso facto*, "unfigurative." While Jane Austen's figurative style has been widely ignored because it is presumed not to exist, a similar neglect of her symbolism is based on the assumption that the structures and implications of her symbolism are all obvious enough. Fortunately, Charles Murrah and Edgar Shannon have not been deterred by this assumption, and their remarks on symbols in *Mansfield Park* and *Emma*, respectively, anticipate several

11. Marvin Mudrick, *Jane Austen: Irony as Defense and Discovery* (Princeton, 1952). Compare D. W. Harding, "Regulated Hatred: An Aspect of the Work of Jane Austen," *Scrutiny*, VIII (1940), 346–62. Contrast Donald J. Greene, "Jane Austen and the Peerage," in *Jane Austen: A Collection of Critical Essays*, ed. Ian Watt (Englewood Cliffs, N.J., 1963), 164; and Alistair M. Duckworth, *The Improvement of the Estate: A Study of Jane Austen's Novel* (Baltimore, 1971), 7.

12. Mark Schorer, "Fiction and the Matrix of Analogy," *Kenyon Review*, XI (1949), 539–60.

of my own findings.[13] On the whole, however, they concentrate on symbolism as a rhetorical process in the author-reader relationship, while I am concerned primarily with the less obvious, but crucial, implications of each character's personal and *conscious* relationship with symbolic structures in the novels. As far as individual styles are concerned ("conversation," letter writing, and dialogue), I have attempted to supplement the earlier findings of critics like Babb by emphasizing the integration of each style with the total fictional framework of the respective novels, and by establishing links between Jane Austen's handling of individual styles, and eighteenth-century precedents in this area.[14] Finally, the subject of parody has attracted a host of Jane Austen critics, but in this regard my main purpose has not been to offer a complete, analytical survey of Jane Austen's parody. Instead I am attempting to explore only those areas of her narrative technique which her methods as a parodist have influenced, but which have not been fully dealt with in previous studies—especially (1) the manner in which her parodic insights combine diverse perspectives into the complexity of viewpoints which Karl Kroeber defines as the essence of narrative point of view, and (2) the contribution of parody to the shaping of one of Jane Austen's most important, but least appreciated, structures, the "comic conclusions" of her novels.

In addition to all this, the present study claims to be innovative because its major arguments are based on the premise that Jane Austen is an eighteenth-century novelist. Now this premise is not new, for it is obviously the main motive of studies like Bradbrook's *Jane Austen and her Predecessors* and Henrietta Ten Harmsel's

---

13. Charles Murrah, "The Background of *Mansfield Park*," in *From Jane Austen to Joseph Conrad: Essays Collected in Memory of James T. Hillhouse*, ed. Robert C. Rathburn and Martin Steinmann, Jr. (Minneapolis, 1958), 23–34. Compare Edgar F. Shannon, Jr., "*Emma*: Character and Construction," *PMLA*, LXXI (1956), 637–50.

14. See, for example, Frank W. Bradbrook, "Style and Judgment in Jane Austen's Novels," *Cambridge Journal*, IV (1951), 515–37; Ian Jack, "The Epistolary Element in Jane Austen," in *English Studies Today*, Second Series (Bern, Switzerland, 1961), 173–86.

Jane Austen: A Study in Fictional Conventions (1964), which offer parallels (sometimes inconclusively) between Jane Austen's
fiction and eighteenth-century traditions in fiction and moral
philosophy. But here I seek to establish specific links between individual Jane Austen techniques and her eighteenth-century predecessors as part of my general interest in style, or technique, as
meaning. Hence Jane Austen's moral philosophy can be illumi-
nated if we compare, say, her ironic diction, not only with similar
structures in eighteenth-century satire and novels, but also with
the moral philosophy which consciously explores attitudes towards
word usages in the eighteenth century: the multiple nuances of
"pride" and "prejudice" in her fiction are more accessible if we can
compare such ironic usages with the implications of the terms as
used by a predecessor like David Hume. Similarly, the thematic
significance and the structure of other narrative techniques acquire more meaning if they can be compared with explicit
eighteenth-century commentary on imagery, conversation, or letter
writing. In short, Jane Austen's style is not only integrated with
her meaning, but also with the philosophical traditions which she
inherits from the eighteenth century. This is appropriate enough:
Jane Austen's style and meaning suggest, on the whole, that the
very notion of tradition is central to her moral insights and her
narrative techniques as an ironist. I am not referring here to the
Janeites' narrowly self-serving notion of tradition, but to Jane
Austen's capacity to perceive social traditions in dual terms: on the
one hand, the traditions of behavioral reality, and, on the other,
the revered traditions of moral idealism. And from as early as the
youthful *Love and Freindship*, Jane Austen has consistently exposed this duality in our cherished notions of "traditional morality": her fiction appeals, directly and implicitly, to the ideal,
while at the same time she demonstrates how counter-idealistic
behavior has established itself as *the* prevailing tradition in moral
judgment.

Obviously this does not exhaust the full range of Jane Austen's
narrative techniques. The components of the so-called Johnsonian

sentence, for example, have long been familiar in surveys of her style. But it does seem that these seven categories are the major structures through which Jane Austen develops her themes and demonstrates her indebtedness to the eighteenth century. And what is equally important, these are the areas in which she is most explicit in defining both the moral and rhetorical functions of style. Indeed Jane Austen's sophisticated awareness of her own artistic forms is analogous to the manner in which the consciousness of her fictional individuals is integrated with prevailing modes of communication in each novel. And it is precisely because they bear so directly upon the novelist's self-awareness and major themes that these selected structures form an "ivory" tablet which affords us an unobstructed view of her "fine" brushwork.

CHAPTER II

Verbal Disputes

IN ONE OF his comments on the ambiguous usages of eighteenth-century English David Hume observes drily, "I do not find that in the English, or any other modern tongue, the boundaries are exactly fixed between virtues and talents, vices and defects, or that a precise definition can be given of the one as contradistinguished from the other."[1] These "verbal disputes," as Hume calls them, are also repugnant to John Hawkesworth, especially with regard to a word like "sentimental":

The word *sentimental* is, like continental, a barbarism that has but lately disgraced our language, and it is not always easy to conceive what is meant by it. We have before seen a *Sentimental* Novel, and a *Sentimental* Journey; and now we have Attempts at *Sentimental* Poetry. Our own old English word *sentiment* means only thought, notion, opinion; the French word *sentiment* seems to mean *intellectual sensation*, a sense of conduct and opinion, distinct from the sense of qualities that affect us by the taste, sight, smell, touch, and hearing: it has a place in the cant of our travelled gentry, many of whom shew, by their use of it, that they neither know the meaning of it in English nor French: to the fashionable use of the word *sentiment*, however, we

1. David Hume, *An Enquiry Concerning the Principles of Morals* (1751), Appendix iv, in *The Philosophical Works*, ed. Thomas Hill Green and Thomas Hodge Grose (4 vols.; Aalen, Germany, 1964), IV, 270. Future references to Hume's works are based on this edition.

owe the word *sentimental*, which, from polite conversation, has, at length, found its way to the press.[2]

Susie Tucker's recent study confirms the respective theses of Hume and Hawkesworth: the ambiguities of eighteenth-century word usage are derived from the linguistic evolution of the period.[3] And in turn, this development reflects the intermingling of old and new values, the double standards which Basil Willey nominates as the primary, ready-made materials of satiric irony in the eighteenth century. The old ideals of spiritual immortality and rational virtues had been diluted or abandoned in the frank materialism of an acquisitive age. "Yet—and this is the point—yet the old standards lived on in ghostly fashion, sitting crowned upon the graves of Christianity and Humanism; it was to them that one still instinctively turned, and by them one was still, in theory, supposed to be living. Anyone, then, who still held firmly to them, and yet had the gift of seeing things as they really were, could find all the materials of satire ready to hand: the ideal and the actual in sharp juxtaposition."[4] It is precisely this ironic awareness that informs the satirist's attack on double standards and hypocritical styles: Jonathan Swift's telling contrast between ideal Christianity and institutional religion in the "Argument Against Abolishing Christianity," Slip-slop's vociferous solicitude for her reputation and chastity in Fielding's *Joseph Andrews*, or young Blifil's materialistic perversion of prudence in *Tom Jones*. And in Richard Steele's *Tatler* No. 21, Jack Dimple is really the satiric personification of a popular cliché, the hackneyed debasement of wit to the level of formal gestures and empty phrases.

Obviously these dichotomies create problems of communication, and Jane Austen's sensitivity to such difficulties is demonstrated by Marianne's outburst against clichés in *Sense and Sensibility*.

2. John Hawkesworth, "Occasional Attempts at Poetry by a Man in Business," *Monthly Review*, Series 1, XLI (1769), 390.

3. Susie I. Tucker, *Protean Shape: A Study in Eighteenth-Century Vocabulary and Usage* (London, 1967).

4. Basil Willey, *The Eighteenth-Century Background: Studies on the Idea of Nature in the Thought of the Period.* (London, 1962), 101.

The kind of jargon that arouses Marianne's scorn is also illustrated in the same work by the "common cant of praise" which loosely equates the merely "lovely" with the "beautiful" (p. 46). And when Lady Middleton assumes that Elinor and Marianne are "satirical" because they are "fond of reading" she betrays her shallow, uninformed judgment by devaluing a definitive term: she has condemned the Dashwood sisters "perhaps without exactly knowing what it was to be satirical; but *that* did not signify. It was censure in common use, and easily given" (p. 246). In *Northanger Abbey* Henry Tilney also reflects Jane Austen's keen interest in ambiguous usages. Hence when Catherine Morland declares that she "cannot speak well enough to be unintelligible," his witty retort illuminates the chasm between traditional excellence and the modern shallowness of "fine" language: "Bravo!—an excellent satire on modern language" (p. 133). Taken together, then, these statements in *Northanger Abbey* and *Sense and Sensibility* emphasize Jane Austen's preoccupation with the kind of ambiguous usages that juxtapose multiple, even contrary, meanings. Moreover, both Henry Tilney's witticism and the exposé of Lady Middleton's shallowness demonstrate that, like her eighteenth-century predecessors, Jane Austen exploits these usages for the purposes of satiric analysis. And these verbal ambiguities are integral to the moral and intellectual distinctions that she draws in the novels. Consequently, we will find that the characterization, major themes, and total structure of several works are dominated by multiple usages, by complex and divergent definitions that reflect the novelist's insight into the moral contradictions of society and the individual.

This strategy appears from as early as the juvenilia. *Jack & Alice*, for example, is actually a dramatic study in hypocrisy. The major characters are gradually unmasked, and their personalities are progressively disengaged from the idealistic terminology with which they are initially disguised. Lady Williams is described as one in whom "every virtue met" but the statement is qualified on a purely materialistic basis: "She was a widow with a handsome

Jointure & the remains of a very handsome face." And this ironic exegesis is followed by an equally suggestive series of false antitheses: "Tho' Benevolent & Candid, she was Generous & sincere; Tho' Pious & Good, she was Religious & amiable, & Tho' Elegant & Agreable, she was Polished & Entertaining" (*Minor Works*, p. 13). The ironic ambiguity of a word like "amiable" becomes even clearer when we compare Jane Austen's satiric context with the eighteenth-century meanings listed in Samuel Johnson's *Dictionary*: (1) "pleasing" or "lovely" and (2) "pretending" or "shewing" love. This kind of connotative irony shifts to another traditional ideal when the Johnsons are introduced as "a family of Love," for it turns out that their "many good Qualities" are somewhat diluted by their addiction to "the Bottle & the Dice" (*Minor Works*, p. 13). Here, too, Jane Austen's satiric phrasing is reinforced by additional ambiguities that originate from beyond her immediate context. Thus "family of love" is a well-tried evangelical cliché which ironists like Tobias Smollett sometimes turned against the alleged sensuality of Puritans and Nonconformists. In *Humphry Clinker* (1771) this results in the occasional *double-entendre*, particularly when Winifred Jenkins, a brand-new but suspect evangelical, refers to her fellow-converts as a "family of love."[5]

The double meanings of such definitive terms are central to the self-contradictions and hypocrisies that Jane Austen explores in Lady Williams and the Johnsons. The ambiguous usages of specific verbal patterns are beginning to serve as the basis of the young novelist's themes and structure. This process is more fully developed in *Love and Freindship* where the major thematic ironies are related to the conflicting connotations of the ubiquitous term "sensibility." On one level it denotes the extravagant sentimentality that exposed the popular novel to Jane Austen's ridicule. But on a more satiric level, it represents the ironist's complex insights into everyday contradictions. Jane Austen is aware of "sensi-

---

5. Tobias Smollett, *Expedition of Humphry Clinker*, ed. Lewis M. Knapp, Oxford English Novels (London, 1966), 338.

bility" as an emotional and moral ideal, and simultaneously she perceives the cold-hearted selfishness often cloaked under the term. It is therefore one of the major ironies of the work that Laura should confide to us that she is an altered person whose own misfortunes still affect her, but who cannot now "feel for those of an other" (*Minor Works*, p. 78). For the truth is that neither Laura nor the other professed disciples of sensibility have ever "felt" for anyone apart from themselves. Their crude egotism is the antithesis of the selflessness that Hume attributes to "love" or "friendship," both of which he defines as a "complacency in another, on account of his accomplishments or service."[6] In matters of sensibility Laura's terms of reference are based on selfish ignorance. Hence a "good-tempered, civil and obliging" acquaintance is contemptuously dismissed because, as a country girl, she "could not be suposed to possess either exalted Ideas, Delicate Feelings or refined Sensibilities" (p. 100). Or our heroine's standards may be little more than thinly disguised erotica. Sir Edward is condemned for gross insensibility because he snores (p. 106), and despite his acknowledged erudition and sense, Graham (Miss Macdonald's fiancé) is despised because his hair is not auburn (p. 93).

In keeping with this ironic strategy, *Love and Freindship* actually reverses the thematic development of the popular sentimental novel. Henry Mackenzie's *Man of Feeling*, for example, pits the doctrine of sensibility (embodied by Harley) against an unfeeling and materialistic society. But in *Love and Freindship* a specious form of sensibility embodies, rather than opposes, selfishness, materialism, and stupidity; and it is even contrasted with the implied, and sometimes explicit, dictates of prudence and judgment. Jane Austen's strategy really exploits what John Noorthouck regards as the literary abuse of the term "sensibility." For the eighteenth-century reviewer deplores "the present latitude allowed to the word *sensibility*; under which licentious livers and writers now shelter propensities that used to receive harsher names; but, in the general relaxation of morals and manners, we

6. Hume, *Dissertation on the Passions*, Sect. II, in *The Philosophical Works*, IV.

reconcile ourselves to many indulgences, by softening the language that expresses them!"[7] And this ironic subversion of reason and morality in *Love and Freindship* is complemented by the manner in which the wholesome values of Laura's in-laws are distorted by the unhealthy perspective of the heroine's "sensibility." Sir Edward is frequently accused of materialism and autocracy, yet his choice of Lady Dorothea as his son's fiancée is well in keeping with Edward's erstwhile preferences. Augusta is charged with being cold, but it turns out that she is guilty only of the prudent suggestion that Laura and Edward take steps to support themselves.[8] The traditional order of emotional and moral responses has been inverted. When Laura's parents die, their death is a minor irrelevance, and their meager bequests are a grievous calamity: "I must inform you of a trifling circumstance concerning them which I have as yet never mentioned. The death of my Parents a few weeks after my Departure, is the circumstance I allude to. By their decease I became the lawfull Inheritress of their House and Fortune. But alas! the House had never been their own and their Fortune had only been an Annuity on their own Lives. Such is the Depravity of the World!" (pp. 89–90). And when Sophia repays the hospitable Macdonalds by stealing their money Laura's sensibility reverses the usual roles of accuser and criminal. Sophia is "justly-offended" by the impertinent allegations of the "vile" and "base" Macdonald. He is the "undaunted Culprit" who is required to "exculpate himself from the crime he was charged with" (p. 96).[9] Similarly, Augustus is commended for having "gracefully purloined" money from his "unworthy father's Escritoire";

---

7. John Noorthouck, *"Julius," Monthly Review*, Ser. 2, II (1790), 463.

8. Marvin Mudrick treats Laura as Jane Austen's mouthpiece for an attack on narrow concepts of propriety and order in his *Jane Austen: Irony as Defense and Discovery* (Princeton, 1952), 15–18. But this ignores the ironic technique (to be more fully developed in *Emma*) of presenting situation and character through the defective judgment of the heroine.

9. Compare a similar reversal of roles in Fielding's *Joseph Andrews*. After attacking Parson Adams and Fanny, a robber poses before his captors as the victim. *Joseph Andrews*, ed. Martin C. Battestin, The Wesleyan Edition of the Works of Henry Fielding (Oxford, 1967), 141–42.

and his "disinterested Behaviour" in defrauding creditors is contrasted with the "perfidious Treachery" and "unparalelled Barbarity" of the latter's claims (p. 88).

These episodes demonstrate not only the perverted sensibility of Laura and her friends, but also the hypocrisy and callousness inherent in their concepts of love and friendship. The title of the work must therefore be related to the basic ironies that Jane Austen derives from ambiguous usages: "love" and "friendship," like "sensibility," have become affected perversions with which Laura attempts to mask selfish indifference and treacherous ingratitude. Conversely, the communication of real love and friendship, by the Macdonalds and by Edward's family, is thwarted throughout by Laura's mouthing of moral terms. Hence the ambiguities of evaluative language in general, and the title in particular, are integral to the individual contradictions and external conflicts of *Love and Freindship*. Indeed, the caption of this early work sets a trend in Jane Austen's fiction in that all her conceptual titles incorporate evaluative and moral terms which summarize the ironic contrasts in the novelist's themes.

When Jane Austen returns to this kind of title in *Sense and Sensibility* she continues the main burden of *Love and Freindship* by interweaving the satire against debased sentimental literature with the exposé of sham sensibility in real life. But here Jane Austen has multiplied the ironic ambiguities of the earlier work. Corrupted sensibility is opposed to sterile rationalism and narrow propriety, as well as to the norms of good sense and feeling that Laura maligns in *Love and Freindship*. It is therefore inadequate to view the title of this novel as the simple statement of two opposite and irreconcilable values. Traditional generalizations that sum up the themes of *Sense and Sensibility* as rigid "antitheses" or "concise distinctions" remain half-truths at best, for they miss the complex interrelationship of themes and character in the work.[10] In its positive and more favorable sense the phrase "sense

10. "The crude antitheses of the original structure [Elinor and Marianne] were never quite overcome." A. Walton Litz, *Jane Austen: A Study of Her Artistic*

and sensibility" embodies Jane Austen's concept of two distinct, but compatible, qualities. Elinor Dashwood therefore represents "sense" on the ideal levels of sound reason and controlling judgment; and as her character demonstrates, these faculties are not necessarily inconsistent with sensibility. The spiritual and emotional values of her sensibility operate, in conjunction with sense, as the basis of social sympathy and individual feeling.[11]

Although Elinor's good sense has generally been acknowledged, her strong sensibility has been neglected or minimized by the assumption that she is simply Marianne's antithesis. But Jane Austen actually emphasizes her heroine's emotional capacities very early in the work: Elinor combines "strength of understanding" and coolness of judgment with "an excellent heart," an "affectionate disposition," and "strong feelings" (p. 8). When aroused, her emotions are unmistakably strong, as is evident in the "tears of joy" that greet the news of Edward Ferrars' release from his engagement to Lucy Steele (p. 360). She is no less demonstrative in her compassion for Marianne when the latter is jilted by Willoughby: she "gave way to a burst of tears, which at first was scarcely less violent than Marianne's" (p. 182). Indeed there are occasions when this kind of parallel with Marianne or Mrs. Dashwood comically emphasizes that Elinor is not entirely proof against the excesses of strong feeling or an excited imagination. Thus she is sceptical when Mrs. Dashwood excuses Willoughby's neglect of Marianne by invoking the sentimental cliché of parental

---

Development (New York, 1965), 73. Compare Alan D. McKillop, "The Context of *Sense and Sensibility*," *Rice Institute Pamphlet*, XLIV (1957–58), 68–69; Andrew H. Wright, *Jane Austen's Novels: A Study in Structure* (2nd ed.; London, 1962), 92–93; Howard S. Babb, *Jane Austen's Novels: The Fabric of Dialogue* (Columbus, Ohio, 1962), 51.

11. More recent critics are beginning to recognize the conjunctive implications of Jane Austen's title. According to Joseph Wiesenfarth, for example, the novel is about "the reality of sense and sensibility being integral to every life that is meaningfully human, and it is about the necessity of sense and sensibility blending harmoniously to make life meaningful." Joseph Wiesenfarth, *The Errand of Form: An Assay of Jane Austen's Art* (New York, 1967), 53. Compare Donald D. Stone, "Sense and Semantics in Jane Austen," *Nineteenth Century Fiction*, XXV (June, 1970), 39–40.

autocracy: Willoughby's absence has been in deference to his family's dislike of Marianne. But when Elinor's own emotional interests are involved she does not scruple to comfort herself with the hackneyed optimism that serves Mrs. Dashwood's unperceptive sentimentality; she is "very well disposed" to account for Edward Ferrars' extreme reserve on the basis of "all the candid and generous allowances" that her mother seeks to establish on Willoughby's account: "The old, well established grievance of duty against will, parent against child, was the cause of all" (p. 102). Subsequently, when she is aroused by Willoughby's purported letter of rejection to Marianne, she gives vent to her outrage in the exaggerated style and sentiments of the emotional Marianne: the letter "proclaimed its writer to be deep in hardened villany" and revealed the "depravity" of the mind that dictated it (p. 184).

What Elinor's personality demonstrates, then, is Jane Austen's harmonious integration of sense and sensibility on the ideal level of moral and emotional stability, the level that is eventually attained by Marianne. But at the same time, the title of the novel does denote an antithesis, the conflict between "sense" and "sensibility" in their perverted forms; for when the terms are simply masks for calculating selfishness and rank emotionalism, respectively, they do describe irreconcilable extremes rather than the ideal synthesis represented by Elinor's character. Hence while the initial excesses of Marianne's sensibility are distinguished from Elinor's equanimity, their real opposite is the "sense" projected by John Dashwood. His materialistic judgment is based on the narrow prudence that Elinor detects in Lucy Steele's obsequious flatteries to Lady Middleton (p. 120). His "propriety" is simply a "cold-hearted, and rather selfish" kind of sense that dissociates him from the generally "strong feelings" of the Dashwoods and links him with the "cold insipidity" of Lady Middleton's shallow decorum (pp. 5, 34). Characteristically, he attempts to disguise his real insensitivity with the transparent affectation of feeling. Hence his specious "civility" to Mrs. Jennings and Colonel Brandon is easily exposed for what it is: "His manners to *them*, though calm, were perfectly kind; to Mrs. Jennings most attentively civil; and on Colonel Brandon's coming in soon after himself, he eyed him with a curiosity which seemed to say, that he only wanted to know him to be rich, to be equally civil to *him*" (p. 223). His personal style is also revealing, for its ambiguous structures are based on his inveterate habit of devaluing definitive and idealistic terms to purely economic levels. Accordingly, he extols Mrs. Ferrars' "noble spirit" and "liberality" largely because she has been assisting him with his wife's expenses (p. 224). And he finds that Mrs. Jennings is a "most valuable" woman—her house, income, and standard of living all declare it (p. 226). On the basis of his computations, Marianne was once "handsome" enough to attract a wealthy husband, but unhappiness and illness have reduced the value of her "style of beauty" on his matrimonial stock exchange: "I question whether Marianne *now*, will marry a man worth more than five or six hundred a-year, at the utmost" (p. 227). And in his usual evaluation of family ties, he estimates that Edward Ferrars' alleged disregard of "duty" and "affection" would cost that erring youth "a good thousand a-year" (p. 266).

But even the direct opposition of John Dashwood's sense to Marianne's sensibility is more ironic and less simplistic than it first seems. For Jane Austen emphasizes the anti-social egotism and the subversive tendencies common to both sides. Thus the perversion of both sense and sensibility in John Dashwood's personality closely parallels the effects of the extreme emotionalism that Marianne shares with her mother. Note, for example, her dogmatic denial of Colonel Brandon's "genius," "taste," and "spirit" on the grounds that "his understanding has no brilliancy, his feelings no ardour, and his voice no expression" (p. 51). Her corruption of ideal qualities here is derived from the same kind of "romantic delicacy" that leads Mrs. Dashwood to disregard "common sense, common care, common prudence" (p. 85). And while her emotional excesses subvert ideal standards of feeling and taste in Colonel Brandon's case, they can also equal John Dashwood's "prudent" insinuations in undermining sense and

judgment. Her earlier, opinionated style, for example, is charac-
terized by emphatic assertions of the nonsensical. On one occasion
she pontificates on compatibility: "I could not be happy with a
man whose taste did not in every point coincide with my own. He
must enter into all my feelings, the same books, the same music
must charm us both" (p. 17). On the subject of "old" lovers, she
declares: "A woman of seven and twenty . . . can never hope to
feel or inspire affection again; . . . with me a flannel waistcoat is
invariably connected with aches, cramps, rheumatisms, and every
species of ailment that can afflict the old and the feeble" (p. 38).
Not surprisingly, she has decided views on the subject of opinions:
"At my time of life [seventeen] opinions are tolerably fixed"
(p. 93).

But the series of ambiguities involving Marianne does not end
with Elinor and John Dashwood. The relationship with Mrs.
Jennings is also pertinent to Jane Austen's elaboration on the
ironic complexities of "sensibility." Mrs. Jennings' inelegant style
and crude joviality are offensive to Marianne's overrefined tastes;
but this very vulgarity underlines the generosity that finds expression in familiar phrases of sincere endearment—"my dear,"
"Law, my dear," and "Lord bless me." Her personality can be
summed up in the phrases that describe the comparable temperament of her daughter, Charlotte Palmer: the "openness and
heartiness" of Mrs. Palmer's manner "more than atoned for that
want of recollection and elegance, which made her often deficient
in the forms of politeness; her kindness . . . was engaging; her
folly, though evident, was not disgusting, because it was not conceited" (p. 304). Like Marianne, Mrs. Jennings (and Mrs. Palmer) disregards the niceties of propriety in favor of unrestrained
self-expression; but in the absence of Marianne's excessive sensibility and egotism, her personality incorporates an honest self-
awareness that Marianne lacks. This is particularly true of the
manner in which the hearty widow couches her invitation to the
Dashwood sisters: "I am sure I shall be monstrous glad of Miss
Marianne's company, whether Miss Dashwood will go or not, only

the more the merrier say I, and I thought it would be more comfortable for them to be together; because if they got tired of me,
they might talk to one another, and laugh at my odd ways behind
my back" (p. 154).

The contemptuous indifference of Marianne and Mrs. Jennings
to social propriety emphasizes not only the fundamental links
between them, but also Jane Austen's ironic treatment of propriety
itself as a manifestation of varying degrees of sense. Social decorum, even the kind based on Elinor's balanced judgment, demands a degree of insincerity and compromise that is repugnant
to Marianne:

"But I thought it was right, Elinor," said Marianne, "to be guided
wholly by the opinion of other people. I thought our judgments were
given us merely to be subservient to those of our neighbours. This has
always been your doctrine, I am sure."
"No, Marianne, never. My doctrine has never aimed at the subjection of the understanding. All I have ever attempted to influence has
been the behaviour. You must not confound my meaning. I am guilty,
I confess, of having often wished you to treat our acquaintance in general with greater attention; but when have I advised you to adopt their
sentiments or conform to their judgment in serious matters?"
"You have not been able then to bring your sister over to your plan
of general civility," said Edward to Elinor. (pp. 93–94)

Elinor's "general civility" involves a delicate balance between
personal feeling and the rational restraint demanded by public
norms of polite pretense. When the Steeles discuss Lady Middleton's alleged merits, Marianne refuses to contribute to the ensuing
panegyrics, and "upon Elinor therefore the whole task of telling
lies when politeness required it, always fell." Hence the well-
behaved Miss Dashwood is obliged to speak of Lady Middleton
"with more warmth than she felt" (p. 122).[12] In effect, rational

---

12. Marvin Mudrick notes the ambiguity of Elinor's social decorum, but argues
that the novelist's irony is not directed at Elinor, that at this point the views of
author and reader begin to diverge. *Jane Austen: Irony as Defense and Discovery*,
69–70. But, contrary to Mudrick's argument, Elinor's self-awareness on the subject implies that Jane Austen is treating propriety as ironically as she does sensibility.

norms of polite decorum generate a double-edged irony throughout the novel. On the one hand, Marianne's laudable system of
sincerity has had "the unfortunate tendency of setting propriety
at nought" (p. 56). But on the other hand, social decorum invariably encroaches on individual sensibilities like Elinor's, or in
the case of Lady Middleton's "insipid propriety," may actually be
a substitute for real feeling. Hence the scene of Elinor's polite lies
and Marianne's rude sincerity dramatizes the satiric tensions that
have evolved from the ambiguities of sense and sensibility. The
need for social order is at odds with individual demands for the
free expression of real feeling, but the disruptive tendencies of unrestrained sensibility are counterbalanced by the inherent hypocrisies of decorum. Furthermore, these tensions are symptomatic
of the multiple conflicts which dominate the novel's thematic
structure, and which are reflected in the ambiguous title: "sense"
and "sensibility" are both used on ideal and pejorative levels, from
each of which Jane Austen derives an ironic multiplicity of parallel and contrasting meanings.

The repeated emphasis on taste in the novel is an important clue
to Jane Austen's eighteenth-century antecedents for the complex
treatment of sense and sensibility. Marianne, especially, is always
at the center of discussions on taste, and it soon becomes clear that
her aesthetic standards conform with her moral and emotional
values. On the basis of her excessive sensibility Marianne equates
taste with an irrational ecstasy, a rapturous delight (p. 19). Hence
she accuses Edward of having "no taste for drawing." Elinor's
defense of Edward's "innate propriety" and simplicity of taste
points to the rational kind of judgment that Marianne discounts
(p. 19). At the same time, Edward's frank indifference to the cult
of the picturesque (much to Marianne's incredulity) underscores
both his restraint and Marianne's turbulence in their respective
approaches to aesthetic experience: "I like a fine prospect, but not
on picturesque principles. I do not like crooked, twisted, blasted
trees. I admire them much more if they are tall, straight and
flourishing. I do not like ruined, tattered cottages. I am not fond

of nettles, or thistles, or heath blossoms. I have more pleasure in a snug farm-house than a watch-tower—and a troop of tidy, happy villagers please me better than the finest banditti in the world" (p. 98). Moreover, when the unprincipled Willoughby charms Marianne into a fit of infatuation by alleging that they share aesthetic interests, Jane Austen seems to be emphasizing the links between suspect taste and ethical values. Similarly, Marianne's piano playing at the Middleton's home excites a variety of responses that is indicative of the disparate intellects in her audience —Sir John's boisterous but good-natured inattentiveness, the insipid hypocrisy of his wife's cold "judgment," Colonel Brandon's intelligent appreciation, and the performer's own suspect standards:

> Marianne's performance was highly applauded. Sir John was loud in his admiration at the end of every song, and as loud in his conversation with the others while every song lasted. Lady Middleton frequently called him to order, wondered how any one's attention could be diverted from music for a moment, and asked Marianne to sing a particular song which Marianne had just finished. Colonel Brandon alone, of all the party, heard her without being in raptures. He paid her only the compliment of attention; and she felt a respect for him on the occasion, which the others had reasonably forfeited by their shameless want of taste. His pleasure in music, though it amounted not to that extatic delight which alone could sympathize with her own, was estimable when contrasted against the horrible insensibility of the others. (p. 35)

The moral and intellectual strengths or weaknesses of each are measured on the basis of their musical taste. The generous and well-bred Colonel Brandon presents an ideal balance of sense and sensibility. At one extreme, Sir John's coarse narrowness and Lady Middleton's specious sense represent "want of taste." And at the other extreme, Marianne's unrestrained sensibility produces, not an absence of taste, but a defective one. Altogether the distinction between the three groups is very similar to the arguments with which Edmund Burke defines taste in his *Philosophical Enquiry* (1757):

Whilst we consider Taste, merely according to its nature and species, we shall find its principles entirely uniform; but the degree in which these principles prevail in the several individuals of mankind, is altogether as different as the principles themselves are similar. For sensibility and judgment, which are the qualities that compose what we commonly call a *Taste*, vary exceedingly in various people. From a defect in the former of these qualities, arises a want of Taste; a weakness in the latter, constitutes a wrong or a bad one. There are some men formed with feelings so blunt, with tempers so cold and phlegmatic, that they can hardly be said to be awake during the whole course of their lives. Upon such persons, the most striking objects make but a faint and obscure impression. There are others so continually in the agitation of gross and merely sensual pleasures, or so occupied in the low drudgery of avarice, or so heated in the chace of honours and distinction, that their minds, which had been used continually to the storms of these violent and tempestuous passions, can hardly be put in motion by the delicate and refined play of the imagination. These men, though from a different cause, become as stupid and insensible as the former; but whenever either of these happen to be struck with any natural elegance or greatness, or with these qualities in any work of art, they are moved upon the same principle.[13]

The want of taste in both these categories (the phlegmatic and the gross) is evident in Lady Middleton and Sir John respectively. Moreover Marianne's defect falls within Burke's definition of "a wrong taste" as "a defect of judgment":

And this may arise from a natural weakness of understanding (in whatever the strength of that faculty may consist) or, which is much more commonly the case, it may arise from a want of proper and well-directed exercise, which alone can make it strong and ready. Besides that ignorance, inattention, prejudice, rashness, levity, obstinacy, in short, all those passions, and all those vices which pervert the judgment in other matters, prejudice it no less in this its more refined and elegant province. These causes produce different opinions upon every thing which is an object of the understanding, without inducing us to suppose, that there are no settled principles of reason.[14]

13. Edmund Burke, *A Philosophical Enquiry into the Origin of our Ideas of the Sublime and Beautiful*, ed. J. T. Boulton (London, 1958), 23–24. See Lloyd W. Brown, "Jane Austen and the Sublime: A Note on *Mansfield Park*," *Studies in Burke and His Time*, X (1968), 1041–43.
14. Burke, *Philosophical Enquiry*, 24.

Finally, we may compare Colonel Brandon's appreciative response with Burke's description of a healthy taste, the union of sound judgment and balanced sensibility: "A rectitude of judgment in the arts which may be called good Taste, does in a great measure depend upon sensibility; because if the mind has no bent to the pleasures of the imagination, it will never apply itself sufficiently to works of that species to acquire a competent knowledge in them." Moreover, this ideal is favorably, but half-regretfully, contrasted with the strength and weakness of excessive sensibility—which is rather similar to the manner in which Marianne places her emotional criteria above Brandon's welcome but nonrapturous attention. According to Burke, "though a degree of sensibility is requisite to form a good judgment, yet a good judgment does not necessarily arise from a quick sensibility of pleasure. . . . In the morning of our days, when the senses are unworn and tender, when the whole man is awake in every part, and the gloss of novelty fresh upon all the objects that surround us, how lively at that time are our sensations, but how false and inaccurate the judgments we form of things?"[15] Burke's thesis could be a blueprint for the subtle parallels and contrasts between Marianne's youthful exuberance and Brandon's mature stability. It is quite clear, too, that this is precisely the kind of argument that justifies the unchallenged moral superiority of Mrs. Jennings' (and Marianne's) freewheeling sensibility in the world of John Dashwood and Lady Middleton—and this in spite of the fact that Jane Austen's satire is simultaneously directed against the disruptive excesses of "lively" sensations.

Generally, then, Burke treats sense and sensibility within the same framework of synthesis and antithesis that provides Jane Austen with her ironic structure of multiple meanings. Moreover, Burke's comments on the passions and on cold-hearted phlegmatism demonstrate that he also anticipates Jane Austen in defining morality as taste. So does Shaftesbury. According to the *Characteristics* (1711), "the taste of beauty and the relish of what is

15. *Ibid.*, 24–25.

decent, just, and amiable perfects the character of the gentleman and the philosopher. And the study of such a taste or relish will, as we suppose, be ever the great employment and concern of him who covets as well to be wise and good as agreeable and polite." On the other hand, "if the fancy be florid and the appetite high towards the subaltern beauties and lower order of worldly symmetries and proportions, the conduct will infallibly turn this latter way." And even religious conscience "will make but a slight figure where this taste is set amiss." [16]

In *Pride and Prejudice* we again encounter an ambiguous title with ironic connotations which are rooted in the philosophical assumptions of the novelist's background, and which encompass the psychological and moral tensions of the novel. Here, too, is a very good example of the manner in which ambiguous usages are integrated with the communicative process, for the human relationships unfolded in the work are dominated by problems of communication. Individual insights are repeatedly distorted by the obtrusion of self, by the failure to see people and things as they really are. When this happens neither intimacy nor distance guarantees objectivity and clarity. Elizabeth Bennet fails to foresee the results of Charlotte Lucas' "prudent" views of marriage, just as easily as she is blinded to Darcy's real qualities. Moreover, this perceptual problem is further complicated by the deceptiveness of personality itself: the individual is not always an open book, even for such remarkably unbiased judgments as Jane Bennet's. There is a great difference between the transparent pretensions of Mr. Collins and the deceptive charms of Wickham. Bingley is not the "deep, intricate character" that Elizabeth likes to study, and her ready ability to understand him disconcerts Bingley. But, ironically, this easy penetration of Bingley's character contributes to her confidence in the kind of first impressions that are wholly inadequate in Darcy's case. Indeed Darcy's complex personality demonstrates the attitudinal as well as perceptual roles of pride

16. Anthony, Earl of Shaftesbury, *Characteristics of Men, Manners, Opinions, Times, etc.*, ed. John M. Robertson (Gloucester, Mass., 1963), II, 256, 265.

and prejudice: the distortions of Elizabeth's faulty insights are compounded by Darcy's failings and by his forbidding mask which obscures his more admirable qualities.

All these questions of communication and judgment are reflected in the multiple meanings of the title, for the ambiguities of "pride and prejudice" connote conflicting and parallel meanings that are as varied as the complexities of *Sense and Sensibility*. Both Charlotte Lucas and Mary Bennet, each in her limited way, point to the double significance of the word "pride." Charlotte interprets it in exclusively materialistic terms, claiming that Darcy's family and fortune give him a "*right* to be proud" (p. 20). It is the pedantic Mary who distinguishes between the positive and defective connotations of pride: "Vanity and pride are different things, though the words are often used synonimously. A person may be proud without being vain. Pride relates more to our opinion of ourselves, vanity to what we would have others think of us" (p. 20). Darcy himself subsequently supports Mary's thesis by defining vanity as a weakness, and pride as a quality that can be praiseworthy when allied with "a real superiority of mind" (p. 57). But if, as Mary pontificates, we all cherish feelings of self-regard, how are the ideal and pejorative connotations of pride to be distinguished? The answer seems to lie in the moral values ignored by the pragmatic Charlotte but expressed by Darcy's emphasis on the intellect as a moderating and sensitive agency.

Some clues to Jane Austen's theme are provided by David Hume's philosophical essays. In the *Enquiry Concerning the Principles of Morals* (1751) he compares the ambiguous usages of the English word "pride" with the French "amour propre." The latter means either pride or self-love, and vanity. At the same time "pride" is "commonly taken in a bad sense; but this sentiment seems indifferent, and may be either good or bad, according as it is well or ill founded, and according to the other circumstances which accompany it." In his *Dissertation on the Passions* (1757) he elaborates on some of these accompanying circumstances: pride is "a certain satisfaction in ourselves, on account of some accomplishment or possession, which we enjoy" (Section II). In the *Enquiry Concerning the Principles of Morals* he also states that vanity "seems to consist chiefly in such an intemperate display of our advantages, honours, and accomplishments . . . as is offensive to others, and encroaches too far on *their* secret vanity and ambition."[17] Or, to borrow Elizabeth's comment on Darcy's conduct, "I could easily forgive *his* pride, if he had not mortified *mine*" (*Pride and Prejudice*, p. 20).

Hume's essays are supported here by Smollett's *Humphry Clinker*. Describing the silly Mrs. Baynard, Matthew Bramble distinguishes her destructive vanity from a higher species of self-regard: "She had not taste enough to relish any rational enjoyment; but her ruling passion was vanity, not that species which arises from self-conceit of superior accomplishments, but that which is a bastard and idiot nature, excited by shew and ostentation, which implies not even the least consciousness of any personal merit."[18] In other words, the contrasting values of "vanity" or "pride" follow the distinction between the natural passions of self-love operating without restraint, and those same impulses governed by the moderating judgment. This is the crux of Darcy's argument to the effect that admirable pride depends on "real superiority" of intellect. And it is the very basis of Pope's well-known thesis on self-love in *An Essay on Man* (1734):

> Two Principles in human nature reign
> Self-love, to urge, and Reason, to restrain;
> Nor this a good, nor that a bad we call,
> Each works its end, to move or govern all:
>
> And to their proper operation still,
> Ascribe all Good; to their improper, Ill.
>   Self-love, the spring of motion, acts the soul;
> Reason's comparing balance rules the whole. (II, 53–60)

---

17. Hume, *Enquiry Concerning the Principles of Morals*, Appendix iv and Section VIII; *Dissertation on the Passions*, Section II.

18. Smollett, *Humphry Clinker*, 287.

And again:

> Modes of Self-love the Passions we may call;
> 'Tis real good, or seeming, moves them all;
> But since not every good we can divide,
> And Reason bids us for our own provide;
> Passions, tho' selfish, if their means be fair,
> List under Reason, and deserve her care;
> Those, that imparted, court a nobler aim,
> Exalt their kind, and take some Virtue's name. (II, 93–100)[19]

The distinctions that Hume and his contemporaries attempt to draw between positive and destructive kinds of self-love are comparable with the Christian schema that a modern critic applies to *Pride and Prejudice*. Within the Augustinian pattern of repentance and conversion, the individual's moral education progresses from egocentricity to love: one must learn to free oneself from the tyranny of the ego so as to become capable of disinterested love of something, someone, outside oneself, "if only the Ancient Mariner's sea snakes."[20] All of which leads in turn to the connotations of pride as an altruistic, rather than egocentric, experience. This is the kind of pride that arises from the selfless appreciation of others, Georgiana Darcy's devotion to her brother, for example, or Mrs. Reynolds' loyal adoration of the master of Pemberley. Yet even on this level the term may be ambiguous, for this kind of loyalty can be affected to become a mask for selfish snobbery. Hence we must contrast Georgiana's family pride with that of the overbearing Caroline Bingley or Lady Catherine de Bourgh.

The ambiguities of "pride" are neatly counterbalanced by the multiple implications of "prejudice." First, the second half of Jane Austen's title represents the uninformed judgments that thwart objectivity. Elizabeth's partiality for Wickham is due to ignorance, and so is her hostility towards Darcy. Mrs. Bennet's violent caprices, her abrupt changes from dislike to enthusiasm,

19. Alexander Pope, *The Poems of Alexander Pope*, ed. John Butt, Twickenham edition (11 vols.; London, 1939–61), III, i.

20. Donald J. Greene, "The Sin of Pride: A Sketch for a Literary Exploration," *New Mexico Quarterly*, XXXIV (1964), 20.

are extreme examples of blind, narrow prejudice. So are the suspect
hyperboles of public opinion, particularly in its obsession with
sensational but unrevealing appearances. The encomiums which
Sir William and Lady Lucas shower on Bingley are typical of the
public's myopic exaggerations: "Her report was highly favourable.
Sir William had been delighted with him. He was quite young,
wonderfully handsome, extremely agreeable, and to crown the
whole, he meant to be at the next assembly with a large party.
Nothing could be more delightful!" (p. 9). The gathering at the
Meryton ball is equally preoccupied with outward appearances:
Mr. Bingley was "good looking and gentlemanlike," and had "a
pleasant countenance"; Mr. Hurst merely "looked the gentleman,"
but Mr. Darcy "soon drew the attention of the room by his fine,
tall person, handsome features, noble mien" (p. 10).[21] And the
instability of this public prejudice is demonstrated by the abrupt
change of heart towards Darcy: "He was the proudest, most disagreeable man in the world" (p. 11). Similarly, Wickham is at
first "universally liked," but with the end of his popularity the
hyperboles swing to the opposite extreme: "All Meryton seemed
striving to blacken the man, who, but three months before, had
been almost an angel of light. He was declared to be in debt to
every tradesman in the place, and his intrigues, all honoured with
the title of seduction, had been extended into every tradesman's
family. Every body declared that he was the wickedest young man
in the world; and every body began to find out, that they had always distrusted the appearance of his goodness" (pp. 294–95).

But on a second level, even the most warped and shallow prepossessions may sometimes have a factual, though limited, basis.
Accordingly, the assembly's view of Mr. Hurst is ironically vali-
dated, for the subsequent narrative never elevates him from the
dubious distinction of having "merely looked the gentleman."
Similarly, even Lady Lucas' superficial panegyrics unconsciously

21. Public opinion is also exaggerated, and suspect, in Fielding's work. Young
Blifil, for example, initially "gained the love of every one," while Tom Jones
"was universally disliked." Henry Fielding, *The History of Tom Jones*, Shakespeare Head Edition (Oxford, 1926), I, 100.

point to the agreeable openness that we eventually associate with Bingley's excessive ductility. Finally, on a third level, this blind prejudice must be distinguished from informed and rational bias. To return to David Hume, rational scepticism is not to be confused with instinctive impulses based on sensory perception alone. According to his *Enquiry Concerning Human Understanding* (1748), some philosophical sceptics (especially the Cartesian school) have a valid point when their more "moderate" arguments recommend some "universal doubt, not only of all our former opinions and principles, but also of our very faculties; of whose veracity, say they, we must assure ourselves, by a chain of reasoning, deduced from some original principle, which cannot possibly be fallacious or deceitful." Moreover, scepticism about the senses does not rest simply on the hackneyed old arguments about the "imperfection and fallaciousness of our organs": sensory fallibility is bound up with, and compounded by, what Hume regards as the human being's prepossessive instincts in matters of external appearances. On this point Hume provides a close parallel with the moral arguments that Jane Austen hinges upon the ambiguities of "prejudice." For, as Hume sees it, the real issue is not simply that sensory impressions are imperfect, but that Man is generally predisposed to trust them above all other modes of perception:

It seems evident, that men are carried, by a natural instinct or prepossession, to repose faith in their senses; and that, without any reasoning, or even almost before the use of reason, we always suppose an external universe, which depends not on our perception, but would exist, though we and every sensible creature were absent or annihilated. Even the animal creation are governed by a like opinion, and preserve this belief of external objects, in all their thoughts, designs, and actions.

It seems also evident, that, when men follow this blind and powerful instinct of nature, they always suppose the very images, presented by the senses, to be the external objects, and never entertain any suspicion, that the one are nothing but representations of the other (Section XII, Part i).[22]

22. David Hume, *An Enquiry Concerning Human Understanding*, Section XII, Part i, in *The Philosophical Works*, IV.

Accordingly, on the basis of this contrast between informed prejudice and blind prepossession we should differentiate between Darcy's well-founded contempt of Wickham and his initial disdain for Elizabeth. Similarly, experience forces Jane to abandon her policy of irrational benevolence and to share her sister's prejudice against Caroline Bingley.

Taken together, all these ambiguities can be attributed to what has usually been accepted as the most probable source of Jane Austen's title. In Fanny Burney's *Cecilia* (1782) Dr. Lyster sums up the moral of the story by elaborating on pride and prejudice as moral paradoxes: "if to PRIDE AND PREJUDICE you owe your miseries, so wonderfully is good and evil balanced, that to PRIDE AND PREJUDICE you will also owe their termination."[23] And it is against this complex background of multiple meanings that we should read Elizabeth's soliloquy of self-recognition in *Pride and Prejudice*, after she reads Darcy's revealing letter. Looking back, she discovers that her conduct towards Wickham and Darcy had been "blind, partial, prejudiced, absurd." She had "prided" herself on her abilities and gratified her "vanity" in "useless or blameable distrust." Her folly has been "vanity," for in favoring Wickham and disliking Darcy she had "courted prepossession and ignorance, and driven reason away, where either were concerned." Vanity, or overweening pride, is cured by the humiliating awareness that follows self-knowledge: "How humiliating is this discovery!—Yet, how just a humiliation! . . . Till this moment, I never knew myself" (p. 208).

As in her previous works Jane Austen incorporates these fundamental ambiguities within the structure of the novel. In particular, the central themes of communication and judgment are allowed to shape the novelist's method of introducing her characters. Generally, the personalities in her previous works are presented directly to the reader in the formal outlines of character sketches. The major exceptions are General Tilney (*Northanger Abbey*) and Willoughby (*Sense and Sensibility*). For the gradual unfold-

23. Fanny Burney, *Cecilia* (5th ed., London 1786), V, 303.

ing of their real natures is integral to the maturing consciousness of Catherine Morland and Marianne Dashwood respectively.
What was an exception in the earlier novels is the prevailing
method of *Pride and Prejudice*. Here, most characters are first exposed through incident or dialogue before being summarized by
the narrator—and in this respect the early presentation of Mr. and
Mrs. Bennet sets the pace for the rest of the narrative. This gradual
introduction bears directly upon the themes of communication
and judgment that Jane Austen links to the ambiguities of her
title, for the process permits the dramatization of the perceptual
and attitudinal conflicts in the novel. The reader now sees the
individual both as he is and as he is assessed by others. Our "first
impressions," and those of the characters, are aroused and then
transformed in order to confirm the multiple connotations of
"pride" and "prejudice." As in *Emma*, the structure externalizes
the problems of communication by obliging the reader to be influenced by, even participate in, incidents of misjudgment and
noncommunication.

Even limited, flat characters like Mrs. Bennet, who are often
quite thoroughly exposed on the first encounter, are introduced
with both their own prejudices and the varying kinds of bias that
they arouse in others. The prolonged introduction of Lady Catherine de Bourgh, for example, serves an important function in the
painful realignment of Elizabeth's "prepossessions" and "prejudices." At first Lady Catherine appears indirectly, as the perennial
subject of Mr. Collins' letters and conversation, and as the target
of Wickham's spiteful caricatures of Darcy's circle. And this pro-
tracted introduction is climaxed by the personal meeting with
Elizabeth at Rosings Park. Before that eventual appearance, our
initial impressions of the dowager exemplify Jane Austen's
achievement in presenting characters on the basis of their social
relationships and through the judgments of other personalities.[24]

24. Kroeber suggests that Jane Austen's characters are usually presented through
personal relationships in his *Styles in Fictional Structure: The Art of Jane Austen, Charlotte Brontë, George Eliot* (Princeton, 1971), 34. But this point is more

Our conviction of Lady Catherine's defects, like Elizabeth's preconceptions, is largely inspired by the excessive praises of Mr.
Collins. Elizabeth's prejudices are confirmed by the personal encounter, and the reader's are substantiated, not by the direct
editorializing of a narrator, but by the diverse reactions of the
visitors to Rosings Park. Lady Catherine's grand manner over-
whelms the Lucases: Sir William sits in stupefied silence and
Maria is "frightened almost out of her senses." Elizabeth who is
"quite equal to the scene" is more detached and critical: Lady
Catherine "was not rendered formidable by silence; but whatever
she said, was spoken in so authoritative a tone, as marked her self
importance, and brought Mr. Wickham immediately to Elizabeth's mind; and from the observation of the day altogether, she
believed Lady Catherine to be exactly what he had represented"
(p. 162). Elizabeth's firsthand observations climax a graduated
process that began with Mr. Collins' suspect panegyrics. The immediate effect of this meeting is to provide the one major instance
in which Elizabeth's hostility towards Darcy's family is substantiated by fact. Her prejudice has been confirmed by the "self
importance," or vanity, of Lady Catherine's corrupted pride.
Consequently, Elizabeth's unbalanced bias against Darcy is
strengthened, and proportionately, her unfounded prepossessions
in Wickham's favor have increased. Both of these related attitudes
will contribute to the crucial scene of her quarrel with Darcy,
which, in turn, will precipitate a fundamental reappraisal of her
perceptual values. In effect, the portrayal of Lady Catherine is a
case history that dramatizes the manner in which the gradual unfolding of personality and human relationships is dominated by
the complex interrelationship of proper pride and destructive
vanity, informed prejudice and blind prepossession.

Even the posthumous caption of *Persuasion* is comparable with
the conceptual titles of the preceding novels, for its double meanings are integral to Anne Elliott's character and experiences. In

applicable to *Pride and Prejudice* and subsequent works than to the earlier works
where direct character sketches are just as important.

one sense, the ubiquitous "persuade" implies the exertion of moral and intellectual influence on a weak or indecisive will which is incapable of formulating or adhering to its own judgment. Lady Russell's dominance over the youthful Anne Elliot is illustrative. Anne now regretfully recalls her own former ductility: "Lady Russell, whom she had always loved and relied on, could not, with such steadiness of opinion, and such tenderness of manner, be continually advising her in vain. She was persuaded to believe the engagement a wrong thing—indiscreet, improper, hardly capable of success, and not deserving it" (p. 27). By way of contrast, her mature reflections on the past exemplify "persuasion" as a form of independent but flexible self-criticism: "She was persuaded that under every disadvantage of disapprobation at home, and every anxiety attending his profession, all their probable fears, delays and disappointments, she should yet have been a happier woman in maintaining the engagement than she had been in the sacrifice of it" (p. 29).

Both connotations of "persuade" were familiar to the eighteenth century. Johnson's dictionary notes two interpretations: (1) "To bring to any particular opinion," and (2) "To influence by argument." Some of the distinctions explored by Jane Austen also seem to have interested John Locke in *An Essay Concerning Human Understanding* (1690), especially in his analysis of "Degrees of Assent." He castigates the kind of proud obstinacy that makes Captain Wentworth so objectionable in the earlier half of *Persuasion*:

I cannot but own, that men's sticking to their past judgment, and adhering firmly to conclusions formerly made, is often the cause of great obstinacy in error and mistake. But the fault is not that they rely on their memories for what they have before well judged, but because they judged before they had well examined. May we not find a greater number (not to say the greatest part) of men that think they have formed right judgments of several matters; and that for no other reason, but because they never thought otherwise? that imagine themselves to have judged right, only because they never questioned, never examined, their own opinions?

Locke then looks at the other extreme, represented in *Persuasion*
by the youthful Anne Elliot: "it carries too great an imputation of
ignorance, tightness, or folly for men to quit and renounce their
former tenets presently upon the offer of an argument which they
cannot immediately answer, and show the insufficiency of." Moreover, "we cannot reasonably expect that anyone should readily and
obsequiously quit his own opinion, and embrace ours, with a blind
resignation to an authority which the understanding of man acknowledges not. For however it may often mistake, it can own no
other guide but reason, nor blindly submit to the will and dictates
of another." Reasoned assent, then, is Locke's ideal, and when he
contrasts this with uninformed obstinacy we are left with a fairly
workable blueprint for the earlier conflict between the mature
Anne Elliott and Captain Wentworth:

> At least, those who have not thoroughly examined to the bottom all
> their own tenets, must confess they are unfit to prescribe to others;
> and are unreasonable in imposing that as truth on other men's belief,
> which they themselves have not searched into, nor weighed the argu-
> ments of probability, on which they should receive or reject it. Those
> who have fairly and truly examined, and are thereby got past doubt
> in all the doctrines they profess and govern themselves by, would have
> a juster pretence to require others to follow them: but these are so
> few in number, and find so little reason to be magisterial in their
> opinions, that nothing insolent and imperious is to be expected from
> them: and there is reason to think, that, if men were better instructed
> themselves, they would be less imposing on others.[25]

   By comparison, Jane Austen distinguishes between Anne Elliot's
unmagisterial maturity and the imperious obstinacy of Captain
Wentworth and Louisa Musgrove. Anne carries her level-headed
individuality with the kind of unimposing intelligence that Locke
admires in the well-instructed few. But both Wentworth and
Louisa are domineering in the profession of ill-considered and
rigidly held opinions. Thus although Anne tolerantly refrains

---

25. John Locke, *An Essay Concerning Human Understanding*, ed. Alexander
Campbell Fraser (2 vols.; New York, 1959), Bk. IV, chap. xvi, sects. 3, 4. All
references to Locke's essay are based on this edition.

from comment on the matter, they are vociferously critical of Henrietta Musgrove's indecision towards Charles Hayter. Priding herself on not being "easily persuaded," Louisa declares, "When I have made up my mind, I have made it. And Henrietta seemed entirely to have made up hers to call at Winthrop to-day—and yet, she was as near giving it up, out of nonsensical complaisance!" Wentworth pontificates in agreement:

"I see that more than a mere dutiful morning-visit to your aunt was in question;—and woe betide him, and her too, when it comes to things of consequence, when they are placed in circumstances requiring forti-tude and strength of mind, if she have not resolution enough to resist idle interference in such a trifle as this. Your sister is an amiable creature; but *yours* is the character of decision and firmness, I see. If you value her conduct or happiness, infuse as much of your own spirit into her, as you can. But this, no doubt, you have been always doing. It is the worst evil of too yielding and indecisive a character, that no influence over it can be depended on.—You are never sure of a good impression being durable. Every body may sway it; let those who would be happy be firm" (*Persuasion*, pp. 87–88).

Wentworth's thesis on indecisive characters is a fairly close ren-dering of Locke's strictures against obsequious judgments and blind resignation. And since Henrietta is obviously intended to be a reincarnation of the ductile Anne Elliott of yesteryear, Went-worth's Lockean definitions are aptly stated. All of which contri-butes to the precise balance of Jane Austen's double-edged irony, for in confirming Locke's criticism of weak wills, Wentworth exemplifies the other extreme that Locke attacks—the magisterial bearing of the unreasonable and the obstinate. His uncompromis-ing individualism distorts the concept of rational persuasion into corrupt forms of "resolution," "fortitude," and "firmness"—just as surely as Henrietta and the younger Anne Elliot have debased it into a specious variety of reasoned acquiescence. Moreover Louisa's accident at Lyme is an example of those "circumstances requiring fortitude and strength of mind," but as it turns out, the headstrong energy that Wentworth confuses with "firmness" is no substitute for Anne's gentle but commanding presence. The

Lyme episode is really a dramatic exposé of the real weaknesses of Wentworth's position. He is immobilized by the crisis. But Anne, with all the unimposing firmness that Locke would have admired, assumes unquestioned leadership after Louisa's mishap; and she demonstrates in the process that true individualism combines flexibility with decisive self-awareness. As Anne's post mortem on the accident makes clear, this is the balanced view of "persuasion" that Wentworth must learn to accept. She wonders "whether it ever occurred to him now, to question the justness of his own previous opinion as to the universal felicity and advantage of firmness of character; and whether it might not strike him, that, like all other qualities of the mind, it should have its porportions and limits. She thought it could scarcely escape him to feel, that a persuadable temper might sometimes be as much in favour of happiness, as a very resolute character" (p. 116).

On the whole, therefore, whenever conceptual terms dominate Jane Austen titles they are pointers to the divergent, moral nuances on which she bases her ironic structures. Moreover, as the writings of her eighteenth-century predecessors demonstrate, Jane Austen is really exploiting semantic phenomena which arise from the multiple crosscurrents of her philosophical heritage. "Verbal disputes" about "friendship," "sensibility," "pride," and "persuasion" have been interwoven with the moral psychology of Laura, Marianne Dashwood, Darcy, and Anne Elliot; and they are the foundation stones, so to speak, of the respective novels. Conversely, the very nature of these "disputes" exposes the links between Jane Austen's themes and her rich heritage of eighteenth-century philosophy. Novels like *Sense and Sensibility* and *Persuasion* often define a moral progression from egocentricity to positive humanism, from self-centered passion to dynamic understanding, and from narrow ratiocination to rational sensibility. The individual is judged on the basis of the ability or (in Laura's case) failure to follow this line of development. And in setting up these schemes of moral education, Jane Austen is manifestly within a philosophical tradition (represented on various levels by Locke, Shaftesbury,

and Burke among others) which recognizes the everyday dichotomies between passion and judgment, or love and individualism,
but which has tried, simultaneously, to project the so-called disparities as a complex but workable synthesis.

At the same time, ambiguous usages are crucial to an understanding of thematic developments in those novels which are not
overtly dominated by conceptual terms. Indeed, the themes of
Emma impinge directly upon epistemological and moral problems which are underlined by ironic ambiguities in other novels.
Thus John Locke's description of "Predominant Passions" is as
relevant to Emma Woodhouse's undisciplined fancy as it is to the
functions of "prejudice" and "prepossession" in *Pride and Prejudice*. As we have already noted, a chastened Elizabeth Bennet
acknowledges that her blind prepossessions had prevented her
from recognizing the facts of human nature and social relationships. According to Locke's analysis of predominant passions in
Human Understanding,

Let ever so much probability hang on one side of a covetous man's
reasoning, and money on the other; it is easy to foresee which will
outweigh. Earthly minds, like mud walls, resist the strongest batteries:
and though, perhaps, sometimes the force of a clear argument may
make some impression, yet they nevertheless stand firm, and keep out
the enemy, truth, that would captivate or disturb them. Tell a man
passionately in love, that he is jilted; bring a score of witnesses of the
falsehood of his mistress, it is ten to one but three kind words of hers
shall invalidate all their testimonies. *Quod volumus, facile credimus*;
what suits our wishes, is forwardly believed, is, I suppose, what every
one hath more than once experimented: and though men cannot always openly gainsay or resist the force of manifest probabilities that
make against them, yet yield they not to the argument.[26]

When we turn to *Emma* we find that the heroine's predetermina-
tions about Mr. Elton and Harriet have blinded her to the "manifest probabilities" suggested by the young vicar's behavior. In
retrospect, the half-repentant Emma is forced to admit that she
had taken up the idea of matching Mr. Elton with Harriet, "and

26. *Ibid.*, chap. xx, sect. 12.

made everything bend to it" (p. 134). Emma's distorting fancy goes hand in hand with pride, a managerial disposition to dominate and manipulate others. Hence, in the case of Harriet's misadventure with the gypsies, Emma's imagination is combined with her egocentric passions to form a "ground-work of anticipation" which has little to do with the probable preferences of either Harriet or Frank Churchill. In effect, her musings on Harriet's new matrimonial prospects are a dramatization of Locke's principle of "predominant" passions:

Such an adventure as this,—a fine young man and a lovely young woman thrown together in such a way, could hardly fail of suggesting certain ideas to the coldest heart and the steadiest brain. So Emma thought, at least. Could a linguist, could a grammarian, could even a mathematician have seen what she did, have witnessed their appearance together, and heard their history of it, without feeling that circumstances had been at work to make them peculiarly interesting to each other?—How much more must an imaginist, like herself, be on fire with speculation and foresight!—especially with such a ground-work of anticipation as her mind had already made" (*Emma*, pp. 334–35).

Or, to paraphrase Mr. Knightley's quotation from Cowper, Emma is creating what she herself sees. Significantly, Mr. Knightley recalls *The Task* (IV, 29) because he wishes to escape "Emma's errors of imagination." Thus he does not allow his strong dislike of Frank Churchill to influence him unduly when he tries to decipher "symptoms" of intelligence between Frank and Jane (pp. 343–44). And, appropriately, it is Mr. Knightley who analyzes the egocentric basis of Emma's fancy: "I have done with expecting any course of steady reading from Emma. She will never submit to any thing requiring industry and patience, and a subjection of the fancy to the understanding" (p. 37).

Of course Jane Austen is not attempting to eliminate fancy in favor of the understanding, any more than she tries to banish "sensibility" in *Sense and Sensibility*. What Emma must learn is to combine judgment and imagination on the only basis on which they will cohere. The judgment must be in control. And the subordination of the wayward fancy means, in effect, the suppression of pride. Unaccustomed as she is to acknowledge her own weaknesses, Emma nonetheless recognizes quite early in the novel that the issues of pride and imagination are closely joined. After Mr. Elton proposes, she temporarily resolves to be "humble and discreet," and to repress imagination "all the rest of her life" (p. 142). Obviously Emma's weakness is not identical to the "disorders" suffered by Samuel Johnson's mad astronomer. But the general discussion of imagination in *Rasselas* does have a bearing on Jane Austen's novel. Indeed, when Imlac remarks on the need to control the fancy his phrasing is not dissimilar to Emma's short-lived resolution. According to Imlac, all power of fancy over reason is a degree of insanity, "but while this power is such as we can controul and repress, it is not visible to others." The astronomer's megalomania is really an archetype of that combination of fancy and pride which is so central to Emma's personality. Even a cursory glance at his illusions of power suggests that the kind of managerial instinct that Emma applies to matchmaking has been elevated by the mad astronomer to a grand cosmic scale: "I have possessed for five years the regulation of weather, and the distribution of the seasons: the sun has listened to my dictates, and passed from tropick to tropick by my direction; the clouds, at my call, have poured their waters, and the Nile has overflowed at my command; I have restrained the rage of the dog-star, and mitigated the fervours of the crab."[27]

The issues raised by Emma's vanity are not limited to the epistemological issues which underlie the ironic double meanings of *Pride and Prejudice*, or the moral philosophy of *Rasselas*. Egocentricity is also crucial to the nature of social relationships, and the realization of creative ties depends on Emma's progression from destructive vanity to a more human view of self and society. This is the point of the ironic double meanings that surround the term "amiable" in *Emma*, especially as it applies to Frank

27. Samuel Johnson, *The History of Rasselas, Prince of Abissinia*, ed. R. W. Chapman (Oxford, 1927), 190, 183.

Churchill. In Mr. Knightley's view, the latter can be "amiable only in French, not in English. He may be very 'amiable,' have very good manners, and be very agreeable; but he can have no English delicacy towards the feelings of other people; nothing really amiable about him" (p. 149). Mr. Knightley's distinction between the French and English definitions differentiates between superficial gracefulness and moral principle. Or, to return to Johnson's dictionary, this is a contrast between (1) "pretending" or "shewing" love, and (2) "pleasing." Moreover, Frank's "amiable" vanity, his lack of "delicacy" towards the feelings of others, is similar to the narrow egotism that Emma displays in her match-making and in her general snobbery. Like Elizabeth Bennet, she recognizes her own vanity only through humiliation. The Box Hill fiasco, for example, is the catalyst through which Emma is able to review her social values. In effect, when Mr. Knightley dwells on the ambiguities of "amiable" he is defining the future course of Emma's moral development.

Henry Tilney performs a similar service in *Northanger Abbey* where the double meanings of "nice" are interwoven with the theme of Catherine Morland's education. When Catherine describes *The Mysteries of Udolpho* as a "nice" work, Henry Tilney provocatively assumes that she refers only to the binding. This kind of usage offends what his sister describes as Henry's "propriety of diction": "Oh! it is a very nice word indeed!—it does for every thing. Originally perhaps it was applied only to express neatness, propriety, delicacy, or refinement; people were nice in their dress, in their sentiments, or their choice. But now every commendation on every subject is comprised in that one word" (p. 108). Henry distinguishes between "nice" as the description of a discriminating taste, and the devaluation of the word to the level of general, and meaningless "commendation." Miss Tilney admittedly reminds Henry of an additional definition by saying that discriminating tastes can degenerate into mere pettifogging: "You are more nice than wise." But in spite of her sally, Henry's statements are valid pointers to the moral center of Jane Austen's novel, for his distinction between intellectual excellence and an uncritical judgment is applicable to the thematic development of the work as a whole. The redefinition of "nice" emphasizes that taste is more than an aesthetic faculty. As in *Sense and Sensibility*, it also involves moral and intellectual standards by which life and literature must be judged. All of which is pertinent to the relationship between Catherine's education and the parody of popular fiction in *Northanger Abbey*. For Catherine's indiscriminate taste in novels is the symptom of an immature judgment that is unable to penetrate the selfish hypocrisy of the Thorpes in real life. But as she learns to be "nice" in her relationships with people she is better able to distinguish between appearance and reality. Isabella Thorpe's calculating flattery is exposed for what it is. Similarly, the lines between literary fantasies and experience begin to emerge. The fictional catastrophes of popular novels (which led Catherine to imagine the murder of the late Mrs. Tilney) are no longer confused with the less sensational, but far more insidious and immediate, hardships of real life. General Tilney's villainy lies in greed and crude inhospitality rather than in the bloody improbabilities of Gothic fiction.

The verbal dispute which centers on "nice" in *Northanger Abbey* is comparable with the debate on "manners" in *Mansfield Park*, for in the latter work disparate interpretations of an evaluative term are again faithful to the moral and intellectual divisions explored by Jane Austen. On the one hand, Mary Crawford limits her understanding of "manners" to etiquette and ceremony, but as Edmund points out, these are not the kind of "manners" which the clergy is supposed to form: "And with regard to their influencing public manners, Miss Crawford must not misunderstand me, or suppose I mean to call them the arbiters of good breeding, the regulators of refinement and courtesy, the masters of the ceremonies of life. The *manners* I speak of, might rather be called *conduct*, perhaps, the result of good principles; the effect, in short, of those doctrines which it is their duty to teach and recommend" (p. 93). The divergent values denoted by Mary's "manners" and Edmund's "conduct" validate David Lodge's argument that the narrative of *Mansfield Park* is based on a delicate balance between social graces and moral principle.[28] The dispute between Mary and Edmund is part of a pervasive, moral antithesis which affects all the personal relationships in the novel. The superficial graces of the Crawfords áre distinguished from Fanny Price's moral principles and deep feeling. Sir Thomas Bertram gradually relinquishes the emptiness of social status in favor of emotional and moral values. The sterile education of his daughters is based on an exclusive preoccupation with form and ceremony; but as events prove, this superficial concept of manners tends to be a brittle restraint on their sexual passions. And its fragility is stressed by the striking clauses which describe Julia's chagrin at the setbacks of the Sotherton visit: "The politeness which she had been brought up to practise as a duty, made it impossible for her to escape; while the want of that higher species of self-command, that just consideration of others, that knowledge of her own heart, that principle of right which had not formed any essential part of her education, made her miserable under it" (*Mansfield Park*, p. 91).

Significantly, Johnson records the divergent definitions of "manners" which obviously reflect the conflicting standards within Jane Austen's novel. Among ten definitions, the *Dictionary* lists its moral and intellectual implications and its purely ceremonial meaning: (1) "Character of the mind," (2) "General way of life; morals; habits," (3) "Ceremonious behaviour; studious civility." But as happens so often in Jane Austen's fiction this kind of dichotomy is not postulated in *Mansfield Park* as an acceptable ideal. In spite of traditional regrets to the effect that Jane Austen has exorcised the vitalism represented by the Crawfords, there is no real evidence in the novel to suggest that the novelist projects moral principle as the natural, and desirable, antithesis of attractive manners. Indeed, if we accept Kenneth L. Moler's recent thesis that

28. David Lodge, "A Question of Judgement: The Theatricals at *Mansfield Park*," *Nineteenth Century Fiction*, XVII (1962–63), 276.

Fanny Price does not represent the final morality of the novel,[29] then it becomes fairly clear that both Mary's scintillating gracefulness and Fanny's dour piety fall short of the ideal synthesis that Shaftesbury envisages in the *Characteristics*. For when he discusses the nature of "wit" and "humour," Shaftesbury defines both acuteness of intellect and amenable disposition as moral desiderata. The immorality of a well-bred and witty man is therefore a moral paradox:

> By gentlemen of fashion, I understand those to whom a natural good genius, or the force of good education, has given a sense of what is naturally graceful and becoming. Some by mere nature, others by art and practice, are masters of an ear in music, an eye in painting, a fancy in the ordinary things of ornament and grace, a judgment in proportions of all kinds, and a general good taste in most of those subjects which make the amusement and delight of the ingenious people of the world. Let such gentlemen as these be as extravagant as they please, or as irregular in their morals, they must at the same time discover their inconsistency, live at variance with themselves, and in contradiction to that principle on which they ground their highest pleasure and entertainment.[30]

Finally, the theme of "ordination," Jane Austen's avowed subject in *Mansfield Park*, is related to the double meanings of "manners" (*Letters*, p. 298). Edmund's ordination turns out to be more than a formal ceremony. It is really a form of education for a calling which, to use Edmund's own words, "has the charge of all that is of the first importance to mankind, individually or collectively considered, temporally and externally—which has the guardianship of religion and morals, and consequently of the manners which result from their influence" (p. 92). R. W. Chapman has observed that a term like "environment" would be more apt than "ordination" in Jane Austen's description of her theme, for this would have emphasized the bluntly didactic treatment

---

29. "Jane Austen did not intend Fanny to be the static 'picture of perfection,' the moral paragon that many readers take her to be, and resent her for being." Kenneth L. Moler, *Jane Austen's Art of Allusion* (Lincoln, Nebr., 1968), 146.

30. Shaftesbury, *Characteristics*, I, 89–90.

of religious and moral education in the novel.[31] However, this supposed didacticism is not as obvious as Chapman alleges. Jane Austen's deliberate choice of "ordination" is quite appropriate to the ironic antitheses of *Mansfield Park*. It reflects the contrast between formal ceremony and moral principle, between manners as social graces and manners as conduct. In this respect she is supported by Johnson whose dictionary also notes the distinction between ordination as principle and ordination as ceremony: "Established order or tendency, consequent on a decree," and "the act of investing any man with sacerdotal power." Hence, far from being irrelevant or obscurantist Jane Austen's personal choice of "ordination" in describing her theme goes to the very heart of the moral conflicts on which *Mansfield Park* rests. And what is equally significant, her deliberate phrasing reflects precisely the kind of ambiguous usage that is so fundamental to her ironic treatment of verbal and moral "disputes" throughout her fiction.

31. R. W. Chapman, *Jane Austen: Facts and Problems* (Cambridge, 1948), 194.

CHAPTER III

Imagery

IT HAS TRADITIONALLY been assumed that Jane Austen dislikes and avoids imagery. Her well-known strictures against "novel slang" supposedly demonstrate a personal dislike of figurative language, and this aversion is alleged to have been caused by her exposure to the florid excesses of popular fiction.[1] However, this traditional assumption needs to be reconsidered in the light of Jane Austen's less famous comments in her letters, together with comparable statements in the novels. Of course, she unfailingly ridicules excessive or inappropriate imagery. Her niece Anna Austen is only one of several persons whose novel slang provoked Jane Austen's derision. For example, she dismisses the works of Miss Sydney Owenson with the comment, "If the warmth of her Language could affect the Body it might be worth reading in this weather" (*Letters*, p. 251). The *Plan of a Novel* also includes "elegant" and highly metaphorical language among its targets. Hence the father of the proposed heroine must die in a "fine burst of Literary Enthusiasm" (*Minor Works*, p. 430).

But it should be noted that on no occasion does Jane Austen attack figurative language *per se*. Her real object is the hackneyed and usually florid imagery in cheap, sensational fiction, and the

---

1. Andrew H. Wright, *Jane Austen's Novels: A Study in Structure* (2nd ed.; London, 1962), 188–91; Mary Lascelles, *Jane Austen and her Art* (London, 1939), 111–13; W. A. Craik, *Jane Austen: The Six Novels* (London, 1965), 29.

complete context of her famous injunction to Anna Austen makes this clear: "Devereux Foster's being ruined by his Vanity is extremely good; but I wish you would not let him plunge into a 'vortex of Dissipation.' I do not object to the Thing, but I cannot bear the expression;—it is such thorough novel slang—and so old, that I dare say Adam met with it in the first novel he opened" (*Letters*, p. 404). Jane Austen's Marianne Dashwood also limits herself to the subject of clichés when she explains her detestation of Sir John Middleton's style: "I abhor every common-place phrase by which wit is intended; and 'setting one's cap at a man,' or 'making a conquest,' are the most odious of all. Their tendency is gross and illiberal; and if their construction could ever be deemed clever, time has long ago destroyed all its ingenuity" (*Sense and Sensibility*, p. 45). Moreover, according to Willoughby, Marianne's abhorrence extends to hackneyed metaphors like "a dagger to my heart" and "a thunderbolt" (p. 325). The cavalier treatment that Marianne metes out to Sir John's style may be compared with the narrator's cutting comment on Sir Edward Denham's rhapsodical deliveries in *Sanditon*: his verbiose outpourings on the sea are little more than "the usual Phrases" (*Minor Works*, p. 396).

The basis of Jane Austen's attacks on hackneyed metaphors must be sought in her characteristic preoccupation with communication and meaning. She is primarily interested in figurative language on the basis of its expressive value, and she attacks imagery when it fails to communicate, when, in Marianne's words, it has lost all meaning and "ingenuity." Yet even original structures are likely to be meaningless and absurd when they are forced into service. Thus in a letter to Cassandra, Jane Austen confesses that her style might be hurt by Fanny Knight's generous praise: "I wish the knowledge of my being exposed to her discerning Criticism, may not hurt my stile, by inducing too great a solicitude. I begin already to weigh my words and sentences more than I did, and am looking about for a sentiment, an illustration or a metaphor in every corner of the room. Could my Ideas flow as fast as the rain in the Store closet it would be charming" (*Letters*, p. 256).

Her statement underlines her primary concern that the image should be appropriate, that it should be meaningful.

Indeed, far from conclusively documenting a jaundiced view of imagery as such, Jane Austen's comments link her with some of the most ardent supporters of figurative language in the eighteenth century. Behind her statements lies a formidable body of rhetorical traditions that repeatedly emphasize the need to integrate language with meaning and feeling. The figure must be expressive. It must neither be hackneyed nor forced into context. Jane Austen's closeness to this tradition is evinced by her knowledge of Hugh Blair's *Lectures on Rhetoric and Belles Lettres* (1783). Blair criticizes inappropriate and hackneyed imagery, but his strictures are no more indicative than Jane Austen's of a complete rejection of figurative language. He contends that in order to be beautiful, figures "must always rise naturally from the subject." As he elaborates on this point, we can recall Jane Austen looking for a metaphor in every corner of the room: "we should never interrupt the course of thought to cast about for Figures. If they be sought after coolly, and fastened on as designed ornaments, they will have a miserable effect."[2] Blair's warning is not unique, for it is one of several eighteenth-century defenses of figurative language—among them, Joseph Addison's *Spectator* No. 411, David Fordyce's *Dialogues Concerning Education* (1745), James Beattie's "On Poetry and Music" (1762), and John Langhorne's critical essay on William Collins (1771).[3]

On the whole, then, Jane Austen's personal comments suggest that she is not averse to imagery as such. She is primarily interested in the complete integration of verbal patterns with the multiple

2. Hugh Blair, *Lectures on Rhetoric and Belles Lettres*, ed. Harold F. Harding (3 vols.; Carbondale and Edwardsville, 1965), I, 364. Jane Austen mentions the work in *Northanger Abbey* (p. 108).

3. Joseph Addison, *The Spectator*, ed. Donald F. Bond (5 vols.; Oxford, 1965), III, 535–39; David Fordyce, *Dialogues Concerning Education* (London, 1745), 368–70; James Beattie, *Essays* (Edinburgh, 1776), 540; John Langhorne (ed.), *The Poetical Works of Mr. William Collins* (London, 1771), 145. Some of these treatises are examined by Earl R. Wasserman, "The Inherent Values of Eighteenth Century Personification," *PMLA*, LXV (1950), 435–63.

levels of her irony. And accordingly, her figurative language is
diversified, ranging from the burlesque of florid styles to the
analytic and the emotive. Indeed, far from being "unmetaphorical," Jane Austen's style is remarkable for the aptness of figurative
epigrams that illuminate the essence of situation or personality. In
Mansfield Park, for example, Fanny Price shuns the "toils of
civility" that are a part of any ball (p. 273). And polite society is
also the target in *Northanger Abbey* when Catherine Morland
assumes that an unintended slight to the Tilneys will result in
"rigours of rudeness" (p. 92). Later, Catherine's unexpected return from Northanger Abbey brings her sister Sarah all the
"sweets of incomprehensibility" (p. 234). Sarah's sensations are
echoed by the "sweets of poetical despondence" which attend Anne
Elliot's reverie on autumn (*Persuasion*, p. 85). On a more satiric
note, Robert Ferrars is crucified by the epigrams that pinpoint the
"strong, natural, sterling insignificance" of his face and the "pup-
pyism of his manner" (*Sense and Sensibility*, 220–21). In the
same novel Lady Middleton and Mrs. John Dashwood are left to
share their "insipid propriety of demeanour" (p. 229). Mrs. Elton
descends on Donwell Abbey" in all her apparatus of happiness"
(*Emma*, p. 358). After Darcy's marriage a disappointed Miss
Bingley prudently "paid off every arrear of civility" to his bride
(*Pride and Prejudice*, p. 387). In *Mansfield Park* the fragile
balance between emotional conflict and polite restraints is summed up by the "short parley of compliment" staged at the rehearsals by Henry Crawford and Yates (p. 132). These are the
kinds of incongruities and contradictions which invariably attract
Jane Austen's irony and which are so aptly expressed by the concise paradoxes of her epigrams. This is particularly true of the
"large fat sighings" with which Mrs. Musgrove "mourns" her
unlamented son, Richard. Significantly, the paradoxical phrase is
followed by narrative explanations of the hypocrisies and contradictions which underlie Mrs. Musgrove's mourning. First, the un-
lovable and forgotten Richard is a rather dubious candidate for the
family's concern. And second, Mrs. Musgrove's ostentatious sighs

for "poor Dick" are not consistent with her demeanor of well-fed happiness: "A large bulky figure has as good a right to be deep in affliction, as the most graceful set of limbs in the world. But, fair or not fair, there are unbecoming conjunctions, which reason will patronize in vain,—which taste cannot tolerate,—which ridicule will seize" (*Persuasion*, p. 68).

Critics like Mary Lascelles and Andrew Wright do acknowledge that Jane Austen uses imagery. But they contend that the restriction of her metaphoric style to defective characters confirms rather than contradicts her hostility to figurative language.[4] It is clear that imagery does perform a satiric role in the portrayal of characters like Sir John Middleton, Mrs. Elton, and Mrs. Musgrove; but there seems to be no real basis for the assumption that this satiric usage *demonstrates* the novelist's alleged dislike of imagery. In the first place, if this thesis were applied to *all* the structures that Jane Austen uses for parody and satiric characterization we would be left with the dubious conclusion that she loathes nearly all details of the English language and of her narrative techniques. And in the second, it should be emphasized that "sound" as well as "defective" tastes in Jane Austen's fiction may be dramatized, not simply by figurative language as such, but by the kind of imagery that they employ, or even by the absence of imagery altogether. Hence, Mrs. Palmer (*Sense and Sensibility*) and Mr. Woodhouse (*Emma*) rarely use imagery: their usually unmetaphorical styles reflect their unimaginative and innocuous personalities. On the other hand, the crude and spiteful bearing of Mary Stanhope (*The Three Sisters*) requires the kind of nonfigurative language that demonstrates her ill-temper and semiliteracy. The self-analysis that follows Mr. Watts's proposal is typical: "If I refuse him he as good as told me that he should offer himself to Sophia and if *she* refused him to Georgiana, & I could not bear to have either of them married before me. . . . The only thing I can think of my dear Fanny is to ask Sophy & Georgiana whether they would have him were he to make proposals to them, & if

4. Lascelles, *Jane Austen and her Art*, 112; Wright, *Jane Austen's Novels*, 188.

they say they would not I am resolved to refuse him too, for I hate him more than you can imagine" (*Minor Works*, pp. 58, 60). By contrast, Georgiana's version of the same problem is interspersed with metaphoric structures which are the primary tools of her cool, penetrating intelligence: "An hour ago she[Mary] came to us to sound our inclinations respecting the affair which were to determine hers. . . . I broke silence to assure Sophy that if Mary should refuse Mr Watts I should not expect her to sacrifice *her* happiness by becoming his Wife from a motive of Generosity to me" (p. 61).

Georgiana's witty style demonstrates that from as early as the juvenilia Jane Austen does not assume a dichotomy between sound judgment and metaphoric statement. And in this connection, Georgiana anticipates the sensitive intelligence of Henry Tilney in *Northanger Abbey*. Some of his most penetrating analyses are couched in figurative language, particularly his ironic disapproval of Catherine Morland's charitable disposition towards the treacherous Isabella Thorpe: "Your mind is warped by an innate principle of general integrity, and therefore not accessible to the cool reasonings of family partiality, or a desire of revenge" (p. 219). Elinor Dashwood's summary of Lucy Steele's character lacks the ironic complexity that is so typical of Henry's mocking style, but her metaphorical phrasing is informed by an equally sophisticated intelligence: Elinor could have no lasting satisfaction in the company of a person who "joined" insincerity with ignorance (*Sense and Sensibility*, p. 127). In *Persuasion* Anne Elliot becomes part of this respectable list of figurative analysts in her intelligent and wholly just suspicions of Mr. Elliot's character. She is disturbed at the fact that he is not open, that he never displays "any burst of feeling, any warmth of indignation or delight" at the evil or good of others. This is a decided imperfection, in Anne's view: her early impressions are "incurable." She "prized" the frank, the openhearted, the eager character beyond all others. "Warmth and enthusiasm did captivate her still." At the same time, she distrusts those whose presence of mind "never varied, whose tongue never slipped" (p. 161). And that most respectable of Jane Austen's characters, Mr. Knightley, does not balk at figurative language in some of his forthright pronouncements. Although his criticism of Frank Churchill is colored by subconscious jealousy, the scathing metaphors are completely vindicated by subsequent disclosures. According to Mr. Knightley, duties cannot be performed by "manoeuvring and finessing;" and it is Frank's duty "to pay" the attention of a visit to Mrs. Weston and his father. This would do Frank more good, "raise him higher, fix his interest stronger with the people he depended on than all that a line of shifts and expedients can ever do" (*Emma*, pp. 146, 147). Frank should have been "following his duty, instead of consulting expediency," but he has merely exploited the advantages of "sitting still when he ought to move." He writes a "fine, flourishing letter, full of professions and falsehoods," then persuades himself that he has "hit upon" the best method of preserving peace at home (pp. 148–49).

When we turn to the inept users of imagery we find that they are distinguished from each other as well as from unimaginative persons who shun images. Moreover, the aptness and control of their figurative language fall far short of metaphoric usages by characters like Henry Tilney. In *Sanditon*, for example, Sir Edward Denham's chaotic mentality is far removed from both Mr. Knightley's ordered rhetoric and Mr. Woodhouse's lifeless inanities. Sir Edward's style is self-consciously metaphoric, and his florid delivery incorporates "all the newest-fashioned hard words," especially in his definition of poetic genius: "It were Hyper-Criticism, it were Psuedo-philosophy to expect from the soul of high toned Genius, the grovellings of a common mind.—The Coruscations of Talent, elicited by impassioned feeling in the breast of Man, are perhaps incompatible with some of the prosaic Decencies of Life" (*Minor Works*, p. 398). The rhetorical novelties of Sir Edward's literary enthusiasm are obviously different in kind from the threadbare metaphors of the unimaginative Mr.

Collins. The latter introduces himself to the Bennets in a burst of hoary clichés: he has always wished to "heal the breach" between himself and the Bennets, and he now hopes that they will not "reject the offered olive branch" (*Pride and Prejudice*, pp. 62–63). Mary Bennet is as widely read as Sir Edward Denham, but lacking his florid imagination she is restricted to Mr. Collins' brand of petrified images. Hence, as she sees it, Lydia's elopement is an unfortunate affair, but "we must stem the tide of malice, and pour into the wounded bosoms of each other, the balm of sisterly consolation" (p. 289). On yet another level, in *The Watsons* the eldest Miss Watson prefers more prosaic clichés that are more in keeping with her nonliterary interests. For example, she congratulates herself on having "escaped with a whole heart" from Tom Musgrave's alleged charms (*Minor Works*, p. 316). Finally, in *Persuasion* Lady Russell reworks time-honored figures, particularly those which are linked with the sacrosanct family tree: if Mr. Elliot "really sought to reconcile himself like a dutiful branch, he must be forgiven for having dismembered himself from the paternal tree" (p. 136).

Jane Austen does not simply diversify figurative styles in order to match the variety of judgments represented by these characters. She also varies the structure and function of images which communicate individual feeling. The precise nature of the imagery depends on the personality involved. Elinor Dashwood, whose emotional capacities have usually been disputed, evinces her strong but controlled sensibility in scenes dominated by imagery. She is overcome by the news of Edward Ferrars' engagement, but even "under the first smart of the heavy blow," she determines to "guard every suspicion of the truth" from her family. And when she joins her mother and sisters at dinner, "after she had suffered the extinction of all her dearest hopes," no one could guess that Elinor secretly mourns "over obstacles which must divide her for ever from the object of her love" (*Sense and Sensibility*, p. 141). Subsequently, she contrasts herself with a happy Marianne: "Elinor . . . could not witness the rapture of delightful expectation which filled the whole soul and beamed in the eyes of Marianne, without feeling how blank was her own prospect" (p. 159).

But Elinor's unequivocal and sincere feelings are not the only kind of emotional experiences that are communicated by the metaphoric styles, or portraits, of Jane Austen's characters. In *Love and Freindship* Laura's hollow "sensibility" is repeatedly betrayed by the telltale orotundity of her novel slang, particularly in her appraisal of Augusta's "disagreable Coldness and Forbidding Reserve": Augusta "was neither animated nor cordial; her arms were not opened to receive me to her Heart, tho' my own were extended to press her to mine. . . . Her Heart was no more formed for the soft ties of love than for the endearing intercourse of Freindship" (*Minor Works*, pp. 82–83). Laura's husband uses a similar technique when he denounces Augusta's alleged insensitivity: "And did you then never feel the pleasing Pangs of Love, Augusta? . . . Does it appear impossible to your vile and corrupted Palate, to exist on Love? Can you not conceive the Luxury of living in every Distress that Poverty can inflict, with the Object of your tenderest Affection?" (pp. 83–84).

On the other hand, Marianne Dashwood's genuine but excessive sensibility avoids the grandiloquent clichés which serve Laura's insincerity. At the same time her sincere excesses invest her typical images with the dangerous energy of her strong feelings. Thus she complains that Edward Ferrars' figure is "not striking," and that his eyes lack "all that spirit, that fire, which at once announce virtue and intelligence." And his reading of Cowper's poetry is intolerable: "To hear those beautiful lines which have almost driven me wild, pronounced with such impenetrable calmness, such dreadful indifference!" (*Sense and Sensibility*, pp. 17, 18). The effect of Marianne's imagery is an ambiguous combination of the emotive and the satiric. Her style is evocative of genuine rather than affected feelings, but, simultaneously, the violent connotations of her language provoke a critical response to her emotional excesses. This kind of dual function is duplicated again and again in the emotive styles of Jane Austen's characters. When Captain Wentworth expresses surprise at Benwick's sudden recovery from Fanny Harville's death, he does so in the familiar rhetoric of sentimentality: "A man like him, in his situation! With a heart pierced, wounded, almost broken! . . . A man does not recover from such a devotion of the heart to such a woman!" (*Persuasion*, p. 183). In one sense, the exclamation is genuinely emotive, for it recaptures the intensity of Benwick's bereavement. But the suggestive extravagance of the images is satiric, for it underlines Wentworth's characteristically rigid and extreme views on emotional or moral stability. He cannot understand how Benwick's sorrow could evolve and eventually give way to new interests—such as marriage with Louisa Musgrove. In the same work Mrs. Smith denounces Mr. Elliot as a "cold-blooded being" who heartlessly deserts those "whom he has been the chief cause of leading to ruin." Her scathing indictment is climaxed by an emotional outburst of conventional metaphors: "He is totally beyond the reach of any sentiment of justice or compassion. Oh! he is black at heart, hollow and black!" (p. 199). Her strong hatred of Mr. Elliot is dramatized by the figurative statements. But the stock images also satirize the understandable emotional excesses of Mr. Elliot's erstwhile victim—and this is subsequently confirmed by the narrator's comment: Mrs. Smith's story proves that Mr. Elliot is unfeeling and unjust, but it "did not perfectly" substantiate her "unqualified bitterness" (p. 208).

Emma Woodhouse's character provides some of the most pointed examples of ambiguous imagery in Jane Austen's fiction. Emma's self-centered and unrealistic point of view is sometimes couched in the appropriate jargon of novel slang. Hence the unfounded conjectures on Jane Fairfax's "secret passion" are delivered in sentimental clichés. Jane is to be congratulated for the "sacrifices" entailed in separation from the Dixons, and "Emma was very willing now to acquit her of having seduced Mr. Dixon's affections from his wife. . . . She might have been unconsciously sucking in the sad poison, while a sharer of his conversation with her friend" (*Emma*, p. 168). Emma's surmise provokes ironically conflicting responses. Her style accurately though unconsciously reflects the intensity of Jane's unhappiness, but it also betrays Emma's characteristic failure to interpret realistically the behavior of people around her. In this case Jane has been "sucking" the "sad poison" of separation from Frank Churchill, and her sacrifices have had nothing to do with the Dixon marriage. It is also noteworthy that when Emma's brief fit of charity has passed, her malicious analysis of Jane's character dispenses with sentimental rhetoric and relies on less emotive, but equally metaphoric phrasing. Thus Jane offends by being a superior pianist, and consequently, appears as a disgusting figure of suspicious reserve: "Wrapt up in a cloak of politeness, she seemed determined to hazard nothing." Nor is the wretched Jane redeemed by complimentary but vague references to Mr. Dixon, for Emma finds that her report is all general commendation and "smoothness" with nothing "delineated" or distinguished. Jane's caution has therefore been "thrown away." Emma has seen its artifice (p. 169).

But when Emma's judgment is again based on an emotional experience the sentimental image reappears with ambiguous results. After the Box Hill picnic Emma ruefully acknowledges the justice of Jane's obvious hostility: "An airing in the Hartfield carriage would have been the rack, and arrow-root from the Hartfield store-room must have been poison" (p. 403). As the mocking echoes of her earlier "poison" metaphor suggest, the phrasing of the present cliché is a satirical reminder of Emma's prior misjudgments. Yet at the same time Jane Austen is exploiting the traditionally emotive functions of the figure to convey the undeniable intensity of Jane's hurt feelings and Emma's own unusual contrition. Moreover, these ambiguous echoes emphasize the causal relationship between Emma's past errors and her present discomfiture. Finally, as Emma is increasingly mortified by former omissions, her affective images become less equivocal. Hence the self-torture of Emma's own conscience shapes the metaphors with which she reviews Jane's recent experiences: "They never could have been all three together, without her having stabbed Jane Fairfax's peace in a thousand instances; and on Box Hill, perhaps, it had been the agony of a mind that could bear no more" (p. 421).[5]

The shifting patterns and emphases of these images are comparable with the metaphors that announce Emma's reappraisal of her relationship with Mr. Knightley. First, there is the great moment of self-recognition: "It darted through her, with the speed of an arrow" that Mr. Knightley must marry no one but herself (p. 408). Once again, the ironic cliché synthesizes the satiric and the affective. It recalls all the fanciful excesses that formerly blinded Emma to reality; and, simultaneously, it dramatizes the genuine shock of Emma's new emotional awakening. The synthesis is more than a rhetorical device. It is also a psychological process, for the pain of present self-discovery has been intensified by the memory of past fantasies and miscalculations. The well-worn "arrow" simile has much the same effect as the "poison" and "sacrifice" images that dominate her relationship with Jane Fairfax: in all cases the hackneyed sentimentality first exposes Emma's romantic shallowness and is later modified to heighten the emotional drama of her very real contrition. It is noteworthy, too, that images relating to herself and Mr. Knightley are similar to the Jane Fairfax sequence in that the ambiguous synthesis of satire and emotion eventually gives way to less hackneyed, and more unequivocably affective, figures. Accordingly, the imagery reflects Emma's increasing mortification as she sits through the

5. Compare Henry Mackenzie's "agony of despair" in *The Man of Feeling*, Oxford English Novels, ed. Brian Vickers (London, 1967), 59. This appears to be one of Jane Austen's favorite metaphors. A variant occurs in *Persuasion* with appropriate overtones of intense, physical pain. After Louisa Musgrove's accident, Captain Wentworth bends over her mostrate form "in an agony of silence" (p. 109). On other occasions Jane Austen uses the structure to ridicule emotional excesses: Marianne Dashwood joins Mrs. Dashwood in an "agony of grief" after Marianne's father's death, and she sits in "an agony of impatience" while awaiting a reunion with Willoughby (*Sense and Sensibility*, pp. 7, 176). Sometimes the emotive connotations of the figure are applied to unlikely personalities—with satirically incongruous effects. Note, for example, Fanny Dashwood's "agonies of sensibility" after the news of Robert Ferrars' marriage (*Sense and Sensibility*, p. 371), and Mrs. Bennet's "agony of ill humour" (*Pride and Prejudice*, p. 130).

interview in which Harriet Smith reveals her new love. Emma now chastises the blindness and madness that "had led her on" to encourage Harriet's attachment to Mr. Knightley. The error has "struck her with dreadful force," but she resolves, in spite of all, to be kind to her friend: "Harriet had done nothing to forfeit the regard and interest which had been so voluntarily formed and maintained" (p. 408). But despite her resolution, she can barely endure Harriet's story: "Her mind was in all the perturbation that such a development of self, such a burst of threatening evil, such a confusion of sudden and perplexing emotions must create" (p. 409). Finally, the reflections which follow Harriet's visit are even more mortifying, particularly when Emma contemplates Mr. Knightley's inevitable humiliation as Harriet's husband. It would be "a union to distance every wonder of the kind." The attachment of Jane and Frank Churchill "became commonplace, threadbare, stale in the comparison, exciting no surprise, presenting no disparity, affording nothing to be said or thought.—Mr. Knightley and Harriet Smith!—Such an elevation on her side! Such a debasement on his!—It was horrible to Emma to think how it must sink him in the general opinion" (p. 413). It is also significant that Mr. Knightley's "future" disgrace is described by the "sinking" metaphor, for this echoes the very figure that expresses Emma's present humiliation: Harriet's confession contains "a substance to sink" Emma's spirit (p. 409). In other words, Emma's personal sensations are being linked metaphorically to Mr. Knightley's real, or imagined, experience. Like the conscience-stricken images that describe Jane Fairfax's "agony" of mind, the present "sinking" metaphor emphasizes the fusion of Emma's emotional experiences with those of persons around her. In both cases this fusion dramatizes Emma's progression from self-centered isolation to a new, human identification with others through love and sympathy. The gradual evolution of her metaphoric style from absurd sentimentality to ambiguous connotations, and finally to unequivocal emotiveness, therefore corresponds with Emma's fundamental education throughout the novel. The subtle shifts in the satiric or emotive emphasis of imagery have become unobstrusive pointers to the moral developments within the novel.

In *Pride and Prejudice* this fundamental relationship between imagery and basic themes is more overt. The Hunsford quarrel between Elizabeth and Darcy illustrates Jane Austen's ability to synthesize divergent metaphoric patterns, and to integrate them with the emotional and moral tensions of her characters. It is noticeable that in the Hunsford scene the figurative styles of both Darcy and Elizabeth express their aroused passions and simultaneously accentuate their long-standing prejudices. Darcy couches his proposal in terms of a reluctant surrender to a debasing passion: he has "struggled," but his feelings will "not be repressed." And he has been inhibited by "the family obstacles, which judgment had always opposed to inclination" (p. 189). The images which accompany Elizabeth's refusal are equally passionate and revealing: Darcy is charged with being the principal means of "dividing" Jane and Bingley, "and of exposing one to the censure of the world for caprice and instability, the other to its derision for disappointed hopes, and involving them both in misery of the acutest kind" (p. 191). He has "reduced" Wickham to poverty by withholding the advantages designed for him (p. 192). Her charges are matched in intensity and metaphoric emphasis by Darcy's rejoinder: "My faults, according to this calculation, are heavy indeed! But perhaps . . . these offences might have been overlooked, had not your pride been hurt by my honest confession of the scruples that had long prevented my forming any serious design. Those bitter accusations might have been suppressed, had I with greater policy concealed my struggles, and flattered you into the belief of my being impelled by unqualified, unalloyed inclination; by reason, by reflection, by every thing. But disguise of every sort is my abhorence" (p. 192). Finally, there is the climactic conclusion provided by Elizabeth's graphic account of her reaction to Darcy's personality: his manners "were such as to form that ground-work of disapprobation, on which succeeding events have built so immoveable a dislike" (p. 193).

Elizabeth's "building" metaphor is an unconscious but telling extension of the motif introduced by Darcy's phrase, "serious design." Their deep divisions have been ironically contradicted by the fact that they have some of their figurative patterns in common. And on a more incisive note, the creative and harmonious connotations of "design" and "built" are pitted against the destructive bitterness of the quarrel. But, to complete the chain of ironic implications, the positive undertones of these images are prophetic of the harmony that ultimately evolves from the present confrontation. In short, Jane Austen has invested one recurrent image with all the subtle variations of feeling (past, present, and future) which impinge on the quarrel. In retrospect, too, the images of expression and repression which dominate Darcy's proposal (and rejoinder) assume a wider significance that goes beyond his immediate self-conflicts. For these figures are really clues to the psychological development of the scene. After Darcy's proposal, the exchanges are marked by the struggle, on both sides, to subdue their passions, to impose some order on language and countenance. Before replying to Darcy's offer, Elizabeth tries "to compose herself to answer him with patience," and despite obvious anger, Darcy is "struggling for the appearance of composure" (pp. 189, 190). But as their mutual aggravations increase, the compulsion to express pent-up emotions supersedes the earlier attempts to follow what Elizabeth calls the "established mode" of polite custom (p. 190). Hence the breakdown of repressive self-control is dramatized by the "quick steps" that accompany Darcy's rebuttal, the "start" with which he receives her charge of ungentlemanly conduct, and by the directness of their final recriminations. It is also pertinent that apart from the opening sentences of Darcy's proposal, the first segment of the interview is presented in reported speech, and this rapidly gives way to the direct statements of the passionate exchanges that follow.

What these metaphoric structures demonstrate on the whole is the fact that the emotional conflicts of the Hunsford encounter are really microcosmic. In the evolving relationships of *Pride and Prejudice* both Elizabeth and Darcy gradually discard the polite decorum that masks their earlier antagonism. Then the frank exchanges at Hunsford provide the emotional catalyst for the reshaping of their respective prejudices. This eventual revaluation is, of course, most dramatic in the case of Elizabeth who is obliged to recant irrational judgments that were made at a time when she "courted" prepossession and when she had "driven" reason away (p. 208). Considered, then, in the wider context of the novel's themes, the images of Darcy's Hunsford proposal typify the discrete role of figurative language in Jane Austen's fiction. In conveying Darcy's prejudice and passion the images do not simply achieve Jane Austen's usual synthesis of the satiric and the affective. They also establish an organic relationship between the manner of Darcy's proposal and the general development of Jane Austen's narrative structure. Darcy's style on this occasion reflects, in turn, his internal conflicts, the dramatic crisis of the Hunsford quarrel, and finally, the evolving relationships that are central to the novel's themes. Once again, the individual's figurative style is relevant not only to the ironies of the human personality but also to the unfolding of theme and structure.

This kind of complexity demonstrates that imagery is a versatile structure in the self-expression of Jane Austen's characters. Its effects are derived, not from the alleged prejudices of the novelist herself, but from the expressive relationship of each figure to the individual's judgment or emotional values, and to the thematic implications of his moral experience. The versatility that is so noticeable in the case of individual styles also applies to Jane Austen's narrative commentary. Her metaphoric analysis of character and situation communicates a wide range of emotions as well as ironic insights. And once again we can see how each metaphoric structure is integrated with general themes, as well as with immediate contexts. In *Sanditon* the striking figurative patterns

of the narrator's more detailed comments reflect the kind of idio-
syncratic exaggerations that Jane Austen satirizes in the enthu-
siasts. Enthusiasm is a pervasive sickness in *Sanditon*—from Sir
Edward's literary and sexual fantasies to Mr. Parker's self-
appointed role of economic "Projector," and the "spirit of restless
activity" that dominates the sisters of the latter. The disease mani-
fests itself in the energetic hypochondria of the Parker sisters and
in the ironic symbolism of Sanditon itself as a health-resort.
Appropriately, therefore, Jane Austen's narrative comments are
frequently couched in images of ill health. Not even the "sober-
minded" Charlotte Heywood is immune to this kind of commentary. Hence after a short period of Sir Edward's agreeable
attentions she realizes that his real target is Clara Brereton—a discovery that "gave an hasty turn to Charlotte's fancy, cured her of
her halfhour's fever, & placed her in a more capable state of judg-
ing . . . of *how* agreable he had actually been" (*Minor Works*, p.
395). Even peripheral characters like the Beauforts are linked to
the sickness imagery. Thus their snobbish satisfaction with "the
Circle in which they moved" elicits the narrator's caustic observation: "to the prevalence of which rototory Motion, is perhaps to be
attributed the Giddiness & false steps of many" (p. 422). As for
Sir Edward Denham, his problem lies in his being "very full of
some Feelings or other, & very much addicted to the newest-
fashioned hard words" (p. 398). And in a more detailed analysis
of his character Jane Austen combines the prevailing disease motif
with a series of spectacular images that satirically echo Sir Edward's extravagant style. He has "read more sentimental Novels
than agreed with him." His fancy had been "early caught" by
Richardson's most exceptionable scenes, while "such Authors as
have since appeared to tread in Richardson's steps" had "occupied
the greater part of his literary hours, & formed his Character." The
villain's graces, spirit, sagacity and perseverance "outweighed"
all his absurdities and atrocities with Sir Edward: "With him
such Conduct was Genius, Fire & Feeling.—It interested & in-
flamed him" (p. 404).

The sick enthusiasm of the Parkers is due to excessively strong imaginations and "quick" feelings. While Mr. Parker "found vent for his superfluity of sensation as a Projector, the Sisters were perhaps driven to dissipate theirs in the invention of odd complaints" (p. 412). The hypochondria of the sisters takes the form of a neurotic delicacy that is often belied by another enthusiastic symptom—their zeal for being useful. Accordingly, Jane Austen occasionally exposes the sham of their "delicate" constitutions by envisioning their zealous schemes as vigorous physical activity. Thus the reference to nervous complaints is countered by the energetic connotations of "driven," "dissipate," and (the projector-scientists') "invention." Diana is subjected to similar irony during her attempts to recruit Mrs. Griffiths as a Sanditon guest. Her activities are envisaged as a vigorous military campaign, complete with reconnaisance and trenches: she had sent "a few polite lines of Information to Mrs. G. herself—time not allowing for the circuitous train of intelligence which had been hitherto kept up,—and she was now regaling in the delight of opening the first Trenches of an acquaintance with such a powerful discharge of unexpected Obligation" (p. 414).

Jane Austen's figurative commentary is just as faithful to the subtle tensions and emotional fluctuations of the other fragment, *The Watsons.* The apprehension with which Emma Watson begins her visit to the Edwards family is appropriately described in violent terms suggesting physical agitation and movement: she feels "the awkwardness of rushing into Intimacy on so slight an acquaintance." But during the actual visit the turbulent suggestions of this image are replaced by the unobtrusive and conventional figures that describe the "formal Civility" of the occasion: "some very, very languid remarks on the probable Brilliancy of the Ball, were all that broke at intervals a silence of half an hour." Then "Mr. Edwards proceeded to relate every other little article of news which his morning's lounge had supplied him with" (*Minor Works*, pp. 322, 323). On the other hand, the highest concentration of dramatic images occurs in the analysis of Emma's increasing sense of total isolation within her family. This, the most intense moment of the fragment, is far removed from the bland politeness of the Edwards' drawing room, and Emma's unhappiness is aptly described in a succession of highly affective and complex images. In her father's room "Emma was at peace from the dreadful mortifications of unequal Society, & family Discord —from the immediate endurance of Hard-hearted prosperity, low-minded Conceit, & wrong-headed folly, engrafted on an untoward Disposition." For the time being she has "ceased to be tortured" by these mortifications, and reading helps to produce "the dissipation of unpleasant ideas." Once she was the favorite of an uncle "who had formed her mind." But now she was "a burden" on her family, "an addition in an House, already overstocked," and surrounded by inferior minds. The change "had been such as might have plunged weak spirits in Despondence" (pp. 361–62).

This kind of suggestive commentary has an equally fundamental role in the crucial moments of the major novels.[6] Catherine Morland's earlier naiveté feeds on the menacing gloom of the Gothic novel, and on the sinister atmosphere that she attributes to Northanger Abbey and its owner. But this suggestive darkness is dispelled, together with her Gothic illusions, as Catherine's insights mature. Thus the description of the late Mrs. Tilney's room emphasizes all the gaiety and light which are so contrary to Catherine's foreboding and which dramatize her new perceptions. The sunlight "gaily poured" through the windows, and after her initial shock a "succeeding ray of common sense added some bitter emotions of shame" (*Northanger Abbey*, p. 193). Similarly, when she is rudely awakened to General Tilney's real character, the analysis of her new awareness echoes both the torment of present discovery and the insubstantiality of earlier, Gothic misjudgments. Her bedroom "in which her disturbed imagination had tormented her on her first arrival, was again the scene of agitated spirits and unquiet slumbers." This present "inquietude" has more "sub-

6. Compare Karl Kroeber, *Styles in Fictional Structure: The Art of Jane Austen, Charlotte Bronte, George Eliot* (Princeton, 1971), 64–84.

stance;" her anxiety "had foundation in fact, her fears in probability" (p. 227).

The complex interrelationship of themes in *Sense and Sensibility* is reflected in the metaphoric patterns which form the basis of the narrator's judgments. Mrs. Dashwood's excessive sensibility requires hyperboles: "in sorrow she must be equally carried away by her fancy, and as far beyond consolation as in pleasure she was beyond alloy" (p. 8). The equally deep emotions of Edward Ferrars and Elinor also call for affective imagery, but being more controlled the feelings of each are counterbalanced by an antithetical awareness. The narrator's metaphorical comments are shaped accordingly. Elinor, for example, is assured by John Dashwood that although she is still unsuitable to be Mrs. Ferrars' daughter-in-law, she is a lesser evil when compared with Lucy Steele. Her reactions to this backhanded compliment are mixed. She has heard enough "if not to gratify her vanity and raise her self-importance, to agitate her nerves and fill her mind" (p. 297). Even Edward's ecstasy after his engagement to Elinor must be qualified by recollections of a past indiscretion. "He had more than the ordinary triumph of accepted love to swell his heart, and raise his spirits. He was released without any reproach to himself, from an entanglement which had long formed his misery" and he was now "elevated at once" to security with another woman (p. 361). In one sense the restrictive motif of the entanglement metaphor simultaneously accentuates and qualifies Edward's happiness. But in keeping with Jane Austen's ironic interweaving of themes, this metaphoric analysis of Edward's true sensibility also echoes and contradicts the imagery of freedom that previously describes John Dashwood's hypocritical pretensions to real feeling. In contemplating an invitation to his sisters John really feels that this was "an attention, which the delicacy of his conscience pointed out to be requisite to its complete enfranchisement from his promise to his father" (p. 253).

This organic relationship between figurative commentary and narrative structure also obtains in the case of the very elaborate

metaphor which announces Edward's reconciliation with his
mother. The figurative comedy of death and rebirth is a macabre
means of satirizing Mrs. Ferrars' repulsive and totally unfeeling
personality:

> Her family had of late been exceedingly fluctuating. For many years
> of her life she had had two sons; but the crime and annihilation of
> Edward a few weeks ago had robbed her of one; the similar anni-
> hilation of Robert had left her for a fortnight without any; and now,
> by the resuscitation of Edward she had one again.
> In spite of his being allowed once more to live, however, he did not
> feel the continuance of his existence secure, till he had revealed his
> present engagement; for the publication of that circumstance, he
> feared, might give a sudden turn to his constitution, and carry him
> off as rapidly as before. (p. 373)

But the image is also integrated with the structural development
of the novel, for it recalls the somber themes of death and inheritance which underlie the narrative from the opening paragraph.
Moreover, the Dashwood family fortunes are also influenced
throughout by the formidable Mrs. Ferrars herself, for Edward's
status (and consequently Elinor's) is subject to her whims. Hence
the "resuscitation" image is linked to another figure which mockingly invests Mrs. Ferrars with royal power. Edward "was admitted to her presence, and pronounced to be again her son," then
"after such an ungracious delay as she owed to her own dignity
... she issued her decree of consent to the marriage of Edward and
Elinor" (pp. 373-74).

In *Mansfield Park* the narrative commentary owes its metaphoric patterns to the ubiquitous conflict between formalized
externals and natural feelings. Note, for example, the contrast between Fanny's inner turbulence and the rigid civility of the ball
given in her honor. The "first great circle" of Sir Thomas and his
guests is unendurable, and the sight of so many people "threw her
back into herself." But with the entrance of the Crawfords and
the Grants civil restraint is replaced by uninhibited sincerity, the
stiff correctness of a geometrical pattern ("great circle") is dis-
pensed with: "The stiffness of the meeting soon gave way before

their popular intimacies" (p. 273). Elsewhere this metaphoric contrast between order and energy is applied on a more satiric level. When the bustling improprieties of the theatricals disrupt the tranquillity of Mansfield Park, the analysis of personal motives metaphorically suggests frenzied physical activity. Yates arrives "on the wings of disappointment, and with his head full of acting." He arouses interest in *Lover's Vows* because of "an itch for acting so strong among young people" (p. 121). And the scheme attracts Henry Crawford "to whom, in all the riot of his gratifications, it was yet an untasted pleasure" (p. 123). Edmund is "driven" by "the force of selfish inclinations" to participate after having "descended from that moral elevation which he had maintained before" (p. 158).

One of the recurrent ironies in Emma Woodhouse's experiences is the fact that her fertile imagination is often surpassed by the realities to which she blinds herself. Accordingly, the narrator's analysis of Emma's actual world occasionally incorporates spectacular patterns of imagery which dramatize the shock values of reality. The collapse of her schemes for Mr. Elton's marriage, and the humiliation occasioned by the vicar's proposal, leave them both in a "state of swelling resentment, and mutually deep mortification." Their "straight-forward emotions left no room for the little zigzags of embarrassment" (*Emma*, p. 132). And when Mr. Weston's indiscriminate hospitality forces Emma to share the Box Hill picnic with the Eltons, "the forbearance of her outward submission left a heavy arrear due of secret severity in her reflections on the unmanageable good-will of Mr. Weston's temper" (p. 353). The contrast between Emma's dreamworld and reality is also dramatized by the description of Mrs. Goddard's school. It is a place where "a reasonable quantity of accomplishments were sold at a reasonable price, and where girls might be sent to be out of the way and scramble themselves into a little education." And this must be distinguished from an "elegant" seminary which represents the kind of artificiality and grotesquerie that characterize Emma's daydreams. These seminaries "combine liberal acquirements with elegant morality upon new principles and new systems;" and they are simply places where "young ladies for enormous pay might be screwed out of health and into vanity" (pp. 21–22).

Even the expected visit of the Sucklings is linked metaphorically to the main themes of the novel. The Sucklings share Mrs. Elton's overwhelming vulgarity, and Jane Austen emphasizes this by exploiting the figurative possibilities of their highly suggestive surname. In the process the Sucklings are reduced to the level of their own marketable commodities: "After being long fed with hopes of a speedy visit from Mr. and Mrs. Suckling," the people of Highbury are disappointed by a postponement. "No such importation of novelties could enrich their intellectual stores at present," and so they are restricted to other topics in "the daily interchange of news" (p. 352). The commerce motif also satirizes Emma's egocentricity, for it joins Mrs. Goddard's school and "the yeomanry" in emphasizing all the mundane realities which Emma futilely tries to exclude from her narrow world. Even the peripheral or absent characters like the Sucklings have therefore been unified with the exploration of Emma's consciousness. And what is also significant, this unity has been effected through the network of multiple implications that Jane Austen invariably constructs with her figurative style.

CHAPTER IV

Symbolism

ON THE WHOLE, symbolism is more recurrent in *Mansfield Park*, *Emma*, and *Persuasion* than it is in her earlier works. But she does experiment with symbolic structures in the juvenilia and early novels. Symbolic names, for example, seem to have aroused her interest in *Frederic & Elfrida* where the farcical nonsense of character and situation is reflected in the description of the locale as the "sweet village" of Crankhumdunberry. This kind of phonetic suggestiveness also applies to the village of Pammydiddle, for the infantile name confirms the pettiness and irrationality that Jane Austen depicts in *Jack & Alice*. One could, presumably, make a case for symbolic meanings in several of the names that Jane Austen uses in the earlier half of her career, and it is also clear that in the last three novels she expands upon the kind of complex or overt symbols exemplified by the place-names of the juvenilia. In the mature works she also prefers forms that derive their symbolic significance from a variety of sources—phonetic structure and historical or social usages—rather than from the more familiar labels of "morality" and "humours" characters. In *Emma* names like "Suckling" and "Bragge" do belong to the latter category. But even here Jane Austen devises a subtle modification of her own, for the real significance of the names is applied obliquely. Since neither of the characters actually appears, the total effect of the labels is directed at Mrs. Elton, whose disagreeable personality is the real target of this satiric symbolism.

"Emma" itself accords with Jane Austen's interest in the phonetic symbolism of names. Mr. Weston's conundrum on the name at the Box Hill picnic is really Jane Austen's way of emphasizing the tonal qualities which seem to associate "Emma" with the quintessence of perfection. The novelist's personal comments on the symbolic mystique of names actually include the comic lament, "There were only 4 dances, & it went to my heart that the Mrs. Lances (one of them too named Emma!) should have partners only for two" (*Letters*, p. 236).[1] Emma Woodhouse has therefore been given a first name that is a direct contradiction of her glaring imperfections, a contrast that is effectively, albeit unconsciously, demonstrated by Mr. Weston at Box Hill:

"I doubt it's being very clever myself," said Mr. Weston. "It is too much a matter of fact, but here it is.—What two letters of the alphabet are there, that express perfection?"

"What two letters!—express perfection! I am sure I do not know."

"Ah! you will never guess. You, (to Emma), I am certain, will never guess.—I will tell you.—M. and A.—Em—ma.—Do you understand?"

Understanding and gratification came together. It might be a very indifferent piece of wit; but Emma found a great deal to laugh at and enjoy in it—and so did Frank and Harriet.—It did not seem to touch the rest of the party equally; some looked very stupid about it, and Mr. Knightley gravely said,

"This explains the sort of clever thing that is wanted, and Mr. Weston has done very well for himself; but he must have knocked up every body else. *Perfection* should not have come quite so soon." (p. 371)

The ironic symbolism of Emma's name seems to be a further development of the strategy that Jane Austen employs in *Mansfield Park*. Henry Crawford's character, for example, belies those

1. On the basis of the *Letters* it also appears that Jane Austen associates "Charlcombe" with "a little green Valley" (p. 64), and "Newton Priors" with the comical and the absurd (pp. 402, 420).

ideal qualities which Jane Austen associates with the sound, "Henry"—in which she may very well have been influenced by her fondness for her brother Henry Austen (*Letters*, p. 348). The historical or social connotations of names are also pertinent to the running feud between Mary Crawford and Fanny Price. Mary's sprightly sense of the graceful and the lively abhors "the sound of Mr. *Edmund* Bertram" because it is "so formal, so pitiful, so younger-brother-like" (*Mansfield Park*, p. 211). And in this respect her terms of reference are quite similar to Jane Austen's, for the novelist's personal correspondence spurns "Mr. Edmund," together with "Mr. John" and "Mr. Thomas" (*Letters*, p. 348). But, as usual, Mary's attractive witticism is flawed by a mercenary interest. "Mr. Edmund" is an unwelcome reminder of the younger brother's lowly economic status. On the other hand, Fanny is true to type in regarding the name as a symbol of feeling and morality. While Mary looks at the familial connotations of the name, Fanny emphasizes the ethical values of its historical symbolism: "To me, the sound of *Mr.* Bertram is so cold and nothing-meaning—so entirely without warmth or character!—It just stands for a gentleman, and that's all. But there is nobleness in the name of Edmund. It is a name of heroism and renown—of kings, princes, and knights; and seems to breathe the spirit of chivalry and warm affections" (*Mansfield Park*, p. 211).[2]

The kind of chivalric significance that Fanny solemnly attributes to "Edmund" is not entirely new in Jane Austen's fiction. The *Letters* confirm the novelist's personal association of nobility with "Lesley" (p. 400), and in the juvenilia *Lesley Castle* ironically juxtaposes these noble overtones and the prosaic (sometimes ignoble) experiences of the dim-witted and the selfish. But it is in *Persuasion* that we find the most sustained use of a chivalric name for the development of intensely ironic conflicts. The Elliot name is the essence of aristocratic breeding, and its pedigree has

2. Donald J. Greene has noted the recurrence of historically aristocratic names in Jane Austen's fiction. "Jane Austen and the Peerage," in *Jane Austen, A Collection of Critical Essays*, ed. Ian Watt (Englewood Cliffs, N.J., 1963), 154–65.

been appropriately enshrined in the *Baronetage* by Sir Walter.
The "noble" implications of the name are dual, opposing Anne's
quiet and unassuming gentility to Sir Walter's repulsive bravado.
Moreover, the specious grandeur of the class-conscious Sir Walter
is undercut by the real worth and substance of the self-made
Captain Wentworth. Similarly, Sir Walter's pretensions are nulli-
fied by the heroic stature accorded to the bearer of the "lowest"
and most "common" of names—Mrs. Smith. And, as usual, Jane
Austen is at pains to draw our attention to the expressive or communicative process that she is describing. Ironically, it is through
Sir Walter that this emphasis is made. He is characteristically contemptuous of Mrs. Smith's name and of all its "low" associations,
and contrasts them with the grand implications of "Elliot":

"A Mrs. Smith. A widow Mrs. Smith,—and who was her husband?
One of the five thousand Mr. Smiths whose names are to be met with
every where. And what is her attraction? That she is old and sickly.—
Upon my word, Miss Anne Elliot, you have the most extraordinary
taste! Every thing that revolts other people, low company, paltry
rooms, foul air, disgusting associations are inviting to you.... A widow
Mrs. Smith, lodging in Westgate-buildings!—A poor widow, barely
able to live, between thirty and forty—a mere Mrs. Smith, an every day
Mrs. Smith, of all people and all names in the world, to be the chosen
friend of Miss Anne Elliot, and to be preferred by her, to her own
family connections among the nobility of England and Ireland! Mrs.
Smith, such a name!" (pp. 157–58)

But in spite of Sir Walter's facile sneers the "every day" Mrs.
Smith embodies what Jane Austen describes as "the choicest gift
of Heaven"—"elasticity of mind" and the "power of turning
readily from evil to good" (p. 154).

Sir Walter's consciousness of these names as symbols is a typical
feature of Jane Austen's narrative use of labels. In using Sir Walter
to stress the referential possibilities of "Elliot" and "Smith," the
novelist continues her usual strategy of calling the mechanics of
any given structure—in this instance, name symbolism—to the
reader's attention. And in so doing Jane Austen has internalized
the symbolic process. Characters like Sir Walter, Fanny Price, and

Mary Crawford consciously interpret and react to the significance of names; and their evaluation, or misinterpretation, of each symbol is symptomatic of personal morality and feeling. In other words, the symbolic communication of meaning to the reader has become, simultaneously, a moral experience for each individual in Jane Austen's fictive world. And when we turn from the name symbols to other representative structures it is still possible to detect this fusion of the individual's consciousness with the mechanics of communication. Two of the few symbols in the earlier works are illustrative. In the youthful fragment *Catharine* the bower represents Catharine's isolation. It serves as the repository of her childhood memories and compensates for the loneliness of the present by linking her with absent friends. And what is most significant, the bower's role as a symbol has been shaped by Catharine's consciousness, by her "warm" imagination and by her emotional needs:

Besides these antidotes against every disappointment, and consolations under them, she had another, which afforded her constant releif in all her misfortunes, and that was a fine shady Bower, the work of her own infantine Labours assisted by those of two young Companions who had resided in the same village—. To this Bower, which terminated a very pleasant and retired walk in her Aunt's Garden, she always wandered whenever anything disturbed her, and it possessed such a charm over her senses, as constantly to tranquillize her mind & quiet her spirits—Solitude & reflection might perhaps have had the same effect in her Bed Chamber, yet Habit had so strengthened the idea which Fancy had first suggested, that such a thought never occurred to Kitty who was firmly persuaded that her Bower alone could restore her to herself. Her imagination was warm, and in her Freindships, as well as in the whole tenure of her Mind, she was enthousiastic. This beloved Bower had been the united work of herself and two amiable Girls, for whom since her earliest Years, she had felt the tenderest regard. . . . In those days of happy Childhood, now so often regretted by Kitty this arbour had been formed, and separated perhaps for ever from these dear freinds, it encouraged more than any other place the tender and Melancholy recollections of hours rendered pleasant by *them*, at one [*sic*] so sorrowful yet so soothing! (*Minor Works*, pp. 193–94)

In effect, the bower has become the center for two ironically juxtaposed arguments. For in stressing the bower as the symbol of her loneliness and past happiness, Catharine inadvertently projects it as the emblem of the enthusiastic imagination which has contributed to her isolation from the everyday world. And in so doing, she has endowed it with all the masochistic impulses represented by her craving for "Melancholy recollections." Catharine sets out to define the nature of the dominant symbol on a basis that will engage the sympathies of the reader; but Jane Austen has modified her heroine's exercise in symbology in order to suggest additional connotations that Catharine herself would not consciously or willingly communicate to the reader. Moreover, this ironic exploitation of her "internal" symbolist anticipates Jane Austen's achievement in *Northanger Abbey* where we find the second major symbol of the early works. In one sense the Gothic style of Northanger Abbey is an architectural representation of Catherine Morland's fantasies. The building's imposing size becomes a physical projection of the overwhelming Gothic presentiments that Catherine brings to the abbey itself. However, the building is comparable to the bower in *Catharine* in that, here too, the symbolic suggestions are not confined to the conscious motives, or rationalization, of the fictive symbolist. Hence, in this case the real importance of Northanger Abbey includes, but is not limited to, the "Gothic" expressiveness which Catherine attributes to it. It is also significant by virtue of the various attitudes that seize upon it as an outlet for expression, be it Catherine Morland's heightened expectations of Gothic horror, or General Tilney's unctuous self-congratulations. The abbey has been endowed with its own individual personality, and the primary function of this identity lies in its stubborn resistance to the patterns of Gothic meaning that Catherine strives to force upon it. Simultaneously, the aura of imaginative splendor which overexcites Catherine serves to rebuff the crass materialism of the building's owner. In effect, Northanger Abbey is a satiric projection of the highly subjective nature of the symbolic process itself. Particularly in the cases of Catherine and General Tilney, it is emblematic of the way in which means of communication like symbols can also be psychological and moral experiences.

Such clearly defined and complex symbols are rare in Jane Austen's early fiction. It is in *Mansfield Park* that her use of symbolism really begins to fulfill the promise of *Northanger Abbey*. Thus the dominance of the abbey in the earlier novel is comparable with the prominence of the theatre in the narrative structure and personal relationships of *Mansfield Park*. The most obvious of these theatre symbols is, of course, *Lovers' Vows*, for the personalities of the amateur actors are dramatized by their respective parts in the play. Maria's performance as Agatha emphasizes the sexuality that leads to Agatha's initial downfall and to the eventual disgrace of the future Mrs. Rushworth. Yates's personality is frequently associated with his theatrical role, even off-stage. Mary Crawford, in particular, invariably refers to him as Baron Wildenhaim—a significant connection in view of the moral rehabilitation experienced by both Yates and the baron. The relationship between Edmund Bertram and Mary is closely paralleled by their performances as Anhalt and Amelia, respectively. Like his *Lovers' Vows* counterpart, Edmund explains the moral principles of marriage, but the symbolism is ironic here, for Mary rejects Edmund's values while Amelia eagerly accepts Anhalt's. Rushworth's role as Count Cassel is also ironic. Edmund and Rushworth are both defective as prospective sons-in-law, but while Baron Wildenhaim rejects Cassel's suit, the equally perceptive but less scrupulous Sir Thomas fails to intervene in Maria's marriage.

These symbolical relationships are further underlined by the close integration of the play and Jane Austen's narrative during the theatricals. For the rehearsals constitute a distinct drama in which the roles and plot of *Lovers' Vows* are used to camouflage the very real emotional tensions at Mansfield Park. First, the casting of roles exposes the hidden conflicts and intrigues of the group, particularly the rivalry between Maria and Julia for the attentions of Henry Crawford. Secondly, as the rehearsals get underway, the ulterior motives of the "actors" become more obvious despite their theatrical masks. Fanny Price who represents the audience notes that Maria acts "too well" in her intimate role with Henry who is "considerably the best actor of all" (p. 165). She is also chagrined to observe Mary Crawford's obvious pleasure in the ambiguous relationship that the latter now experiences with Edmund, as a result of the *Lovers' Vows* roles. Altogether, the emblematic significance of the play is shaped by the impulse that Jane Austen explores in *Catherine* and *Northanger Abbey*—the individual's instinct to symbologize, to project objects or incidents as the embodiment of his feelings or status. And in this instance the symbolist's professed equations are undercut by the far more revealing implications of ulterior motives. Hence the keen rivalry for the role of Agatha is ostensibly sparked by the usual identification of the actor's ego with the "leading" role: Agatha is a choice part and is attractive for reasons of prestige. But, as we have seen, the real motives of the Bertram sisters are far more questionable; and the specious equations based on questions of prestige are eventually subordinated to the far more real symbolism that Jane Austen derives from the sexual links between Agatha and the Bertram sisters.

Finally, the drama of the rehearsals is climaxed by Sir Thomas' unexpected return home. Both the new and old emotional tensions at Mansfield Park are intensified by the skillful postponement of the inevitable. Sir Thomas relaxes with his family before repairing to his "own dear room" (p. 181) which has been converted to a theatre in his absence. And the suspense is heightened by the maddeningly effective irrelevancies of Lady Bertram's unlikely raptures (she actually feels "how dreadfully she must have missed" him) and of Mrs. Norris' bustling interference: "Sure, my dear Sir Thomas, a basin of soup would be a much better thing for you than tea. Do have a basin of soup" (pp. 179, 180). Meanwhile, an oblivious Yates playing Baron Wildenhaim rants away in the theatre, and a flippant remark, made earlier by Mary Crawford, now assumes an ominous note: "Could Sir Thomas

look in upon us just now, he would bless himself, for we are re-
hearsing all over the house. Yates is storming away in the dining
room" (p. 169). When Sir Thomas does enter the theatre the
dramatic interruption of Yates's solitary rehearsal emphasizes the
kind of human drama that the theatricals symbolize in the novel.
For this scene, the very last in the drama of the rehearsals, ironically projects the interchangeability of theatrical and social identities—the very kind of reciprocity which the amateur actors use
as the basis of their selfish symbolic equations and which Jane
Austen simultaneously exploits to satirize the real connections
between *Lovers' Vows* and the personalities at Mansfield Park.
Sir Thomas' astonished reaction befits his unwitting stage debut,
his "making part of a ridiculous exhibition in the midst of theatrical nonsense" (p. 183). And Yates's shock can be adequately expressed only with what is for once a genuine histrionic gesture:

At the very moment of Yates perceiving Sir Thomas, and giving perhaps the very best start he had ever given in the whole course of his
rehearsals, Tom Bertram entered at the other end of the room; and
never had he found greater difficulty in keeping his countenance. His
father's looks of solemnity and amazement on this his first appearance on any stage, and the gradual metamorphosis of the impassioned
Baron Wildenhaim into the well-bred and easy Mr. Yates, making his
bow and apology to Sir Thomas Bertram, was such an exhibition,
such a piece of true acting as he would not have lost upon any account. It would be the last—in all probability the last scene on that
stage; but he was sure there could not be a finer. The house would
close with the greatest eclat. (pp. 182–83)

In this piece of "true acting" it becomes clear that the symbolism
of the theatricals goes beyond the straightforward equations of the
Lovers' Vows roles with the aspiring actors, and beyond the representation of the human drama at Mansfield Park. What is
also involved here is the symbolical function of acting itself. For
in the society of Mansfield Park acting is at once representational
and factual. It simultaneously embodies the sincere and the pretended. Herein lies the clue to the psychological effectiveness with
which Jane Austen establishes the moral equation of her own char-

acters with the *Lovers' Vows* personalities. The moral ambiguities inherent in acting as such become a vehicle for the examination of all the contradictions, double motives, and deceptions of the theatricals. This partly accounts, too, for the controversial nature of the theatricals themselves. As Lionel Trilling argues, the staging of the play becomes suspect because of "a traditional, almost primitive feeling" about acting. There is the fear that the actor's personality may be affected by his fictional role, that "the impersonation of any other self will diminish the integrity of the real self."[3] In this connection, it is important to note that many of the arguments during the rehearsals center on the individual's specious application of the line of reasoning outlined by Trilling. According to Yates, for example, the role of the cottager's wife is socially unsuited for Julia Bertram: it is a "trivial, paltry, insignificant part" which would be insulting to Julia and which had been fit only for the governess at Ecclesford (p. 134).

The ambiguities symbolized by acting are particularly significant in Henry Crawford's case: they emphasize the strong combination of sincerity and impersonation that forms his character. His role as Frederick in *Lovers' Vows* is typical. On one level the intimacy with Maria Bertram is simulated to meet the requirements of the Agatha-Frederick plot; but on another level, it is an actual flirtation. Similarly, though on a less reprehensible level, his attempts at reform are sincere in themselves, but they are also part of an elaborate performance aimed at Fanny. Hence his "continued attentions" adapt themselves "more and more to the gentleness and delicacy of her character" (p. 231). His "dramatic" performance as a reader, for example, demonstrates the inherent ambiguities of his relationship with Fanny. And, once again, it is noteworthy that Jane Austen prefers a highly dramatic presentation for symbolic episodes of this kind:

The King, the Queen, Buckingham, Wolsey, Cromwell, all were given in turn; for with the happiest knack, the happiest power of jumping and guessing, he could always light, at will, on the best scene, or the

3. Lionel Trilling, "*Mansfield Park*," *ibid.*, 132.

best speeches of each; and whether it were dignity or pride, or tenderness or remorse, or whatever were to be expressed, he could do it
with equal beauty.—It was truly dramatic.—His acting had first taught
Fanny what pleasure a play might give, and his reading brought all
his acting before her again; nay, perhaps with greater enjoyment, for
it came unexpectedly, and with no such drawback as she had been
used to suffer in seeing him on the stage with Miss Bertram.

Edmund watched the progress of her attention, and was amused
and gratified by seeing how she gradually slackened in the needle-
work, which, at the beginning, seemed to occupy her totally; how it
fell from her hand while she sat motionless over it—and at last, how
the eyes which had appeared so studiously to avoid him throughout
the day, were turned and fixed on Crawford, fixed on him for minutes,
fixed on him in short till the attraction drew Crawford's upon her, and
the book was closed, and the charm was broken. (p. 337)

In short, the moral ambiguities of acting are a framework for the
exposé of all the tensions and double meanings of the scene:
Fanny's half-fearful and half-fascinated approach to the theatre
in general, her gradual progression from loathing Henry to a
perceptible ambivalence; and, on Henry's side, the incipient transformation from cold-blooded rake to warm-hearted admirer.

In fact Henry's assumed roles are invariably subverted or transformed by the sincere features of his performances. His calculated
pretense of affection for Fanny is succeeded by real love. The
improprieties of his interest in Maria are too obvious to be contained by the theatrical masks of *Lovers' Vows*, and are apparent
even to the obtuse Rushworth. Later, when he feigns the revival
of that earlier interest he is trapped into an elopement with Maria.
Consequently, Henry's experiences tend to demonstrate that there
is a corollary to the proposition that the actor's self may be undermined by the process of impersonation: the role itself is shaped,
and even subverted, by the performer's ego. It is the latter, no less
than the former, thesis that provides some insight into the controversy of the theatricals. The moral ambiguities of acting arise
from the suspect motives of the actors as well as from the possible
dangers of the parts themselves. Hence the participation of the
Bertram sisters is questionable, partly because of the moral and

social issues that are enunciated, appropriately enough, by the solemn Fanny Price: "Agatha and Amelia appeared to her in their different ways so totally improper for home representation —the situation of one, and the language of the other, so unfit to be expressed by any woman of modesty, that she could hardly suppose her cousins could be aware of what they were engaging in" (p. 137). But the impropriety also arises from the questionable motives of the sisters. Their choice of roles, and the casting generally, have little to do with taste or acting ability. When Julia rejects the part of Amelia on social and moral grounds, she is simply disguising her chagrin over having lost "Agatha" (and the role's titillating fringe benefits) to Maria: "I am *not* to be Agatha, and I am sure I will do nothing else; and as to Amelia, it is of all parts in the world the most disgusting to me. I quite detest her. An odious, little, pert, unnatural, impudent girl" (p. 136). Moreover, when Edmund objects to the theatricals he emphasizes not only the "*general*" moral questions, but also external considerations which have a direct bearing on the status and attitudes of some participants—the "imprudence" of a performance during Maria's engagement, and the danger of appearing indifferent to Sir Thomas' absence from home (p. 125).

It should also be noted that when Edmund himself finally succumbs his real motives are no more histrionic than Henry's or Julia's. Like Julia's rejection of "Amelia," Edmund's objection to Charles Maddox as Mary Crawford's partner is dressed up with the usual rhetoric of propriety and moral decency: Charles Maddox's entry will be "the end of all the privacy and propriety which was talked about at first," and "the excessive intimacy which must spring from his being admitted among us in this manner, is highly objectionable, the *more* than intimacy—the familiarity. I cannot think of it with any patience—and it does appear to me an evil of such magnitude as must, *if possible*, be prevented." But as Edmund elaborates on the problems of "intimacy" and "familiarity," it becomes quite clear that "evils" of the moment have little to do with ethical judgment. They are simply the invention of Edmund's jealous possessiveness regarding Mary Crawford: "To think only of the licence which every rehearsal must tend to create. It is all very bad! Put yourself in Miss Crawford's place, Fanny. Consider what it would be to act Amelia with a stranger" (pp. 153, 154).

On the surface, it would appear that Fanny certainly does not wish to be in Miss Crawford's place—in an intimate role opposite Edmund Bertram. We have already noted her strictures against the general improprieties of theatricals and the specific defects of both "Agatha" and "Amelia." Besides, it is to her penetrating observations that we owe our most direct insight into the petty motivations behind the rehearsals: "Fanny looked on and listened, not unamused to observe the selfishness which, more or less disguised, seemed to govern them all, and wondering how it would end" (p. 131). However, the crisis created by Edmund's entry into the rehearsals reveals that not even the moralistic Fanny is entirely immune to these kinds of ulterior motives. For when the play threatens Fanny's own personal interests, when the roles of Anhalt and Amelia throw Edmund and Mary into some kind of exclusive intimacy, Fanny's *moral* considerations are subordinated to much more selfish reactions. Her jealousy of Mary Crawford is as real, and dominant, as Edmund's sexual misgivings about the effects of Charles Maddox's possible "familiarity" with Mary:

She was full of jealousy and agitation. Miss Crawford came with looks of gaiety which seemed an insult, with friendly expressions towards herself which she could hardly answer calmly. Every body around her was gay and busy, prosperous and important, each had their object of interest, their part, their dress, their favourite scene, their friends and confederates, all were finding employment in consultations and comparisons, or diversion in the playful conceits they suggested. She alone was sad and insignificant; she had no share in any thing; she might go or stay, she might be in the midst of their noise, or retreat from it to the solitude of the East room, without being seen or missed. She could almost think any thing would have been preferable to this. (pp. 159–60)

On the whole, then, Fanny's "moral" objections to the theatricals are ambiguous. She is partly sincere in her ethical strictures, but she is also an actor, using moral judgments to mask her general loneliness and her jealousy of Mary Crawford. The pious stance is, in one sense, a disguise for the emotional needs that have been accentuated by the general effusions and intimacies (proper and otherwise) of the rehearsals. And Fanny's limited but very real acting in this regard is analogous to the multiple, private performances that are embraced by the theatricals as a whole: the moral ambiguity of *Lovers' Vows* as theatre, and the suspect nature of acting itself, have been combined by Jane Austen to serve as a symbolic ambience for the reprehensible double-dealing of Henry and the Bertram sisters, Edmund's self-contradictions, and Fanny Price's inner conflicts. Neither are these kinds of ambiguities confined to the immediate issues of acting and the theatricals. They are also pertinent to the novel's portrayal of the central conflict between social form and natural feeling. Public roles, for example, become choice parts in a continuing series of theatricals that involve the opposition of divergent values and the double standards of hypocrisy. Hence the elaborate "etiquette" of Maria Bertram's wedding is really a miniature drama based on the polite impersonations of social "propriety":

It was a very proper wedding. The bride was elegantly dressed—the two bridemaids were duly inferior—her father gave her away—her mother stood with salts in her hand, expecting to be agitated—her aunt tried to cry—and the service was impressively read by Dr. Grant. Nothing could be objected to when it came under the discussion of the neighbourhood, except that the carriage which conveyed the bride and bridegroom and Julia from the church door to Sotherton, was the same chaise which Mr. Rushworth had used for a twelvemonth before. In every thing else the etiquette of the day might stand the strictest investigation. (p. 203)

The entire scene is invested with all the superficial elegance of the "proper" or formal occasion, complete with the neighborhood audience and critics. But the very nature of the personalities involved has transformed the stilted ceremony into a dramatic conflict between etiquette and hidden motives. And however flawless the decorum of the day might have been, the private feelings and inner dramas of the performers are more vulnerable to "the strictest" investigation. Hence "elegantly" is an ironic contradiction of Maria's recent improprieties with Henry Crawford. For the sake of prestige and wealth Sir Thomas has ignored signs that the present match with Rushworth is undesirable, and this betrayal of parental responsibility lends an ironic thrust to an apparently simple ceremonial detail, "her father gave her away." When our attention is drawn to the incongruity of Lady Bertram's expected agitation and to Mrs. Norris' unlikely susceptibility to tears, it becomes clear that this is more than the broadening of comic effect. It is the climactic exposure of the fact that "the etiquette of the day" is nothing but an elaborate imposture, a self-conscious adoption of specific roles by individual hypocrites.

With the subject of Dr. Grant's reading we are brought, as we so often are in *Mansfield Park*, to the fundamental issues of religion and moral principle as they are represented by the clerical order. Thus Dr. Grant's "impressive" reading, the ceremonial and public aspect of his office, must be contrasted with those personal defects which are acidly summarized from time to time by Mary Crawford. In fact the entire subject of Dr. Grant's "performance" has a direct bearing on the moral significance of acting, particularly in relation to the issues which are explored in the novel through Henry Crawford's talents as a reader. Henry characteristically regards a preacher's sermon as he would the reading of a Shakespearean play. The sermon is an elaborate and pleasing artifice which should be limited to the polished few—"to the educated; to those who were capable of estimating my composition." Altogether, Henry the preacher would be a highly accomplished actor to whom technique is everything. A "thoroughly good sermon, thoroughly well delivered, is a capital gratification. I can never hear such a one without the greatest admiration and respect, and more than half a mind to take orders and preach myself. There is

something in the eloquence of the pulpit, when it is really eloquence, which is entitled to the highest praise and honour" (p.
341). In other words, Jane Austen has combined the symbolism of
the actor with that of the priesthood in order to emphasize the
distinction between two concepts of "ordination." Henry's preoccupation with "real" eloquence, like Dr. Grant's success as an
"impressive" reader, hinges on a superficial view of the clergy:
preachers are skillful artists whose polished performances are con-
ducive to the kind of decorous ceremonial implied by a limited
interpretation of "ordination."

It is Edmund who offers a definition of the sermon which combines art with moral value:

"Even in my profession"—said Edmund with a smile—"how little
the art of reading has been studied! how little a clear manner, and
good delivery, have been attended to! I speak rather of the past, however, than the present.—There is now a spirit of improvement abroad;
but among those who were ordained twenty, thirty, forty years ago,
the larger number, to judge by their performance, must have thought
reading was reading, and preaching was preaching. It is different now.
The subject is more justly considered. It is felt that distinctness and
energy may have weight in recommending the most solid truths; and,
besides, there is more general observation and taste, a more critical
knowledge diffused, than formerly; in every congregation, there is a
larger proportion who know a little of the matter, and who can judge
and criticize." (pp. 339–40)

On one level Edmund's strictures on poor reading are comparable
not only with Henry Crawford's artistic standards, but also with
Jonathan Swift's "Letter to a Young Gentleman Lately enter'd
into Holy Orders" (1721). In decrying the awkwardness of poorly
read sermons, Swift's *Letter* goes so far as to suggest that instead
of being read sermons should be memorized and then delivered
with dramatic realism and gracefulness. But on another level
Swift's persona, a "Person of Quality," is closer to Henry Crawford in that they both tend to emphasize the artistry of delivery
almost to the exclusion of what Edmund calls "solid truths." When

Swift writes in *propria persona* there is a shift of emphasis. Thus without entirely discounting the importance of style, the sermon "Upon Sleeping in Church" comes closer to Edmund's ideal when it attacks those whose pettifogging about technique has replaced any interest in the moral functions of both sermon and preacher. Unlike Jane Austen's Henry Crawford, Swift does not view the preacher simply as a performer. The primary aim of the sermon is not artistic perfection but moral teachings: "Refinements of Stile, and Flights of Wit, as they are not properly the Business of any Preacher, so they cannot possibly be the Talents of all. In most other Discourses, Men are satisfied with sober Sense and plain Reason; and, as Understandings usually go, even that is not over frequent."[4] On the whole, therefore, Swift's treatment of style in sermons is predicated on the same distinctions that Jane Austen draws in *Mansfield Park* between the preacher as performer and the clergyman as moral agent, between Henry Crawford's one-sided preferences for "eloquence" and Edmund's combination of "distinctness" with "truths."

Altogether then, the combined symbols of acting and the priesthood explore divergent implications of "ordination," and in the process they elucidate the continuing contrast between moral conduct and superficial formality in the novel. As we have already seen, this conflict applies to the Bertram sisters' impatience of control, especially the confinement imposed by authority and moral standards. And their rebellion consequently gives rise to another symbolic structure. Hence, in the episode of the Sotherton visit the iron gate leading to the park represents the kind of external controls that both Maria and Julia find so irksome. Maria desires to pass through to the park "that their views and their plans might be more comprehensive." But the gate is locked, Rushworth has forgotten the key, and he is obliged to return to the house for it (pp. 97–98). During his reluctant absence, Maria and Henry Craw-

4. Jonathan Swift, *Prose Works*, ed. Herbert Davis (14 vols.; Oxford, 1939–62), IX, 71–72; 217.

ford engage in a dialogue that conveys all the suggestions of liberty and cheerfulness, as opposed to the restraint and authority represented by the locked gate:

> "Naturally, I [Maria] believe, I am as lively as Julia, but I have more to think of now."
>
> "You have undoubtedly—and there are situations in which very high spirits would denote insensibility. Your prospects, however, are too fair to justify want of spirits. You have a very smiling scene before you."
>
> "Do you mean literally or figuratively? Literally I conclude. Yes, certainly, the sun shines and the park looks very cheerful. But unluckily that iron gate, that ha-ha, give me a feeling of restraint and hardship. I cannot get out, as the starling said." As she spoke, and it was with expression, she walked to the gate; he followed her. "Mr. Rushworth is so long fetching this key!"
>
> "And for the world you would not get out without the key and without Mr. Rushworth's authority and protection, or I think you might with little difficulty pass round the edge of the gate, here, with my assistance; I think it might be done, if you really wished to be more at large, and could allow yourself to think it not prohibited."
>
> "Prohibited! nonsense! I certainly can get out that way, and I will." (p. 99)[5]

Maria's disregard for the barrier, at Henry's suggestive instigation, represents both her general impatience at moral restraint and the related issue of her eventual elopement with Henry. Moreover, Rushworth's pitiful key, symbol of the ill-fated marriage that failed to disguise Maria's impatience with respectable restraints, merely becomes the prefiguration of his subsequent cuckoldry.

The tensions between feeling and social standards here arise from the general distinction between nature and artifice, and this

---

5. The starling reference is based on Laurence Sterne's *Sentimental Journey* (1768). Significantly, Sterne is discussing social and moral forms of restraint, symbolized by the bird's cage and by the Bastille. *A Sentimental Journey through France and Italy by Mr. Yorick*, ed. Gardner D. Stout, Jr. (Berkeley, Calif., 1967), 197–200. Charles Murrah also discusses the symbolic significance of the ha-ha episode: "The Background of *Mansfield Park*," in *From Jane Austen to Joseph Conrad, Essays Collected in Memory of James T. Hillhouse*, ed. Robert C. Rathburn and Martin Steinmann, Jr. (Minneapolis, 1958), 32–34.

prevailing conflict is also explored through symbolism. Mansfield Park itself represents the quiet elegance and harmony which Fanny worships in nature. On the other hand, the elaborate artifice of the man-made town is associated with physical chaos and discomfort. In Portsmouth even the sun is affected by the urban malaise: to Fanny sunshine appears to be "a totally different thing in a town and in the country. Here, its power was only a glare, a stifling, sickly glare, serving but to bring forward stains and dirt that might otherwise have slept. There was neither health nor gaiety in sun-shine in a town." The general sleaziness is represented in the Price home: "She sat in a blaze of oppressive heat, in a cloud of moving dust; and her eyes could only wander from the walls marked by her father's head, to the table cut and knotched by her brothers, where stood the tea-board never thoroughly cleaned, the cups and saucers wiped in streaks, the milk a mixture of motes floating in thin blue, and the bread and butter growing every minute more greasy than even Rebecca's hands had first produced it" (p. 439). The symbolic artifices of the "improver" join the town as the antithesis of the natural and the truly harmonious. At Sotherton, for example, the rigid uniformity of the lawn, the bowling green, and the terrace corresponds with the artificial grouping of the Mansfield Park visitors and their hosts into three parties of three persons each:

The lawn, bounded on each side by a high wall, contained beyond the first planted aerea, a bowling-green, and beyond the bowling-green a long terrace walk, backed by iron palissades, and commanding a view over them into the tops of the trees of the wilderness immediately adjoining. It was a good spot for fault-finding. Mr. Crawford was soon followed by Miss Bertram and Mr. Rushworth, and when after a little time the others began to form into parties, these three were found in busy consultation on the terrace by Edmund, Miss Crawford and Fanny, who seemed as naturally to unite, and who after a short participation of their regrets and difficulties, left them and walked on. The remaining three, Mrs. Rushworth, Mrs. Norris, and Julia, were still far behind. (p. 90)

In short, the "improver's" artificial forms of harmony have become symbols of discordance, of the deep-seated animosities which have divided members of the Mansfield Park circle.

Fanny's aversion to artifice of all kinds is matched by her enthusiasm for nature as a form of harmony that transcends manmade forms: "Here's harmony! . . . Here's what may leave all painting and all music behind, and what poetry only can attempt to describe. Here's what may tranquillize every care, and lift the heart to rapture! When I look out on such a night as this, I feel as if there could be neither wickedness nor sorrow in the world; and there certainly would be less of both if the sublimity of Nature were more attended to, and people were carried more out of themselves by contemplating such a scene" (p. 113). Fanny's phrasing suggests that Jane Austen is invoking some familiar eighteenth-century theories of the sublime. Edmund Burke for one defines the aesthetic properties of poetry by remarking that the mind is "hurried out of itself" by complex imagery.[6] Significantly, Burke makes this point in comparing the sublime effects of both poetry and nature; and like Fanny, he also relegates other art forms like painting to "the pleasure of imitation." Joseph Addison, too, adheres to the popularized versions of Longinian aesthetics by stressing the mind-enlarging properties of the sublime. Hence, Fanny's ejaculation recalls *Spectator* No. 412 in which Addison suggests that the imagination is naturally attracted to the great and the stupendous: "Our Imagination loves to be filled with an Object, or to grasp at any thing that is too big for its capacity."[7] And *Spectator* No. 414 anticipates Fanny by arguing that art lacks the sublime properties ("Vastness and Immensity") of nature—a traditional assumption that is also shared by William Cowper's *Task*: "Lovely indeed the mimic works of Art,/But Nature's works far lovelier."[8] By investing Fanny's apostrophe with echoes of eighteenth-century theories of the sublime, Jane Austen has

6. Edmund Burke, *A Philosophical Enquiry into the Origin of our Ideas of the Sublime and Beautiful*, ed. J. T. Boulton (London, 1958), 62.

7. Joseph Addison, *The Spectator*, ed. Donald F. Bond (Oxford, 1965), III, 540.

8. William Cowper, *Poems*, ed. Hugh l'Anson Fausset (London, 1931), 316–17.

endowed the nature symbol in *Mansfield Park* with associations of emotional depth and spiritual grandeur which are pitted in the novel against the narrow egotism that passes for refinement in the Bertram family. Hence, when Edmund leaves Fanny, at the end of the apostrophe, to join in a glee with other members of the household, he is moving from a world of natural harmony to a company of artificial personalities who are appropriately engaged in an inferior kind of man-made harmony, and whose defects originate with their narrow feelings, their incapability of being "carried more out of themselves." In effect, the sublime implications of the nature symbol project taste as an index to the moral psychology of character. Fanny Price's aesthetic sensibilities are closely linked to her strong sense of moral principle, to her abhorrence of "wickedness" and "sorrow." And as we have already seen in the case of *Sense and Sensibility* Jane Austen echoes Burke's *Enquiry* and Shaftesbury's *Characteristics* in associating a morally defective judgment with an inadequate or moribund taste. Therefore, Mary Crawford, Fanny's perennial antithesis, admits a total indifference to the emotional and aesthetic experiences which so frequently move Fanny. While Fanny's response to nature takes the form of a selfless identification with the cosmos, Mary characteristically declines to be "carried" or "hurried" out of her self. *Her* interest in nature is frankly, and narrowly, self-assertive: "I see no wonder in this shrubbery equal to seeing myself in it" (pp. 209–210).[9]

Fanny's emotional responses must, of course, be defined in relation to those who are not her moral opposites. We need to examine, in this respect, the implications of the tripartite symbol created by William Price's cross and the two chains presented to Fanny by Edmund and Henry respectively.[10] The fact that Edmund's is the chain that fits the cross demonstrates the crucial feature of Fanny's emotional experiences. Edmund's special place

---

9. See Lloyd W. Brown, "Jane Austen and the Sublime: A Note on *Mansfield Park*," *Studies in Burke and His Time*, X (1968), 1041–43.
10. Compare Murrah, "The Background of *Mansfield Park*," p. 29.

in her heart has initially been secured by the parallels that she has drawn between Edmund and William. From the beginning of Fanny's stay at Mansfield Park, Edmund appears as a kind of brother-substitute, one who helps her to write her first letter "with all the good will that her brother could himself have felt," and whose general kindness causes her to love him "better than any body in the world except William" (pp. 16, 22). Similarly, Henry Crawford shrewdly gains her good opinion by his efforts on William's behalf. Fanny's sexual interests are influenced by her love for her brother, because "even the conjugal tie is beneath the fraternal." According to the narrator, "Fraternal love, sometimes almost every thing, is at others worse than nothing. But with William and Fanny Price, it was still a sentiment in all its prime and freshness, wounded by no opposition of interest, cooled by no separate attachment, and feeling the influence of time and absence only in its increase" (p. 235). Hence only Edmund's chain can fit William's cross, and Crawford's gift is worn only when it ceases to be a threat to this symbolic union. Edmund's chain and William's cross are "memorials of the two most beloved of her heart, those dearest tokens so formed for each other by every thing real and imaginary." Crawford's necklace is worn "when it was no longer to encroach on, to interfere with the stronger claims, the truer kindness of another" (p. 271).

In using symbols to analyze the psychological traits of her heroine Jane Austen continues to explore the relationship between individual consciousness and the process of symbolizing. As we have already seen in the case of Fanny Price and other characters, personal morality and tastes may be dramatized by the individual's instinct to manufacture or define modes of symbolic expression. The exploration of Fanny's emotional responses points to subsequent developments in *Emma* where symbolism is even more closely interwoven with the subtleties of character and situation. The excesses of Emma's wayward imagination invariably compound the complexities of individual relationships, including Frank Churchill's secret engagement, the mystery surrounding

Jane Fairfax's personal life, and the ill-fated matrimonial ambitions of Harriet Smith and Mr. Elton respectively. The built-in ambiguities of individual attitudes and the natural limitations of her own perception have been exaggerated by Emma's willful preoccupation with her fanciful schemes. In viewing the situations and characters through her eyes the reader is confronted with a series of unnecessary mysteries and magnified puzzles; and accordingly, the dominance of the riddle symbol is related directly to the integration of plot and Emma's imagination.

To return to Mr. Weston's conundrum on Emma's name, the flattering riddle is ironic because it presents such an obvious contrast with Emma's glaring imperfections, both at Box Hill and elsewhere. But the conundrum is also important because, as a riddle, it represents the hidden and the mysterious—in this case, the secret relationships and intrigues, the underlying tensions and barely concealed hostilities which make a shambles of the Box Hill picnic. Similarly, Frank Churchill's suggestive word puzzles, suspect only in the eyes of the acute Mr. Knightley, reflect the double-dealing that marks his relationship with both Jane Fairfax and Emma. Or, in Mr. Elton's case, the short-lived intimacy with the Hartfield family is linked to the charade in particular and riddles of all kinds in general. The charade on "courtship," for example, dramatizes the ambiguous nature of the relationship that has evolved between the vicar, Emma, and Harriet, primarily because the vicar's real intentions have been disregarded or misinterpreted. And the puzzle elucidates the manner in which Emma's imagination converts the obvious into a mystery, the disastrous facility with which she makes everything "bend" to the preconceived idea. Thus, although she is struck by the applicability of the phrase "soft eyes" to Harriet, she is undeterred by the inappropriate description "ready wit" and decides that only a blind lover would attribute wit to Harriet (pp. 71–72). It is this typical misjudgment that heightens the ironic contrast between Emma's ready grasp of the literal meaning of the charade and Harriet's "confusion of hope and dulness," for the ultimate significance of the puzzle has been just as effectively obscured for Emma by her own confusion of hope and conceit. This connection between cipher and wayward fancy is subsequently reiterated when Emma decides that Jane Fairfax is "a riddle," for the supposed mysteries of Jane's private attachments have been compounded by Emma's imagination (p. 285).

Emma's self-centered imagination is also responsible for her isolation. Her stubborn fantasies cut her off from reality, and the egotistic attempts to control others are directly related to her vaunted determination to remain detached and uninvolved. Hence she revels in the self-appointed role of matchmaker at the same time that she loudly denies any personal interest in marriage. And altogether her schematic detachment and her general isolation are symbolized by Hartfield itself—the reader has to be reminded that "in spite of its separate lawn and shrubberies and name" it actually belongs to the village of Highbury (p. 7). The weather, too, symbolically emphasizes Emma's isolation, especially in the crucial moments of self-recognition. After the embarrassing revelations of Mr. Elton's proposal, Emma is confined to her home by bad weather and becomes "a most honourable prisoner" (p. 138).

Moreover, the weather is generally used as a barometer of the emotional crises of the narrative. Gloomy weather is usually associated with melancholy spirits, bright sunshine with cheerfulness and gaiety. And variations are occasionally introduced for ironic effects. Hence there is a "very fine day" for the disastrous Box Hill picnic, and the pleasant weather is combined with "all the other outward circumstances of arrangement, accommodation, and punctuality" to augur "a pleasant party" (p. 367).[11] This kind of nature symbolism goes beyond the direct moral equations of *Mansfield Park*. It also effects what amounts to the mutual impregnation of emotion and environment.[12] And this close relationship is demonstrated by three of the more intense

11. Compare Edgar Shannon, Jr., "*Emma*: Character and Construction," *PMLA*, LXXI (1956), 647.
12. Walter Allen, *The English Novel* (New York, 1954), 100–101.

episodes in the novel. First, Emma's disappointment in the abortive Smith-Elton match is linked with the gloom of night, and the return of her natural cheerfulness with the light of morning: "To youth and natural cheerfulness like Emma's, though under temporary gloom at night, the return of day will hardly fail to bring return of spirits. The youth and cheerfulness of morning are in happy analogy, and of powerful operation; and if the distress be not poignant enough to keep the eyes unclosed, they will be sure to open to sensations of softened pain and brighter hope" (pp. 137-38). Subsequently, Emma's conscience-stricken reflections on her past relationship with Jane Fairfax partake of the gloom and violence of a stormy evening: "The evening of this day was very long, and melancholy, at Hartfield. The weather added what it could of gloom. A cold stormy rain set in, and nothing of July appeared but in the trees and shrubs, which the wind was despoiling, and the length of the day, which only made such cruel sights the longer visible" (p. 421). Finally, on the next day when the weather has changed, the tranquility and brilliance of the day interact with her hopes for future "serenity"—soon to materialize with Mr. Knightley's unexpected declaration of love: "The weather continued much the same all the following morning; and the same loneliness, and the same melancholy, seemed to reign at Hartfield—but in the afternoon it cleared; the wind changed into a softer quarter; the clouds were carried off; the sun appeared; it was summer again. With all the eagerness which such a transition gives, Emma resolved to be out of doors as soon as possible. Never had the exquisite sight, smell, sensation of nature, tranquil, warm, and brilliant after a storm, been more attractive to her. She longed for the serenity they might gradually introduce (p. 424)."

The integration of human experience and physical environment is continued in *Persuasion* where the seasons, especially autumn, dominate the mood and symbolical texture of the narrative. The prevailing connotations of autumn are typified by Anne Elliot's reverie during a walk to Winthrop: "Her *pleasure* in the walk must arise from the exercise and the day, from the view of the last smiles of the year upon the tawny leaves and withered hedges, and from repeating to herself some few of the thousand poetical descriptions extant of autumn, that season of peculiar and inexhaustible influence on the mind of taste and tenderness, that season which has drawn from every poet worthy of being read, some attempt at description, or some lines of feeling" (p. 84). The mood is dispelled by the mundane details of the Winthrop farm:

> Anne could not immediately fall into a quotation again. The sweet scenes of autumn were for a while put by—unless some tender sonnet, fraught with the apt analogy of the declining year, with declining happiness, and the images of youth and hope, and spring, all gone together, blessed her memory. She roused herself to say, as they struck by order into another path, "Is not this one of the ways to Winthrop?" But nobody heard, or, at least, nobody answered her.
>
> Winthrop, however, or its environs—for young men are, sometimes, to be met with, strolling about near home, was their destination; and after another half mile of gradual ascent through large enclosures, where the ploughs at work, and the fresh-made path spoke the farmer, counteracting the sweets of poetical despondence, and meaning to have spring again, they gained the summit of the most considerable hill, which parted Uppercross and Winthrop, and soon commanded a full view of the latter, at the foot of the hill on the other side.
>
> Winthrop, without beauty and without dignity, was stretched before them; an indifferent house, standing low, and hemmed in by the barns and buildings of a farm-yard. (p. 85)

In one sense the contrast between the poetics of autumn and the prosaic realities of Winthrop is intended to be anticlimactic, a satiric thrust at the formulaic sentiments of reflective poetry. But Jane Austen is also presenting the antithesis between autumn as the season of maturity and reflection, and spring as the symbol of youthful activity, between fulfillment and promise. At the same time there is a counterbalancing sense of continuity—the promise of spring after autumn and winter. And this seasonal continuity is reflected in Anne Elliot's development. First, there is the youthful happiness of her former engagement to Wentworth, then the pain of estrangement and the growing-pains which culminate in

Anne's maturity, and finally, the joys of eventual reconciliation as well as the promise of a new life together.

However, as the relationship between Anne and Wentworth illustrates, mature reason or "persuasion" is often confused with obduracy and pride. And by the same token a distinction must be maintained between the uses of autumn as the symbol of both true and specious "maturity." Hence, while Anne sees the season as a projection of reflective reason and spiritual fulfillment, Wentworth typically obscures the symbolism when he defines "firmness" (or to be more exact, stubbornness) by referring to the traditional symbol of autumnal maturity—the nut:

"Here is a nut," said he, catching one down from an upper bough. "To exemplify,—a beautiful glossy nut, which, blessed with original strength, has outlived all the storms of autumn. Not a puncture, not a weak spot any where.—This nut," he continued, with playful solemnity,—"while so many of its brethren have fallen and been trodden under foot, is still in possession of all the hapiness that a hazel-nut can be supposed capable of." Then, returning to his former earnest tone: "My first wish for all, whom I am interested in, is that they should be firm. If Louisa Musgrove would be beautiful and happy in her November of life, she will cherish all her present powers of mind." (p. 88)

Wentworth is correct in associating autumnal maturity with resilience, but as usual he has confused firmness with obduracy. He lacks the flexibility that Anne has learnt to combine with strength. And in this instance, too, we can observe how, once again, Jane Austen has internalized the symbolical process; for the distinctions between Anne and Wentworth at this stage have been demonstrated, not simply by emblematic equations, but also by the manner in which they themselves formulate symbols to project their respective temperaments.

Altogether then, the autumn symbols of *Persuasion* are a part of Jane Austen's fusion of feeling and environment, whether it is on the level of Wentworth's headstrong pride or on the basis of Anne's gentle awareness. And this interpenetration of character and ambience is also typical of several other symbols in the novel.

Uppercross, for example, greets Anne with the cheerless scenery of a "dark November day" when she returns from the near tragedy of the Lyme visit:

> If Louisa recovered, it would all be well again. More than former happiness would be restored. There could not be a doubt, to her mind there was none, of what would follow her recovery. A few months hence, and the room now so deserted, occupied but by her silent, pensive self, might be filled again with all that was happy and gay, all that was glowing and bright in prosperous love, all that was most unlike Anne Elliot!
>
> An hour's complete leisure for such reflections as these, on a dark November day, a small thick rain almost blotting out the very few objects ever to be discerned from the windows, was enough to make the sound of Lady Russell's carriage exceedingly welcome; and yet, though desirous to be gone, she could not quit the mansion-house, or look an adieu to the cottage, with its black, dripping, and comfortless veranda, or even notice through the misty glasses the last humble tenements of the village, without a saddened heart.—Scenes had passed in Uppercross, which made it precious. It stood the record of many sensations of pain, once severe, but now softened; and of some instances of relenting feeling, some breathings of friendship and reconciliation, which could never be looked for again, and which could never cease to be dear. She left it all behind her; all but the recollection that such things had been. (p. 123)

As a record of "many sensations" Uppercross is comparable with the season symbols in that it adjusts itself to the cyclical nature of emotional experiences. It recalls Anne's fluctuating moods in the past (particularly with regards to Wentworth), dramatizes her present anguish, and promises the inevitable renewal of friendship and high spirits. Hence the present cycle will be completed, despite the forbidding associations of the "comfortless" surroundings. And with the Christmas season that follows, the "domestic hurricane" of the Musgrove festivities fulfills Anne's prediction of a "happy and gay" Uppercross. The brooding darkness and deathlike stillness of November have given way to lights, color, and bustling vitality:

On one side was a table, occupied by some chattering girls, cutting up silk and gold paper; and on the other were tressels and trays, bending under the weight of brawn and cold pies, where riotous boys were holding high revel; the whole completed by a roaring Christmas fire, which seemed determined to be heard, in spite of all the noise of the others. Charles and Mary also came in, of course, during their visit; and Mr. Musgrove made a point of paying his respects to Lady Russell, and sat down close to her for ten minutes, talking with a very raised voice, but, from the clamour of the children on his knees, generally in vain. It was a fine family-piece. (p. 134)

As a "place" symbol, Lyme is similar to Uppercross because both localities are "records" of the cycle of changing human emotions. Before Louisa Musgrove's accident, Lyme represents the vitality and freshness of youth. The high spirits of Louisa, "the most eager of the eager," are matched by the usual bustle of Lyme— "the remarkable situation of the town, the principal street almost hurrying into the water, the walk to the Cobb, skirting round the pleasant little bay, which in the season is animated with bathing machines and company" (pp. 94, 95). But even before Louisa's mishap, the natural environment of Lyme is a pointed reminder of the usual juxtaposition of youth and age, happiness and tragedy. Hence the surrounding scenery of freshness and growth is, simultaneously, a monument to the inexorable march of time. Anne and her companions are fascinated by Charmouth's "high grounds and extensive sweeps of country, and still more its sweet retired bay, backed by dark cliffs, where fragments of low rock among the sands make it the happiest spot for watching the flow of the tide, for sitting in unwearied contemplation;—the woody varieties of the cheerful village of Up Lyme, and, above all, Pinny, with its green chasms between romantic rocks, where the scattered forest trees and orchards of luxuriant growth declare that many a generation must have passed away since the first partial falling of the cliff prepared the ground" (pp. 95–96).

The time motif which is so prominent in the autumn symbols and in the Lyme scenery runs through most of the major symbolical structures of *Persuasion*. The Uppercross mansion therefore represents not just the cycle of human emotions and experiences, but also the related passage of time. It combines the generation of past tastes and styles with the current mania for "improvements," and the earlier Musgroves are represented by portraits which seem "to be staring in astonishment" at the activities of their descendants. And even among the living, there is a suggestive contrast between the generations—"father and mother were in the old English style, and the young people in the new" (p. 40). Moreover, the "old-fashioned square parlour" and the generally "old English style" of the mansion must be distinguished from the modern "prettinesses" of Uppercross cottage. At the same time, the "improvements" represented by the cottage are counterbalanced by the signs of age and decrepitude which mark its interior and occupant. Mary Musgrove, who has lost her "bloom," is "lying on the faded sofa of the pretty little drawing-room, the once elegant furniture of which had been gradually growing shabby, under the influence of four summers and two children" (pp. 36, 37). The "bloom" metaphor is not peculiar to this context, for it joins all the other major symbols in dramatizing the coincidental cycles of time and experience. As such it is associated with all three Elliot sisters. Mary's bloom has been lost early, and permanently—emphasizing the stunting of her emotional and intellectual faculties. Sir Walter Elliot fondly believes that Elizabeth is as "blooming" as ever (p. 6). But Sir Walter's self-serving compliment to his *alter ego* is no comfort to Elizabeth. Her claims to good sense and social consequence are continuously undermined by palpable evidence of her narrow-mindedness; hence her pretensions to youthful beauty are undercut by a series of sweeping, parallel statements which ruthlessly emphasize the passage of time. And the revolutions of the time cycle are contrasted with the depressing standstill in Elizabeth's womanhood, a *stasis* that satirically accords with the vaunted permanence of her youthful "bloom":

It sometimes happens, that a woman is handsomer at twenty-nine than she was ten years before; and, generally speaking, if there has been neither ill health nor anxiety, it is a time of life at which scarcely any charm is lost. It was so with Elizabeth; still the same handsome Miss Elliot that she had begun to be thirteen years ago. . . .

Elizabeth did not quite equal her father in personal contentment. Thirteen years had seen her mistress of Kellynch Hall, presiding and directing with a self-possession and decision which could never have given the idea of her being younger than she was. For thirteen years had she been doing the honours, and laying down the domestic law at home, and leading the way to the chaise and four, and walking immediately after Lady Russell out of all the drawing-rooms and dining-rooms in the country. Thirteen winters' revolving frosts had seen her opening every ball of credit which a scanty neighbourhood afforded; and thirteen springs shewn their blossoms, as she travelled up to London with her father, for a few weeks annual enjoyment of the great world. (pp. 6–7)

On the other hand, Anne's flexible disposition and her capacity for change and development are paralleled by the fluctuating time symbolism of the bloom metaphor. Her bloom vanishes early as a result of her disappointment in love. But even before she is reconciled with Wentworth her wholesome disposition is reflected in the youthful color that reappears from time to time. At Lyme, for example, her spirits are bouyed by "the delight of the fresh-feeling breeze," and her features reveal "the bloom and freshness of youth restored by the fine wind" (pp. 102, 104).

Time, then, is not simply a setting or background in *Persuasion* but an experience that is integral to the emotional and moral development of character. The static nature of personalities like Elizabeth's is emphasized by the continuous flux and change represented by time. But in Anne's case that cyclical progression is symptomatic of intellectual and emotional maturity, and of the contrasting patterns of sorrow and cheerfulness which accompany real growth. Thus when Wentworth disparages Anne's "altered features" (pp. 60–61), he ignores the far more important, nonphysical changes that have taken place. And Mrs. Smith, who has been visited with all the ill health and anxiety that have escaped Elizabeth over the years, has acquired a remarkable degree of fortitude and insight. In comparison, Elizabeth's bloom is ironic, for it embodies the perpetuation of her adolescent shallowness and conceit. Indeed it is one of the persistent ironies of the novel that those who are most apprehensive about time and old age, are the very ones whose moral and intellectual faculties have remained impervious to time and experience. For their vanity renders them insensitive to the kind of suffering through which age and disadvantages remould or strengthen the characters of Anne and Mrs. Smith.

This brings us to the symbolic role of the *Baronetage*, for the "favourite volume" of Sir Walter Elliot links him ironically to the time motif. First, it is a veritable monument to time in the novel, for it chronicles the history of the Elliot family through a series of entries spanning half of a century, including the events of the narrative. But, secondly, it also represents the absurd vanity and narrow-mindedness which blind Sir Walter to the realities that are unfolded over the years. Vanity, as the narrator observes, is the beginning and the end of his character (p. 4). His egotism readily lends itself to a crude form of self-dramatization as he parades before his own eyes. Consequently, he frequently thinks of himself in the third person: "He considered the blessing of beauty as inferior only to the blessings of a baronetcy; and the Sir Walter Elliot, who united these gifts, was the constant object of his warmest respect and devotion" (p. 4). The *Baronetage* is crucial to this self-adulation, for it sets forth Sir Walter Elliot of Kellynch Hall in all his ancestral glory—for Sir Walter's unfailing admiration. And this literary looking-glass is complemented by the very real mirrors which have proliferated in his dressing room, and which are literally the physical projection of the baronet's obsession with self. Appropriately, the symbolism of the mirrors is stressed by Admiral Croft whose unselfish commonsense makes him the very antithesis of his landlord. Hence, he detests the mirrors on the very grounds that make them indispensable to Sir

Walter: "Such a number of looking-glasses! oh Lord! there was no getting away from oneself" (p. 128). On the whole, then, the *Baronetage* embodies the integration of time and personality which is so fundamental to the themes of *Persuasion*. And in this respect it is related to the cyclical structure that all the other time symbols, including autumn, have contributed to the narrative form of *Persuasion*. As we have already seen, most of these symbols illustrate the cycles of change and continuity by which individual growth, or *stasis*, is measured. Coincidentally, the *Baronetage* symbolizes the resulting form of Jane Austen's narrative: it describes a circular process in that it is literally opened and closed at the beginning and conclusion of the story—first to recount the history of Sir Walter's family, and finally, to record Anne's marriage. And in so doing, the *Baronetage* becomes yet another monument to the ironic self-consciousness with which Jane Austen evolves her comic structures; for just as she exploits names, or Northanger Abbey, as projections of the symbolical process itself, so it is that with the *Baronetage* Jane Austen symbolizes the nature and direction of her total narrative form in *Persuasion*.

CHAPTER V

Conversation

THE SELF-CONSCIOUSNESS with which Jane Austen's characters use or define symbols in the novels brings us to the subject of individual styles, for personal "conversation" is predicated on the same general basis that applies to symbolic usages: each person's mode of communication corresponds with his moral and emotional values. In an apparent paraphrase of Cowper, Jane Austen describes John Thorpe's endless "effusions" as "talk" rather than "conversation" (*Northanger Abbey*, p. 66).[1] The distinction that she makes here is important for the proper understanding of the structure and function of individual styles in her fiction. As Jane Austen makes clear elsewhere in *Northanger Abbey*, "conversation" is much more than a verbal exchange, in the looser twentieth-century sense. Thus she notes that Mrs. Allen and Mrs. Thorpe habitually engage in "what they called conversation, but in which there was scarcely ever any exchange of opinion, and not often any resemblance of subject" (p. 36). The real import of "conversation" in Jane Austen's novels is the definition of individual tastes and ethics as they are evinced by social intercourse. These standards of conversation are measured against high ideals. Even Mr. Elliot, whose good sense and wit make him an admirable

1. Compare Cowper's *Conversation* (1782): "Words learn'd by rote a parrot may rehearse, / But talking is not always to converse." William Cowper, *Poems*, ed. Hugh l'Anson Fausset (London, 1931), 267.

conversationalist, is reprimanded by his cousin Anne for equating "good company" with mere birth and manners—to the exclusion of intellectual excellence (*Persuasion*, pp. 143, 150). And Emma Woodhouse's insulting conduct at Box Hill can be traced, in part, to her deficiency in matters of feeling, in the sensibility that is a prerequisite for ideal conversation.

In view of these criteria the echoes of Cowper's *Conversation* in *Northanger Abbey* are more than coincidental. Jane Austen's definition of conversation as morality and feeling is a reaffirmation of the standards that are frequently postulated by Cowper and other eighteenth-century writers. Congreve, in the dedication of *The Way of the World* (1700), and Addison, in *Spectator* No. 409 (1712), concur in defining a "man of conversation" as one whose superior tastes and intellect make him an indispensable mentor in matters pertaining to literary and social standards. Richard Steele is another contributor to this thesis, for in *Tatler* No. 21 (1709) he stresses that the hallmark of a man of conversation is the ability to avoid giving offense, to make others feel at ease in his company. Moreover, the most necessary talent in such an individual is a sound judgment.[2] Lord Chesterfield's description of good breeding and conversation is also relevant here. Good breeding, he urges his son, is rooted in sense, not external flourishes: it "does not consist in low bows and formal ceremony; but in an easy, civil, and respectful behaviour." And like Steele, he stresses the point that Jane Austen's Emma ignores at Box Hill: the man of sense bases the art of conversation on "the art of pleasing." Conversely, improper forms of address or clumsy styles reveal "an awkwardness of the mind."[3]

2. William Congreve, *The Way of the World*, in *The Complete Plays of William Congreve*, ed. Herbert Davis (Chicago, 1967), p. 391; Joseph Addison, *The Spectator*, ed. Donald F. Bond (Oxford, 1965), III, 529; Richard Steele, *The Tatler*, ed. George A. Aitken (4 vols.; London, 1898), I, 176. Herbert Davis examines "The Augustan Art of Conversation" in *Jonathan Swift: Essays on his Satire and other Studies* (New York, 1964), 260–76.

3. *The Letters of Philip Dormer Stanhope 4th Earl of Chesterfield*, ed. Bonamy Dobrée (6 vols.; London, 1932), II, 523–24; III, 1035; II, 464. As a matter of fact, Emma dramatically reverses this principle when she permits Frank Churchill

Henry Fielding confirms these social and intellectual standards, but he goes beyond them in order to describe conversation as the human mode of self-expression at all levels of experience. Thus his "Essay on Conversation" which originally appeared in the *Miscellanies* (1743) sets forth three kinds of conversation: men's conversation with (1) God (2) themselves, and (3) each other. These three are closely interrelated. Hence when Fielding analyzes the "social" forms of conversation, he does not limit himself to considerations of "good breeding" and the "art of pleasing." Fielding is also quick to add that this social excellence is deeply rooted in the ideals of religious morality. Thus good breeding can be undermined by pride, folly, arrogance, insolence, and ill-nature. Moreover, the true art of raillery, one of the hallmarks of ideal conversation, is not supposed to be destructive and malicious. In effect, Fielding views it as a social extension of the Christian ideals of brotherhood and charity, as a gentle and sympathetic playing on the peccadilloes of others.[4]

Fielding's comprehensive definition of conversation is similar to Swift's. Like several of his contemporaries, Swift emphasizes that ideal conversation depends on good breeding. And Swift's essay, "On Good Manners and Good Breeding" (first published in 1754), associates his ideal with the intellectual excellence of "the best understandings." In "Hints Towards an Essay on Conversation" (1710), he also shares Fielding's moral bias with regard to standards of manners and conversation. Hence he asserts that conversation is the very symbol of human nature, for it is the great distinction between men and brutes. This accords with the parallel that Swift draws between conversation and morality in "A Proposal for Correcting, Improving and Ascertaining the English Tongue" (1712). According to Swift, the language of a society reflects its mores. Hence, what Swift regards as degenerate con-

---

to demand that *she* should be pleased by others: "I am ordered by Miss Woodhouse to say, that she . . . requires something very entertaining from each of you" (*Emma*, p. 370).

4. *The Works of Henry Fielding,* introd. Edmund Gosse (12 vols.; New York, 1899) XI, 117–172.

versation on the individual's part is interpreted as the outcome of a continuing deterioration in religious morality, and it presages the general collapse of English civilization, a reversion to the brute kingdom.[5]

Even a cursory glance at some individual styles in Jane Austen's novels will reveal the extent to which her methods of characterization are rooted in eighteenth-century concepts of conversation. Mrs. Elton's vulgar directness, particularly the crude familiarity with which she patronizes "Mr. K." or "Mr. E.," is quite in keeping with that "awkwardness of the mind" which Chesterfield sees as the cause of "improper titles and appellations" (*Letters*, II, 464). When Steele, Swift, and Fielding, among others, distinguish between external flourishes and the good breeding of ideal conversation, they provide Jane Austen with a kind of blueprint for the superficially graceful address of defective characters like the Crawfords in *Mansfield Park* and Mr. Elliot in *Persuasion*. Similarly, the reiterated emphasis, throughout the eighteenth century, on conversation as the art of pleasing is very pertinent to Emma Woodhouse's relationship with Miss Bates. For the "witty" retort that humiliates Miss Bates at the Box Hill picnic violates the humane and conciliatory concept of raillery which Fielding outlines in his essay on conversation, and which Swift enunciates in "Hints."[6] And the moral emphasis that we find in Fielding and Swift when they describe the "art of pleasing" is also relevant to Jane Austen's fiction. On the one hand, there are morally sound but crude characters, like Mrs. Jennings, whose style offends against the norms of "good" or polite manners, but never against the feelings of others or the established codes of moral conduct. On the other hand, there are defective personalities, like Lucy Steele, whose moral shortcomings are evinced by decorous but spiteful style; or those, including Mary Crawford, who enjoy thoughtless, but polished, witticisms at the expense of friends and

5. Jonathan Swift, *Prose Works*, ed. Herbert Davis (Oxford, 1939–62), IV, 5–21, 94, 217.
6. *Ibid.*, 91–92.

family. And this is the kind of distinction that Frank W. Brad-brook blurs when he generalizes that coarseness of expression in Jane Austen's novels leads invariably to breaches of conduct.[7]

However, the function of an individual's style in Jane Austen's fiction is not confined to the expression of personal mores. The very standards that are implicit in ideal conversation—sense, sensibility, moral excellence—also serve as a frame of reference for the novelist's presentation of experience as a whole. Hence, each individual style, whatever its weaknesses or strengths, is more than self-revelatory. It also impinges on the wider themes of each novel and, consequently, on the structural development of the work. Like ambiguous usages, or any of the other verbal patterns that we have already examined, the individual's style has a communicative role that is not limited to its immediate context. It is integrated with the total development of each novel's theme and structure. In *Northanger Abbey* even the placid inanities of Mrs. Allen's feeble conversation are functional in this wider sense. Her style dramatizes the prosaic routine of everyday reality, the kind of reality that is so far removed from the barbaric splendor of Catherine's Gothic dreamworld. Mrs. Allen's "perfect serenity" of style is unruffled even by the discomfort of having no "large acquaintance" at Bath (p. 22). When her enthusiasm is aroused it is on account of nothing more exciting than the latest fashions: "Miss Tilney was in a very pretty spotted muslin, and I fancy, by what I can learn, that she always dresses very handsomely" (p. 68).

Neither is Mrs. Allen the only character whose conversation is linked to the themes of Catherine's education. For example, the pointed contrast between General Tilney's style and the self-expression of the Thorpes has a direct bearing on Catherine's problems in relating the real and imaginary levels of her experience. General Tilney's ingratiating addresses to Catherine are almost exclusively in the form of understatement, a technique that often proclaims the defective personality in Jane Austen's fiction.

---

7. Frank W. Bradbrook, "Style and Judgment in Jane Austen's Novels," *Cambridge Journal*, IV (1951), 515–37.

His "disparaging" panegyric on the Woodston parsonage is typical: "We are not calling it a good house. . . . We are not comparing it with Fullerton and Northanger—We are considering it as a mere Parsonage, small and confined, we allow, but decent perhaps, and habitable; and altogether not inferior to the generality; —or, in other words, I believe there are few country parsonages in England half so good" (p. 213). The hypocrisies of his understatements are more obvious in reported speech, for the narrator is then free to undercut his transparent apologetics. Thus, in descanting on the beauties of his "dining-parlour," he "acknowledged that it was by no means an ill-sized room; and further confessed, that, though as careless on such subjects as most people, he did look upon a tolerably large eating-room as one of the necessaries of life" (p. 166). Beyond its betrayal of General Tilney's real personality, the understatement serves the wider purpose of ironically confirming Catherine's Gothic misgivings about him. Altogether, it projects an image of unctuous insinuation, in the best tradition of the villainous role to which Catherine's fancy has already assigned the general. The irony is intensified by the contrast with the hyperbolic styles which are preferred by both Isabella and John Thorpe. Catherine has presumed a dichotomy between the diabolical general and the "open" gaiety of her Bath friends; and this assumption has been mockingly confirmed by the opposition of styles. But in truth the general's real villainy, his selfish greed, is also the primary motive of the Thorpes. Hence, the conversational styles of the latter are just as suspect as General Tilney's telltale understatements. Isabella, for example, greets Catherine with "a hundred things" to discuss, namely, the weather, a hat, and *The Mysteries of Udolpho* (p. 39). Or the endearing superlatives with which she bombards all and sundry may be indiscriminately applied, in the same breath, to the human and the inanimate: Miss Andrews, she reports, is a "sweet girl," one of the "sweetest creatures" who is making "the sweetest cloak" (p. 40). The hyperbole is also typical of John Thorpe's conceited self-interest, and it is particularly effective when he dishonestly exaggerates the Morland family income—to no less a person than that master of hypocritical understatement, General Tilney:

> Thorpe, most happy to be on speaking terms with a man of General Tilney's importance, had been joyfully and proudly communicative;— and being at that time not only in daily expectation of Morland's engaging Isabella, but likewise pretty well resolved upon marrying Catherine himself, his vanity induced him to represent the family as yet more wealthy than his vanity and avarice had made him believe them. With whomsoever he was, or was likely to be connected, his own consequence always required that theirs should be great, and as his intimacy with any acquaintance grew, so regularly grew their fortune. The expectations of his friend Morland, therefore, from the first over-rated, had ever since his introduction to Isabella, been gradually increasing; and by merely adding twice as much for the grandeur of the moment, by doubling what he chose to think the amount of Mr. Morland's preferment, trebling his private fortune, bestowing a rich aunt, and sinking half the children, he was able to represent the whole family to the General in a most respectable light. (pp. 244–45)

Finally, Jane Austen emphasizes the intrinsic similarities between General Tilney and the Thorpes by using indirect speech to heighten the hypocrisies of their contrasting styles. Consequently, the indirect reporting of John Thorpe's inventory of the Morland estate is comparable with the oblique presentation of General Tilney's encomiums on Northanger Abbey.

Henry Tilney's style is also a part of the general framework which is comprised of personal conversation in the novel, and which is centered on Catherine Morland's evolving consciousness. In fact Henry's predominant role in the shaping of Catherine's perceptions is paralleled by the degree to which the range of his conversational techniques conforms with the thematic and structural developments of the novel. And in view of the prevailing parodic motif, it is not surprising that his style frequently partakes of the burlesque. His parody of Ann Radcliffe's *Romance of the Forest* is well known (*Northanger Abbey*, pp. 158–60). But it is not a self-contained literary exercise on Henry's part, for his technique provides an ironic frame of reference for Catherine's subsequent development. For example, when he gives prophetic details of Catherine's nocturnal exploration at Northanger Abbey, he invokes the kind of comic anticlimax that is so recurrent in the various stages of Catherine's education. First, he envisions Catherine's discovery of a "precious treasure," a roll of manuscripts which cannot be read, however, because her lamp will go out in the darkness (p. 160). And when she actually explores her rooms at the abbey, Catherine does undergo a mortifying anticlimax, for a promising roll of manuscripts turns out to be merely an inventory of linen (p. 172). Secondly, Henry's sense of the anticlimax coincides, in a more general way, with the function of parody in *Northanger Abbey* as a whole. The exorcism of Catherine's Gothic fears brings her abruptly to earth, but the realities to which she returns prove, ironically, to be less anticlimactic than they seem at first. Her post-Gothic perceptions are bathetic by the standards of her former literary tastes, but, simultaneously, these new insights represent a crucial point in Catherine's progression from naiveté to awareness. Altogether then, it is appropriate that Henry's eye-opening lecture on the real nature of evil partakes of an anticlimactic structure, for this method demonstrates both his own conversational technique and Jane Austen's general narrative strategy. He begins with a reassuring reminder of those Anglo-Christian virtues which seem to render Catherine's Gothic fears ludicrous: " 'Remember the country and the age in which we live. Remember that we are English, that we are Christians. Consult your own understanding, your own sense of the probable, your own observation of what is passing around you—Does our education prepare us for such atrocities? Do our laws connive at them?' " Then with the peroration that follows, he effects the anticlimactic exposé of the social evils that are the real antidotes to fears of Gothic crimes: " 'Could they be perpetrated without being known, in a country like this, where social and literary intercourse is on such a footing; where every man is surrounded by a neighbourhood of voluntary spies, and where roads and newspapers lay every thing open?' " (pp. 197–98)

Henry's penchant for parody is also applied to the real foibles of the everyday world. The Bath tourist is among his early victims as he entertains Catherine with an imitation of the typical Bath fop. Forming his features "into a set smile, and affectedly softening his voice," Henry greets Catherine "with a simpering air": "Have you been long in Bath, madam?" (p. 26). He is well acquainted with the typical visitor's affected boredom with the resort: "Bath, compared with London, has little variety, and so every body finds out every year. 'For six weeks, I allow Bath is pleasant enough; but beyond *that*, it is the most tiresome place in the world' " (p. 78). Without realizing it, Henry has a ready-made victim in this regard, for Isabella has been very quick to discover symptoms of her being "immoderately sick" of Bath: "though it is vastly well to be here for a few weeks, we would not live here for millions" (pp. 70–71). The link with Isabella is significant, for Henry's social commentary is really a preview of the selfish artifices that Catherine will encounter in Isabella's world. His parody of social manners is just as prophetic as his comic imitation of Gothic sensationalism. And in both cases, Catherine does not fully appreciate Henry's conscious or unwitting warnings, until after personal disillusionment. The parodic motifs of Henry's conversation therefore coincide with, and synthesize, the effects of Catherine's literary fantasies and the course of her social awareness.

His style is also symbolic of the analytical techniques which the narrative plot brings to bear on Catherine's intellectual development. Catherine's initial naiveté is symptomatic of her generally unanalytical mind. She succumbs to the artifices of the Thorpes as readily as she does to the sensational improbabilities of *Udolpho*. Consequently, her insights must be developed through the analytical process that Jane Austen derives from the narrative structure of *Northanger Abbey*. First, Catherine is confronted with a series of new experiences (the noisy variety of Bath, the flatteries of the Thorpes, the beguiling pleasures of reading novels, and the sinister appearance of General Tilney and Northanger Abbey). Then her first impressions are jolted by "anticlimatic" insights into each subject as she acquires a more realistic view of her environment. Hence, she is gradually conditioned to reshape or abandon initial attitudes by testing and analyzing them in the light of actual experience. As Catherine's analytical powers develop, Isabella's cheerful hyperboles and John's effusions become suspect. She is no longer willing, for example, to take the careless apologies of Isabella's letter at face value when it attempts to explain away the infidelity to Catherine's brother. Her good nature does not permit an outright condemnation of Isabella's double-dealing; but Catherine evinces a new interest in the analysis of human motives and self-expression when she questions the sincerity of Isabella's professed regard for young Morland (pp. 218–19).

Henry Tilney's style is dominated by the experiential strategy that shapes the maturing of Catherine's awareness. The "nice" perception of which Eleanor Tilney playfully accuses him is really a fastidious intellect that refuses to take persons or things at face value. Hence, language, especially the trite and affected kind, must be analyzed on the basis of its fidelity to experience. His dissection of a Catherine Morland ellipsis is typical. When Catherine recalls, in disappointment, that Isabella had "promised so faithfully" to write, Henry deliberately ignores the elliptical nature of the phrase: "Promised so faithfully! A faithful promise! That puzzles me.—I have heard of a faithful performance. But a faithful promise—the fidelity of promising! It is a power little worth knowing, however, since it can deceive and pain you" (pp. 195–96). By taking the ellipsis in a literal sense he has reduced the phrase to an absurd tautology that emphasizes the hypocrisy of Isabella's original promise. Moreover, Henry's satiric commentary analyzes the statement by testing it against the logic of grammar and experience. Thus while "a faithful promise" is grammatically analogous to "a faithful performance," experience offers no logical parallels between the two. Finally, the intensively analytical course of Henry's arguments is marked by his method of gradually conceptualizing Catherine's statement: "promised so faithfully . . . faithful promise . . . the fidelity of promising." In effect, Henry has subjected the single phrase to the same kind of experiential analysis that is integral to the general development of the novel. But here, too, his style is not simply symbolic of the narrative process. It is also incorporated within Catherine's maturing consciousness. Consequently, the exposé of Isabella's "fidelity of promising" hastens the awakening of Catherine's suspicions about her Bath friend.

As we have already seen, the styles of major characters in *Sense and Sensibility* are integral to the themes and structure of the novel. The complex of antitheses and parallels is reflected in the ambiguous relationships of individual styles. Hence Marianne's excessive but sincere emotionalism contrasts with John Dashwood's hypocritical rationalism. But, simultaneously, their styles share the tendency to undermine or corrupt idealistic concepts of sense and feeling. Mrs. Jennings' jocular vulgarity is diametrically opposed to Marianne's delicate sensibilities; but the former's crude style links her with Marianne's dominant virtues— the honest expression of feeling and the contemptuous disregard for the restraints of social propriety. But the scrupulous care with which Jane Austen incorporates individual styles within her narrative fabric appears to be even more striking when it is realized that the conversation of minor characters is just as organic to her thematic developments. Robert Ferrars, for example, is prone to the kind of dogmatic statement that serves Marianne's uncompromising assertiveness:

"I advise every body who is going to build, to build a cottage. My friend Lord Courtland came to me the other day on purpose to ask my advice, and laid before me three different plans of Bonomi's. I was to decide on the best of them. 'My dear Courtland,' said I, immediately throwing them all into the fire, 'do not adopt either of them, but by all means build a cottage.' And that, I fancy, will be the end of it.

"Some people imagine that there can be no accommodations, no space in a cottage; but this is all a mistake. I was last month at my friend Elliott's near Dartford, Lady Elliott wished to give a dance. 'But how can it be done?' said she; 'my dear Ferrars, do tell me how

it is to be managed. There is not a room in this cottage that will hold
ten couple, and where can the supper be?' *I* immediately saw that
there coud be no difficulty in it, so I said, 'My dear Lady Elliott, do
not be uneasy. The dining parlour will admit eighteen couple with
ease; card-tables may be placed in the drawing-room; the library may
be open for tea and other refreshments; and let the supper be set out
in the saloon.' Lady Elliott was delighted with the thought." (pp.
251–52)

This is obviously a burlesque of Marianne's dogmatic style and of
her fanatically picturesque taste in cottages. As an unconscious
imitation of Marianne's style, Robert's "talk" becomes another
ironic means of lampooning her excessive emotionalism. But at
the same time, his crude self-dramatization is alien to the sensitive
Marianne. He parades his shallow ideas with the same degree of
ostentation that characterizes Lucy Steele. In this respect his style
is crucial to the succeeding denouement of the plot, for in order to
be plausible, Robert's sudden elopement with Lucy must be con-
vincingly related to their respective personalities. Consequently,
his crudely egotistic style is comparable with Lucy Steele's carefully staged martyrdom on Edward's behalf: "You [Elinor] can't
think how much I go through in my mind from it altogether. I
only wonder that I am alive after what I have suffered for Edward's sake these last four years. Every thing in such suspense and
uncertainty; and seeing him so seldom—we can hardly meet above
twice a-year. I am sure I wonder my heart is not quite broke"
(p. 133). On the basis of this similarity of styles, it appears that
Jane Austen has exploited Robert's "talk" in order to prepare the
reader for an abrupt marriage that will conveniently release Edward Ferrars. The direct self-revelations of Robert's conversation
is a narrative economy that enables the novelist to project affinities
with Lucy Steele without having to expend disproportionate
space and attention on an ancillary character.

Robert's magisterial absurdities are therefore to be considered
not as isolated instances of comic relief, but as integral units of
Jane Austen's narrative structure. And the same is true of the
abrupt self-contradictions which make Mrs. Palmer so reminiscent

of Addison's "asserter of paradoxes," in *Tatler* No. 155. Mrs. Palmer's style is at its most typical when she elaborates on her intimate "acquaintance" with Willoughby:

"Oh! dear, yes; I know him extremely well," replied Mrs. Palmer—"Not that I ever spoke to him indeed; but I have seen him for ever in town. Somehow or other I never happened to be staying at Barton while he was at Allenham. Mama saw him here once before;—but I was with my uncle at Weymouth. However, I dare say we should have seen a great deal of him in Somersetshire, if it had not happened very unluckily that we should never have been in the country together. He is very little at Combe, I believe; but if he were ever so much there, I do not think Mr. Palmer would visit him, for he is in the opposition you know, and besides it is such a way off. I know why you inquire about him, very well; your sister is to marry him. I am monstrous glad of it, for then I shall have her for a neighbour you know." (p. 114)

And Willoughby's subsequent disgrace prompts an angry series of paradoxical resolutions: "'She was determined to drop his acquaintance immediately, and she was very thankful that she had never been acquainted with him at all. She wished with all her heart Combe Magna was not so near Cleveland; but it did not signify, for it was a great deal too far off to visit; she hated him so much that she was resolved never to mention his name again, and she should tell everybody she saw, how good-for-nothing he was'" (p. 215). On the whole, Mrs. Palmer's style reflects the conflict of tastes and moral values which accounts for the dramatic tensions of *Sense and Sensibility*. Her conversation is divided between the demands of natural feeling and polite hypocrisy. Externally, she is linked to these conflicting demands by her family ties. From her mother, Mrs. Jennings, she inherits an instinct for honesty which prompts her to be candid. In truth, she does not know Willoughby very well, neither will she ever be in a position to punish him effectively for his betrayal of Marianne. But the hypocritical code of social decorum requires that she make a show of knowledgeable sympathy with the Dashwood sisters. Hence her honest impulses are compromised by her unskilled attempts to imitate the impoverished politeness of Lady Middleton's society. The "insipid" demeanor that passes for propriety with the Lady Middletons and the Fanny Dashwoods encourages the self-serving flattery of someone like Lucy Steele. And in Mrs. Palmer's case it gives rise to brief and uneasy spells of benevolent insincerity. By simultaneously attracting and repelling her, this kind of specious sense creates the apparently hopeless self-contradictions of her style. In essence Mrs. Palmer's conversation comically dramatizes the same tensions that underlie Elinor Dashwood's social relationships: their real feelings are opposed by their public obligations to social propriety and its attendant burden of polite lies.

In *Pride and Prejudice*, too, the styles of so-called minor characters are linked to theme and structure. Even Mrs. Bennet's querulous outbursts are relevant. She is addicted to the kind of external details which typify the superficial judgments of "prepossession," particularly in her account of the Meryton ball: Bingley, according to her report, "seemed quite struck with Jane as she was going down the dance. So, he . . . asked her for the two next. Then, the two third he danced with Miss King, and the two fourth with Maria Lucas, and the two fifth with Jane again, and the two sixth with Lizzy, and the Boulanger—" (p. 13). Ironically, Mrs. Bennet's shallowness is comparable with that of her arch-enemy, Miss Bingley; for the latter's carping criticism of Elizabeth Bennet is replete with the very kind of superficial trivia that mesmerize Mrs. Bennet. According to Miss Bingley, Elizabeth's face is "too thin; her complexion has no brilliancy; and her features are not at all handsome. Her nose wants character; there is nothing marked in its lines. Her teeth are tolerable, but not out of the common way" (p. 271). In other words, Jane Austen has emphasized the stylistic links between the personalities of Mrs. Bennet and Miss Bingley in order to dramatize the prepossessive judgments which they share in common and which ironically cut across their strong, mutual dislike.

Appropriately, it is Elizabeth herself whose personality and style pervade the tone of *Pride and Prejudice*. Jane Austen's own comments on the "playfulness" of the novel is well known (*Letters*, pp. 299–300). But this general lightness of tone is usually more apparent than real. The lighthearted posture of the narrator is really a kind of stalking-horse for satiric analysis that easily matches the ruthless incisiveness of *Sense and Sensibility* or *Mansfield Park*. This is fairly evident in the epigrammatic summaries of character and situation. Lucas Lodge is a place where Sir William "could think with pleasure of his own importance" and "occupy himself solely in being civil to all the world" (p. 18). Mr. Collins' stupidity "must guard his courtship from any charm that could make a woman wish for its continuance" (p. 122). As a husband, Mr. Bennet has helped to undermine family discipline by his amused contempt for Mrs. Bennet; "but where other powers of entertainment are wanting, the true philosopher will derive benefit from such as are given" (p. 236). The "light, and bright, and sparkling" style is particularly arresting in Mr. Bennet's case, for the shortcomings being related here bear directly upon the crisis of Lydia's elopement with Wickham. And this satiric strategy is typical, not only of the narrator's commentary in general, but also of Elizabeth Bennet's conversation. Elizabeth's puckish response to a Hunsford visit by Miss de Bourgh is typical: "I expected at least that the pigs were got into the garden, and here is nothing but Lady Catherine and her daughter!" (p. 158). So is her epigrammatic contrast of Darcy and Wickham: "One has got all the goodness, and the other all the appearance of it" (p. 225). The playful archness of her conversation provokes Darcy's discerning comment, "You find great enjoyment in occasionally professing opinions which in fact are not your own" (p. 174). And it is this provocative posture that frequently serves her mocking inversion of traditional values, especially in her comic maxims. Hence the contrast between the weak-willed Bingley and the idiotic Mr. Collins leads her to speculate, "Stupid men are the only ones worth knowing, after all" (p. 154). She is ready with another "moral" in order to dispel doubts about the astonishing engagement to Darcy: "in such cases as these, a good memory is unpardonable" (p. 373). And this mock subversion of conventional standards is comparable with the ironic effects of Jane Austen's own comic maxims, particularly the famous opening sentence of the novel, "It is a truth universally acknowledged, that a single man in possession of a good fortune, must be in want of a wife" (p. 3). Finally, the playful banter of Elizabeth's personal style is akin to the narrative commentary in that a ruthlessly satiric directness is never far beneath the surface. Hence Charlotte Lucas' unexpected engagement provokes the exclamation, "My dear Jane, Mr. Collins is a conceited, pompous, narrow-minded, silly man" (p. 135).

Elizabeth's conversation approximates the ironic penetration of the narrator's judgment whenever her inherently sound intellect is free of unreasonable bias. But there is a discernible change whenever she gives vent to irrational prejudices and unfounded viewpoints, when she is merely prepossessed rather than rational. For example, she tends to lapse into sentimental jargon on the subject of Jane and Bingley. While she justifiably deplores Bingley's apparent ductility with regards to Darcy's influence, she also unfairly loads the case against Bingley by exaggerating the openness of his attachment to Jane. According to Elizabeth, Bingley was once "violently in love" with her sister (p. 140). But as Mrs. Gardiner's rejoinder emphasizes, the phrase is "hackneyed," "indefinite," and superficial: "It is as often applied to feelings which arise from an half-hour's acquaintance, as to a real, strong attachment" (pp. 140–41). Moreover, there is a suggestive parallel between Elizabeth's prejudiced exclamation and the phrasing that Mr. Collins uses in his abortive proposal: "And now nothing remains for me but to assure you in the most animated language of the violence of my affection" (p. 106). As with Marianne Dashwood and John Dashwood, Mrs. Bennet and Miss Bingley, Jane Austen heightens the effect of Elizabeth's lapses by using conversational style to link such failings with those of a moral opposite or archenemy. Thus, the suspect nature of Elizabeth's remarks about Bingley is underlined by the temporary affinity that they establish between herself and one of the most detested members of her circle.

Altogether Elizabeth's use of clichés represents an unthinking acceptance of the trite and the superficial. In this respect, the occasional failing of her conversational techniques reflects the structural pattern of the first half of the novel. At first, Jane Austen presents a facade of superficial appearances and judgments that will be demolished or ironically confirmed by subsequent events: Darcy's repulsive manners, Wickham's genteel charms, and Miss Darcy's intractable pride. Hence the shortcomings of Elizabeth's judgment and conversation conform with Jane Austen's ironic strategy in the first half of the novel. But after the revelations of fact have replaced prepossession and conjecture, Elizabeth's style reflects the mature insights that she acquires in the second half of the narrative. Her natural sense of the comic is more self-critical, less prone to partake of the hackneyed and the superficial. This is particularly true of her attitude towards outworn phrases or postures. She now anticipates and parodies the kind of trite remarks which formerly marred her own style, or which were used by individuals like Wickham to exploit her prejudices. Thus after her Derbyshire trip, she mockingly supplies Wickham with an explanation of his poor reputation at Pemberley: "At such a distance as *that*, you know, things are strangely misrepresented" (p. 327). This shift to parody is also evident in her ironic, rather than uncritical, approach to sentimental jargon in the later stages of the narrative. Consequently, she sums up her marital prospects with Darcy in terms that playfully recall the "violent affection" of previous judgments: "It is settled between us already, that we are to be the happiest couple in the world" (p. 373).

In *Mansfield Park* Mary Crawford's lighthearted conversation is superficially reminiscent of Elizabeth Bennet's style. Mary's spirited imitation of Hawkins Browne's "Address to Tobacco," in anticipation of Sir Thomas' return from the Caribbean, recalls Elizabeth's (and Henry Tilney's) gift for parody (*Mansfield*

Park, p. 161). Like Henry Tilney, Mary imitates social types as well as literary topics. Hence she fearlessly mimics Mrs. Norris' favorite refrain during a brief encounter at the ball in Fanny Price's honor: "Ah! ma'am, how much we want dear Mrs. Rushworth and Julia to-night!" (p. 277). There are also echoes of Elizabeth's deceptive playfulness in Mary's satiric analysis of her acquaintance. The plans for Maria's marriage immediately after Sir Thomas' return remind her of "the old heathen heroes, who after performing great exploits in a foreign land, offered sacrifices to the gods on their safe return" (p. 108). She is unsparing on the subject of Dr. Grant's love of food: "he did not eat any of the pheasant to day. He fancied it tough—sent away his plate—and has been suffering ever since" (p. 171). And in these satiric moods her accurate witticisms are faithful to the "really good feelings by which she was almost purely governed" (p. 147). But this similarity to Elizabeth Bennet's style is limited. Virginia Woolf has remarked that Mary's conversation is usually marred by the sudden, discordant note, and her "talk" becomes "flat" thereafter.[8] This is certainly true of the pun with which she assesses Yates as a potential husband for Julia Bertram: "What a difference a vowel makes!—if his rents were but equal to his rants!" (p. 394). Here the brilliant witticism emphasizes, rather than disguises, the predominantly materialistic standards that govern Mary's judgment and conduct. These standards are frequently postulated in her maxims, comic generalizations that recall those of *Pride and Prejudice* insofar as they imitate society's usual inversion of conventional ideals. But unlike Elizabeth Bennet, Mary identifies her values with the everyday order of priorities. Consequently, she defines marriage on a wholly materialistic basis: everybody should marry "as soon as they can do it to advantage" (p. 43). Similarly, since double-dealing is frequently experienced in marriage, "I feel that it *must* be so." And marriage is "of all transactions, the one

8. Virginia Woolf, *The Common Reader* (London, 1925), pp. 177–78. Compare Lionel Trilling, "*Mansfield Park*," in *Jane Austen, A Collection of Critical Essays*, ed. Ian Watt (Englewood Cliffs, N.J., 1963), 133; and Kenneth L. Moler, *Jane Austen's Art of Allusion* (Lincoln, Neb., 1968), 129.

in which people expect most from others, and are least honest themselves" (p. 46).

The incongruities of Mary's conversation are linked to the dichotomy between artifice and real feeling in *Mansfield Park*. Her graceful style is analogous to the polished formalities with which natural impulses are disguised in the Bertram family. Hence the disagreeable features that appear from time to time in Mary's conversation are not simply symptomatic of the temporary breakdown of her own elegant facade. They are also comparable with the frequent disruption of social propriety when the passions of Maria or Julia shatter the decorum imposed by an artificial upbringing. And in this regard, the ponderous formality of Sir Thomas' conversation is more closely related to Mary's style than would appear on the surface. His general reserve represses the open flow of his daughters' spirits in his presence (p. 19). But when his absence removes this arbitrary and unrealistic kind of moral control, their undisciplined instincts prompt all the indiscretions of the Sotherton trip, the theatricals, and the abortive Rushworth marriage. Sir Thomas' conversational style is an extension of this superficial and ineffective kind of propriety. For the rhetorical order of his massive eloquence is undercut by the selfish materialism that initially mars his character. His lecture to Fanny on Henry Crawford's merits is illustrative:

"Here is a young man of sense, of character, of temper, of manners, and of fortune, exceedingly attached to you, and seeking your hand in the most handsome and disinterested way; and let me tell you, Fanny, that you may live eighteen years longer in the world, without being addressed by a man of half Mr. Crawford's estate, or a tenth part of his merits. . . . And I should have been very much surprised had either of my daughters, on receiving a proposal of marriage at any time, which might carry with it only *half* the eligibility of *this*, immediately and peremptorily, and without paying my opinion or my regard the compliment of any consultation, put a decided negative on it." (p. 319)

While Mary Crawford's style shares affinities with Sir Thomas' personality, it is poles apart from Fanny Price's conversation. And aptly so, for this accords with the manner in which Mary's worldly cynicism is counterbalanced by Fanny's pious romanticism. Mary echoes and accepts the standards established by social practice, rather than the ideals that are theoretically supposed to govern everyday conduct. And this makes her the effective agent of Jane Austen's irony, for Mary's frank materialism is the realistic perspective that enables us to see society and manners as they really are. The central irony, then, of Mary's style is the fact that a *faux pas* which betrays her moral shortcomings is, simultaneously, the indispensable means for the satiric exposé of society. And it does appear to be indispensable when one accepts the realistic logic that pervades the characterization of Mary Crawford: life as it is can be most clearly seen, and most effectively ostracized, when it is presented through spokesmen who owe their allegiance to the real rather than to the ideal. Mary's personality and conversation arouse ambivalent responses on the same grounds that make satiric realism both attractive and disturbing: the aesthetic pleasures of imitation are counterbalanced by the shock of moral self-recognition. On the other hand, Fanny's conversation is rooted in the norms of traditional morality. And the ambiguity that surrounds Mary's style has its corollary in Fanny's personality. Fanny espouses, or pays lip-service to, ideals which are desirable on ethical grounds but which often seem incongruous or irrelevant because they are so far removed from the realities of life as it is. Hence, the psychological barrier that exists between Fanny's morality and the real world is dramatized by the sentimental heritage on which her character has been based. For example, she suffers from a constitutional debility that leaves her at a disadvantage in comparison with Mary, either in walking (at Sotherton) or in horseback riding. And this fragile physique and her tearfulness emphasize that Fanny is typical of the other-worldly, sentimental heroine, just as Mary is a prototype of the knowing cynic. Fanny's judgments tend to be self-consciously literary and are based on the idealistic or sentimental interpretation of popular writers. The depredations of the improver, for example, move her to quote Cowper's eulogy to the "fallen avenues" of nature in *The Task* (*Mansfield Park*, p. 56). Her disappointment with the architecture and atmosphere of the Sotherton chapel stirs recollections of Scott's *Last Minstrel* pp. 85–86). Samuel Johnson's *Rasselas* and Cowper's *Tirocinium* are both pressed into service when she is homesick for Mansfield Park (pp. 392, 431). And the poetic apostrophe is always at hand during moments of sentimental reflection, particularly when she recalls the "dear old, grey poney" with which she began her riding lessons (p. 27).[9] In effect, Fanny's literary idealism exposes the heartlessness of Mary Crawford's worldly brilliance; but, in turn, Mary's satiric realism counteracts Fanny's sentimental piety.

The network of relationships between Mary Crawford's conversation and other personalities in *Mansfield Park* is typical of the organic function of individual styles in Jane Austen novels. But this technique is really perfected in *Emma* where the heroine's consciousness dominates the presentation of character and action. And because of this dominance Emma's style dramatizes the defects which bring her in conflict with some persons and make her comparable with other members of her circle. Emma recalls Henry Tilney, Elizabeth Bennet, and Mary Crawford in that she is an accomplished parodist. She silently mimics the "Exactly so" of Mr. Elton's gallant "paradings" (p. 49), and the "Very true, my love" with which her sister usually pacifies John Knightley (p. 113). But as with Mary Crawford, this gift has been perverted to serve questionable purposes. In Emma's case, it dramatizes thoughtless arrogance, especially in her imitation of Miss Bates' style at the Coles' party. The subject is Miss Bates' imaginary gratitude for Mr. Knightley's "great kindness" in marrying Jane

9. As Frank W. Bradbrook notes, there is some satire directed against Fanny's self-conscious idealism, "Sources of Jane Austen's Ideas about Nature in *Mansfield Park*," *Notes & Queries*, CCVI (1961), 222–24. Fanny's eulogy to her dead pony may be based on Jane Austen's parody of the popular "animal" poems of the late eighteenth century. Cowper who appears to be Fanny's favorite poet, composed a formidable number of such verses, ranging from the comic to the sentimental. Among the latter there are epitaphs on Lady Throckmorton's bull finch and on her dog, Fop. Cowper, *Poems*, 125–26, 162–63.

Fairfax: " 'So very kind and obliging!—But he always had been such a very kind neighbour!' And then fly off, through half a sentence, to her mother's old petticoat. 'Not that it was such a very old petticoat either—for still it would last a great while—and, indeed, she must thankfully say that their petticoats were all very strong!' " (p. 225).

At other times this arrogance takes the form of an aggressive dogmatism. Her lectures to Harriet Smith are interspersed with maxims on marriage and society: "I lay it down as a general rule, Harriet, that if a woman *doubts* as to whether she should accept a man or not, she certainly ought to refuse him" (p. 52). Defending her snobbish indifference to the yeomanry she pontificates that the farmer does not need her help, "and is therefore in one sense as much above my notice as in every other he is below it" (p. 29). The precise antithesis of this statement is typical of the so-called Johnsonian structures which exaggerate her dogmatic deliveries. Her ringing denunciation of marriage is couched in a series of sweeping, parallel statements: "Fortune I do not want; employment I do not want; consequence I do not want" (p. 84). This kind of repetitive emphasis also appears in her heartless description of Miss Bates as "so silly—so satisfied—so smiling—so prosing —so undistinguishing and unfastidious—and so apt to tell every thing relative to every body" (p. 85). Her dogmatism heightens the absurdities of her undisciplined imagination, particularly when, like Marianne Dashwood, she asserts the wholly conjectural or the imaginary with all the absoluteness of fact. Consequently, Harriet Smith is assured that there can be no doubt of "your being a gentleman's daughter" (p. 30). An indignant Mr. Knightley is told, "There can scarcely be a doubt that her [Harriet's] father is a gentleman—and a gentleman of fortune" (p. 62). And she is equally assertive in her fanciful conjectures on Mr. Elton's attachment to Harriet's portrait: "It is his companion all this evening, his solace, his delight. It opens his designs to his family, it introduces you among them, it diffuses through the party those pleasantest feelings of our nature, eager curiosity and warm prepossession. How cheerful, how animated, how suspicious, how busy their imaginations all are!" (p. 56).

Emma's dogmatism links her, ironically, with her worst enemy, Mrs. Elton. For in some respects the vicar's wife is a grotesque caricature of Emma's worst faults, especially her self-centered complacency and her magisterial determination to manage and dominate the affairs of others. Consequently Emma's arrogant assertiveness is often reproduced in Mrs. Elton's conversation, including the occasion on which the latter proposes a joint leadership of Highbury society: "I hope we shall have many sweet little concerts together. I think, Miss Woodhouse, you and I must establish a musical club, and have regular meetings at your house, or ours. Will not it be a good plan? If *we* exert ourselves, I think we shall not be long in want of allies. Something of that nature would be particularly desirable for *me*, as an inducement to keep me in practice" (p. 277). And this ironic link between Emma and a character whom she despises is paralleled by the similarity between herself and those whom she patronizes. Hence, Emma is contemptuously amused by Harriet Smith's sentimental cache of "*Most precious treasures*" (pp. 338–39). But Harriet's mementos of the ill-fated intimacy with Mr. Elton are also tangible reminders of Emma's own absurdities, the sentimental fantasies which lead her to initiate a match between Harriet and Mr. Elton, or to conjure up the "sweet, sad poison" of Jane Fairfax's illicit passions. Similarly, Emma's contempt for Miss Bates' foibles is counteracted by the fact that in awkward moments, Emma herself lapses into the staccato delivery which she usually derides in Miss Bates. Hence, in formulating lame excuses for having neglected the spinster's family Emma finds that any intimacy would have been disagreeable, "a waste of time—tiresome women—and all the horror of being in danger of falling in with the second rate and third rate of Highbury" (p. 155). This similarity is satirically incongruous, for the narrow selfishness that has inspired Emma's embarrassed self-defense is directly opposed to Miss Bates's "universal good-will and contented temper" (p. 21). Emma's broken sentences express the shamefaced recognition—and simultaneous denial—of insensitivity towards Jane Fairfax. On the other hand, Miss Bates's incomplete structures are expressive of her diffusive generosity, the "desultory good-will" which allows her to love everybody and to be "interested in every body's happiness, quick-sighted to every body's merits" (p. 21).

In fact, the comparisons with Miss Bates's style are not limited to Emma's conversation, for the spinster's delivery is central to a distinct network of ironically juxtaposed personalities. Miss Bates's long-winded account of Frank Churchill's kindness to her family demonstrates her benevolent disposition as well as the more obvious absurdities:

"What was I talking of?" said she, beginning again when they were all in the street.

Emma wondered on what, of all the medley, she would fix.

"I declare I cannot recollect what I was talking of.—Oh! my mother's spectacles. So very obliging of Mr. Frank Churchill! 'Oh!' said he, 'I do think I can fasten the rivet; I like a job of this kind excessively.'—Which you know shewed him to be so very. . . . Indeed I must say that, much as I had heard of him before and much as I had expected, he very far exceeds any thing. . . . I do congratulate you, Mrs. Weston, most warmly. He seems every thing the fondest parent could. . . . 'Oh!' said he, 'I can fasten the rivet. I like a job of that sort excessively.' I never shall forget his manner." (pp. 237–38)

Ironically, Mrs. Elton falls back on an incongruous version of Miss Bates's "medley" whenever she wishes to affect universal goodwill. The "apparatus of happiness" with which the vicar's wife descends on Donwell Abbey is illustrative:

"The best fruit in England—every body's favourite—always wholesome.—These the finest beds and finest sorts.—Delightful to gather for one's self—the only way of really enjoying them.—Morning decidedly the best time—never tired—every sort good—hautboy infinitely superior—no comparison—the others hardly eatable—hautboys very scarce—Chili preferred—white wood finest flavour of all—price of strawberries in London—abundance about Bristol—Maple Grove—cultivation—beds when to be renewed—gardeners thinking exactly different—no general rule—gardeners never to be put out of their way—delicious fruit—only too rich to be eaten much of—inferior to cherries—currants more refreshing—only objection to gathering strawberries the stooping —glaring sun—tired to death—could bear it no longer—must go and sit in the shade." (pp. 358–59)

But the unconscious adoption of Miss Bates's style is not always incongruous. The broken sentences emphasize Mr. Knightley's indignation against Frank Churchill, for the traditionally emotive aposiopesis expresses the speaker's genuine concern at Frank's supposed unfaithfulness to Emma: " 'Time, my dearest Emma, time will heal the wound.—Your own excellent sense—your exertions for your father's sake—I know you will not allow yourself —. Her arm was pressed again, as he added, in a more broken and subdued accent, 'The feelings of the warmest friendship—Indignation—Abominable scoundrel!' " (p. 426).

Altogether, then, the emotional values represented by Miss Bates's personality and conversation have become the central point of reference in the evaluation of feeling in the novel. And her comic absurdities are a kind of mask that Jane Austen uses to disguise this moral function. Neither does this entirely account for ironic roles that are assigned to Miss Bates's conversation; for if her emotional strengths are utilized as moral criteria, her mental limitations are just as important in the general framework of Jane Austen's narrative commentary. On the whole, Jane Austen intensifies the effect of her satiric commentary by presenting it as the unintentional irony of intellectually limited characters like Miss Bates. Prior to *Emma* this technique is not frequently in evidence, and appears only in Catherine Morland's unconscious satire on "fine language" (*Northanger Abbey*, p. 133), and in Lady Bertram's ingenuous reminders to Mrs. Norris about the latter's comfortable income (*Mansfield Park*, pp. 28–30). But in *Emma*, Miss Bates is joined by Harriet Smith and Mr. Woodhouse as the unwitting agents of satiric analysis. For example, Miss Bates is blissfully unaware of the ironic incongruity that she effects when she extends her uncritical benevolence to Mr. Elton and his future wife: "It is such a good thing when good people get together

—and they always do. Now, here will be Mr. Elton and Miss Hawkins; and there are the Coles, such very good people" (p. 175). Harriet Smith's naiveté is unwittingly ironic when she, too, remarks on the compatibility of the Eltons: Mrs. Elton "does seem a charming woman, just what he deserves. Happy creature!" (p. 272). And the unconscious ironies of both Miss Bates and Harriet become more explicit at Box Hill when Frank Churchill delivers his sarcastic toast to the Eltons: "Happy couple! . . . How well they suit one another!" (p. 372). Miss Bates's undiscriminating generosity becomes more incisively ironic when it is applied to Emma, especially in connection with the Box Hill picnic. In reprimanding Emma's rudeness to Miss Bates, Mr. Knightley's deliberate strictures are more than equaled by the characteristic goodwill of Miss Bates herself: "I must make myself very disagreeable," Miss Bates comments after Emma's insult, "or she would not have said such a thing to an old friend" (p. 371). Subsequently, when a conscience-stricken Emma visits the Bates family she is again subjected to the unintended satire of her hostess's reflections on the ill-starred picnic: "I cannot say that any of them seemed very much to have enjoyed it. However, *I* shall always think it a very pleasant party, and feel extremely obliged to the kind friends who included me in it" (p. 381). Nor does Emma obtain relief when she returns home, for there Mr. Woodhouse demonstrates *his* links with Miss Bates: "Dear Emma has been to call on Mrs. and Miss Bates, Mr. Knightley, as I told you before. She is always so attentive to them!" (p. 385).

Jane Austen's emphasis on unwitting, rather than conscious, irony in *Emma* is only partially explained on the basis of Miss Bates's obvious incapacities as a deliberate satirist. The unintentional effects of Miss Bates's conversation, together with the styles of Harriet Smith and Mr. Woodhouse, are also derived from the major psychological issues that influence satiric judgment in *Emma*. Initially, Emma is unconscious of her society and the realities of her environment because she is hampered by imagination and pride. Hence her love for Mr. Knightley remains largely subconscious at first, disguised by the traditional feuds of the inverted courtship. It rises to the surface, momentarily, only when her possessive regard is threatened by rumors of Jane Fairfax's rivalry. Before Harriet's confession forces Emma to conscious awareness, Mr. Knightley's real significance is revealed only through ironic implication, by Emma's inadvertent betrayal of her subconscious affections: "A Mrs. Knightley for them all to give way to!—No—Mr. Knightley must never marry. Little Henry must remain the heir of Donwell" (p. 228). Moreover, when Emma tries to dominate human relationships without knowing anything about them, the truths to which she blinds herself are often implied to the reader—Mr. Elton's real interest in Hartfield, or the telltale signs of a secret understanding between Frank and Jane. And the implications of the truth are ironically juxtaposed, first with Emma's smug blindness, and subsequently with her embarrased awareness.

In other words, ironic implication is a predominant narrative principle in *Emma*, and it is related directly to the moral psychology of the heroine's character. It is through implication and satiric innuendo that Jane Austen keeps the reader alert to the subconscious or external realities which Emma has obscured from herself. Miss Bates's unwitting role as a satiric agent is analogous to Jane Austen's exploitation of Emma's subconsciousness in order to imply the heroine's real, but unacknowledged, impulses. Secondly, Miss Bates's reportorial style mirrors the way in which the narrative as a whole is gradually unfolded through implication. She is a "great talker upon little matters" who is "full of trivial communications and harmless gossip" (p. 21). Mary Lascelles has already demonstrated how much of the apparent trivia is really information that is crucial to the development of the plot (*Jane Austen and her Art*, pp. 177–78). But the *manner* as well as the content of Miss Bates's "trivial communications" is also relevant; for like the general development of the novel's structure, her reportage proceeds on the basis of implication. When she comments on Mr. Elton's forthcoming marriage, for example, the typical medley of incomplete sentences becomes an innocent but subtle recapitulation of the vicar's former intimacy with Emma:

"A Miss Hawkins.—Well, I had always rather fancied it would be some young lady hereabouts; not that I ever—Mrs. Cole once whispered to me—but I immediately said, 'No, Mr. Elton is a most worthy young man—but'—In short, I do not think I am particularly quick at those sort of discoveries. I do not pretend to it. What is before me, I see. At the same time, nobody could wonder if Mr. Elton should have aspired —Miss Woodhouse lets me chatter on, so good-humouredly. She knows I would not offend for the world." (p. 176)

Miss Bates's hints inadvertently embarrass Emma with mortifying proof that Mr. Elton's real object at Hartfield had always been obvious, even to those who, like Miss Bates, are not "particularly quick at those sort of discoveries." Moreover, the innuendos of the incomplete sentences reflect the very process of implication and ironic suggestion through which Mr. Elton's motives had initially been revealed to the reader. The "incessant flow" with which Miss Bates makes her entrance for the Crown Inn ball is comparable, for on that occasion the recurrent minutiae about Frank Churchill imply a degree of intimacy that prepares for the eventual disclosure of his involvement with Jane Fairfax. And with a totally unconscious touch of irony, Miss Bates disguises these hints by prefacing them with precisely the kind of irrelevant chitchat (about Jane and Mr. Dixon) which distracts Emma from the real truth:

"Thank you, my mother is remarkably well. Gone to Mr. Woodhouse's. I made her take her shawl—for the evenings are not warm—her large new shawl—Mrs. Dixon's wedding present.—So kind of her to think of my mother! Bought at Weymouth, you know—Mr. Dixon's choice. There were three others, Jane says, which they hesitated about some time. Colonel Campbell rather preferred an olive. My dear Jane, are you sure you did not wet your feet?—It was but a drop or two, but I am so afraid:—but Mr. Frank Churchill was so extremely—and there was a mat to step upon—I shall never forget his extreme politeness.—Oh! Mr. Frank Churchill, I must tell you my mother's spectacles have never been in fault since; the rivet never came out again. My

mother often talks of your goodnature. Does not she, Jane?—Do not
we often talk of Mr. Frank Churchill? Ah! here's Miss Woodhouse.
(pp. 322–23)

Here, too, the structure of Miss Bates's conversation is a microcosm
of Jane Austen's narrative form. The innocent details about Frank
Churchill are subtle pointers to facts of crucial importance; and
the universal gratitude which recalls Mr. Dixon's thoughtfulness
is an ironic parallel to Emma's reprehensible suspicions about
Jane's romantic misadventures. Moreover, the strategy whereby
Jane Austen juxtaposes factual experience and Emma's fantasies
is reproduced by the effects of Miss Bates's seemingly chaotic
style: we are led from the misleading side issue of the Dixons, to
the real drama represented by Frank Churchill, then, appropriately, to Emma Woodhouse herself.

   The pervasive influence of Miss Bates's style, particularly in relation to Emma's development, attests once again to the fundamental roles of "flat" styles in Jane Austen's fiction. The harmless
Miss Bates is a major agent of Jane Austen's satire by virtue of
the multiple suggestions that the novelist derives from the apparently "simple" conversational style. Miss Bates represents both
the climax and the conclusion of a technique that can be traced
back to *Northanger Abbey*. Few of the individual styles of *Persuasion* are as comically obtrusive as the conversation of Mrs.
Palmer or Miss Bates. Sir Walter Elliot and Admiral Croft are
exceptions, but on the whole, there is less emphasis on the network
of ironic associations which Jane Austen achieves in the previous
novels by carefully interrelating individual styles with each other
and with the total narrative framework. For these structural functions are served largely by Jane Austen's increasing interest in the
kind of comprehensive symbolism that we have already examined
in *Persuasion*.

CHAPTER VI

The True Art
of Letter Writing

IN A LETTER to her sister Cassandra, Jane Austen observes, "I have now attained the true art of letter-writing, which we are always told, is to express on paper exactly what one would say to the same person by word of mouth; I have been talking to you almost as fast as I could the whole of this letter" (*Letters*, p. 102). As usual, Jane Austen's flippant tone fails to disguise the seriousness of her literary judgment, for the remark really demonstrates her interest in the letter as an extension of conversation. The true art of letter writing is analogous to the polite traditions of conversation. This parallel is crucial to an understanding of the function of letters in her fiction. Occasionally, Jane Austen's personal correspondence notes the importance of letters in the straightforward dissemination of facts (*Letters*, pp. 181, 244); and this role is fairly evident in the novels. Mr. Collins' visit to Longbourn is heralded by his letter to Mr. Bennet, and during her stay at Portsmouth Fanny Price's main sources of information on the Mansfield Park family are letters from Mary Crawford and Lady Bertram. But as Jane Austen's own comparison of letter writing with conversation makes clear, she is more interested in letters (in fiction and in real life) as the direct transmission of personal values and feeling. In essence, epistolary styles are as integral to the theme and structure of each work as individual conversation.

And this concern with the expressive values of the letter is evinced by the novelist's generous praise of Fanny Knight's style: "Such Letters, such entertaining Letters as you have lately sent!—Such a description of your queer little heart!—Such a lovely display of what Imagination does. . . . You are the Paragon of all that is Silly & Sensible, common-place & eccentric, Sad & Lively, Provoking & Interesting.—Who can keep pace with the fluctuations of your Fancy, the Capprizios of your Taste, the Contradictions of your Feelings?—You are so odd!—& all the time, so perfectly natural—so peculiar in yourself, & yet so like everybody else!" (*Letters*, p. 478). But in *Mansfield Park* Henry Crawford's letters fall far short of the standards represented by Fanny Knight. In spite of Fanny Price's prejudices against the Crawfords, it is still possible to accept her judgment that Henry's indifferent performance as a letter writer argues serious defects in his emotional faculties: "I cannot rate so very highly the love or good nature of a brother, who will not give himself the trouble of writing any thing worth reading, to his sisters, when they are separated" (p. 64). Similarly, Lady Bertram's letters reflect the selfish indolence that has immunized her against feeling. Lacking any really expressive functions, her letters usually magnify the trivial and the irrelevant. Hence they are written in "a very creditable, common-place, amplifying style, so that a very little matter was enough for her" (p. 425).

Like her views on conversation, Jane Austen's concept of epistolary self-revelation is comparable with those of her eighteenth-century predecessors, especially Samuel Richardson. In *Clarissa* there are several reminders of Richardson's faith in the letter as a kind of confessional. This belief is voiced by Belford who asserts that the style of those "writing of and in the midst of *present* distresses is *much more* lively and affecting" than the "dry" and "unanimated" narrative that describes "dangers surmounted." Even Lovelace is forced to admit the phenomenon of a man's conscience being able to "force his fingers to write whether he will or not," and to run him upon a subject which "he more than once, at the very time, resolved not to think of."[1] Richardson's personal correspondence partially supports the thesis propounded in his novels. Writing to Sophia Westcomb, he declares that epistolary styles vary as much as faces, "and are indicative, generally beyond the power of disguise, of the mind of the writer!"[2] In his essay on Richardson's letters, John Carroll has noted that the novelist personally tends to obscure or oversimplify the limitations of the letter as a form of emotional self-expression: "Richardson ignores the psychological barrier against complete exposure of the self (the writing closet cannot easily be turned into a confessional) and the desire of the letter-writer to present himself in a favorable light." And curiously, unlike his creations, Richardson "does not take account of the suppressions and evasions that may affect the style of the least designing of correspondents."[3] Carroll's point is well taken, and he is supported by Samuel Johnson whose "Life" of Pope views "epistolary intercourse" as a temptation to "fallacy" and "sophistication."[4] However, Johnson's comment does imply a crucial corollary. For in spite of painstaking efforts to create a desirable image of himself, the letter writer unconsciously betrays his real personality in the very process of self-flattery and beguiling "sophistication." Obviously this is the implication of Johnson's uncomplimentary penetration of what he regards as the facade raised by Pope the letter writer. In effect, the writing of a letter is at once an act of confession and an experience in conflict. The writer's instinct to project a favorable image of himself is counteracted by the letter's inherent tendency to be self-expressive. The process of spontaneous self-revelation is not wholly negated by deliberate efforts at concealment—it is simply transformed into unconscious self-betrayal. Hence Lovelace's exclamation on the

1. Samuel Richardson, *Clarissa, or the History of a Young Lady*, Shakespeare Head Edition (8 vols.; Oxford, 1930), VII, 77; VIII, 145. Richardson quotes Belford in his preface where the novelist makes a general defense of the epistolary form (I, xiv).

2. Samuel Richardson, *Selected Letters*, ed. John Carroll (Oxford, 1964), 64.

3. *Ibid.*, 33–34.

4. Samuel Johnson, *Lives of the Poets*, ed. G. B. Hill (3 vols.; Oxford, 1905), III, 206–208.

compulsion of conscience is really a highly dramatized insight with which Johnson may well have agreed.

Jane Austen's treatment of epistolary styles attests to her awareness of these psychological subtleties. Her emphasis on the self-expressiveness of Fanny Knight's letters is matched by her exploitation of epistolary styles, in the novels, as the means of unintended self-betrayal. Hence the irony of Mr. Collins' self-conscious style, both as a letter writer and as a conversationalist, lies in the fact that his native stupidity is repeatedly dramatized by the very orotundity that is meant to demonstrate intelligence. Johnson's thesis is even more effective when it is applied to the highly self-conscious "amplifications" of Lady Bertram's "commonplace" letters, or to the kind of letter writer that Henry Tilney castigates for a "general deficiency of subject, a total inattention to stops, and a very frequent ignorance of grammar" (*Northanger Abbey*, p. 27). These "confessional" and self-betraying functions which Jane Austen's fictional letters inherit from Richardson do not exhaust the potential of epistolary forms in her novels. The third role, which Richardson also develops, is quite as important. Specifically, the letter writer not only engages in some kind of self-portrayal, but he also contributes his style and judgment to the presentation of other characters. A very notable example of this in Richardson's fiction would be Pamela's portrait of Mr. B. His major qualities—intemperance, sexual attractions, aristocratic pride, and general failings as an employer—are presented in turn through Pamela's strong moral sense, her equally strong sexual instincts, individualism, and a peasant's pride in the integrity of her class. But this technique is not exclusive in *Pamela*. After all, the heroine also acts as a reporter and narrator and, as such, frequently allows us unedited transcripts of Mr. B.'s words and actions. Her young master's personality is conveyed to the reader on two levels—through the self-revelations of *his* letters and through Pamela's conscious judgment. In *Clarissa* this epistolary technique comes even closer to Jane Austen's achievement. For in his second novel Richardson uses the greater and more continuous interplay of correspondents to present Solmes from several viewpoints, without resorting to the reportorial impartiality of a part-time narrator. Solmes is never really allowed to expose himself to the reader in the manner of Lovelace or on the basis of Mr. B.'s unedited declarations. Indeed Solmes is not simply an independent psychological entity, but also a combined projection of all the hostile reactions to his personality. Anna Howe's contemptuous irony, Clarissa's sexual revulsion, and Lovelace's outraged pride—all these are the perceptual and emotional reactions to Solmes, and he literally owes his only identity in the novel to them. Thus, in Solmes's case, Richardson is allowing his letter writers to use their correspondence not only for personal communication, but also for the establishing of specific identities beyond themselves.

Like Richardson, Jane Austen uses this interplay of individual judgments to project the identity of a separate character, from as early as the juvenilia. Hence Mr. Watts (*Three Sisters*) is comparable with Solmes in that both have been presented through the prejudices of others. Mary and Georgiana Stanhope agree, for once, on Mr. Watts's repulsiveness, on his jealousy and his domineering ill-temper. And this parallel between Mr. Watts and Richardson's Solmes complements Jane Austen's general parody of the family rivalries in *Clarissa*.[5] In fact Jane Austen's earlier experiments with the epistolary mode are closely integrated with the parodies which dominate the juvenilia. The journal-like form of Laura's unilateral correspondence in *Love and Freindship* parodies the structure of *Pamela*, and, more probably, the popular, sentimental imitators of Richardson's first novel. And in *Lesley Castle* Jane Austen plays a literary game with the letter as self-revelation. The work is partly a burlesque study of letter writing *per se*, as is evident in the correspondence of Miss Lutterell and Mrs. Marlowe. The former echoes the Richardsonian thesis on the letter as a confessional: "I assure you that it will be a great

5. Generally, the relationship between Jane Austen's three women, especially *vis à vis* Mr. Watts, is similar to the opening scenes of *Clarissa*. Arabella Harlowe's selfish jealousy with regards to Lovelace's short-lived courtship anticipates Mary Stanhope's fearful suspicions of her sisters.

releif to me to write to you and as long as my Health and Spirits will allow me, you will find me a very constant correspondent. ... The Possibility of being able to write, to speak, to you of my lost Henry will be a luxury to me, and your goodness will not I know refuse to read what it will so much releive my Heart to write" (*Minor Works*, p. 132). Miss Lutterell's intentions are not wholly absurd. Her faith in the expressiveness of the epistolary form has a respectable precedent, and her interchangeable use of "to write" and "to speak" is very much in accord with Jane Austen's personal definition of letter writing. But the therapeutic "luxury" that Miss Lutterell seeks from her correspondence suggests that Jane Austen is satirizing the sentimental abuses of Richardson's techniques, and Mrs. Marlowe's rejoinder makes the parody more obvious: "I think the melancholy Indulgence of your own sorrows by repeating them and dwelling on them to me, will only encourage and increase them, and that it will be more prudent in you to avoid so sad a subject" (*Minor Works*, p. 134). In short, Jane Austen is not decrying the epistolary tradition as such, but as in the case of imagery, she characteristically dissociates a literary medium from popular abuse while simultaneously exploiting it for the purposes of her own art.

Those goals are in evidence from the juvenilia, and they include, above all, her early interest in the psychological roles of the epistolary form. In *Love and Freindship*, for example, the epistolary form is not simply a parodic device. It is also carefully integrated with the kind of personality that Laura reveals herself to be. Laura begins with the ostensible purpose of personal aggrandizement and self-flattery. Her letters to Marianne are to be guidelines for moral conduct and discretion: "I will gratify the curiosity of your [Isabel's] Daughter; and may the fortitude with which I have suffered the many afflictions of my past Life, prove to her a useful lesson for the support of those which may befall her in her own" (*Minor Works*, p. 77). Obviously, Laura intends that by inspiring Marianne with fortitude and prudence her letters will be monuments to her own tested "virtues." But, as we have already seen, the values that Laura postulates in the guise of love and friendship are really the selfish perversions of those ideals. Her subversive ego communicates itself, appropriately, through the kind of unilateral correspondence that leaves her at center-stage. And the attempts to present herself as the sentimental heroine *par excellence* are continually undermined by the repeated betrayal of her cynical materialism and selfish pride. Moreover, and this is Jane Austen's fundamental strategy throughout, Laura's self-betrayals are most obvious, and her perverted values are most glaring, in the very letters that attempt self-justification. Thus when she defends Sophia's "accidental" and "dignified" theft of Macdonald's money (pp. 95–96), or when she extols Augustus' indifference to his debts (p. 88), she demolishes her own pretensions to genuine sensibility. The retreat to the Highlands is a final, egotistical gesture. For in emphasizing the romantic sensibility that leads her to Scotland, Laura hypocritically includes her alleged grief for what she once described as the "trifling circumstance" of her parents' death (p. 89): "I took up my Residence in a romantic Village in the Highlands of Scotland where I have ever since continued, and where I can uninterrupted by unmeaning Visits, indulge in a melancholy solitude, my unceasing Lamentations for the Death of my Father, my Mother, my Husband and my Freind" (pp. 108–109). The present interest in "melancholy," in "romantic" nature, and "solitude" is very similar to her antisocial interpretation of love, friendship, and sensibility. For Laura has veritably transformed these idealistic terms into the rhetoric of self-interest. And the final effect of the metamorphosis is a series of ironic juxtapositions: idealistic terms are yoked with materialistic realities, literary sentimentality with social insensitivity, and self-justification with self-betrayal. Or, to paraphrase Samuel Johnson, Laura's egotistic "sophistication" as a letter writer accords with the incongruities and the contradictions that Jane Austen satirizes in *Love and Freindship*. The inherent, psychological conflicts of letter writing have become the foundation for parody, social satire, and characterization.

Jane Austen's juvenilia offer several parallels to the kind of self-betrayal that is represented by the letters in *Love and Freindship*. In *Jack & Alice* Lady Williams' letters counsel principled conduct in one sentence, then discount morality in the next: " 'Why do you hesitate my dearest Lucy, a moment with respect to the Duke? I have enquired into his Character & find him to be an unprincipaled, illiterate Man. Never shall my Lucy be united to such a one! He has a princely fortune, which is every day encreasing. How nobly will you spend it!' " (*Minor Works*, p. 27). This is, admittedly, a rather crude version of the contradictions on which Jane Austen constructs Laura's letters in *Love and Freindship*. The conflict between sensibility and materialism, between sentimental rhetoric and cynical action, is awkwardly obvious in Lady Williams' case. But in both works the objective is the same: the ironic exposure of the heroine's hypocrisy is predicated upon the manner in which the letter writer's instinct for self-justification is counteracted by the inevitable revelations of the epistolary mode. Thus in *Love and Freindship* the ironic contrasts emanate from Laura's misuse of definitive or evaluative terms, from her habit of exploiting idealistic terminology as a camouflage for selfish impulses. But in *Jack & Alice* Lady Williams favors an exclamatory rather than an analytical style, and her letter is comparatively free of definitive terms. Hence her hypocrisy is expressed in the form of excited self-contradiction. This may not be the most realistic method in the world, but it is consistent with Lady Williams' habitual style. Her letter is comparable with her conversational techniques in the nonepistolary section of the work, a parallel that takes us once again to Jane Austen's personal comparison of letters and conversation. Note, for example, the "persuasive arguments" with which Lady Williams urges Lucy to visit Bath: "Lady Williams insisted on her going—declared that she would never forgive her if she did not, and that she should never survive it if she did" (p. 24).

On the whole, then, both *Love and Freindship* and *Jack & Alice* demonstrate that the young Jane Austen is scrupulously exact in integrating the idiosyncrasies of each writer, and the general principles of letter writing, with prevailing satiric themes. This also applies to *The Three Sisters* where Jane Austen's narrative centers on the conflicting personalities of Mary and Georgiana Stanhope. And accordingly, the epistolary style of each is sharply distinguished from the other. Georgiana's letters are analytical. Her sentences are carefully constructed to conform with the ironic interplay of ideas and judgments. Her account of Mary's engagement, for example, is given in a complex sentence of subordinate and coordinate clauses which counterbalance the motives of the contracting parties: "Our neighbour Mr Watts has made proposals to Mary: Proposals which she knew not how to receive, for tho' she has a particular Dislike to him (in which she is not singular) yet she would willingly marry him sooner than risk his offering to Sophy or me which in case of a refusal from herself, he told her he should do, for you must know the poor Girl considers our marrying before her as one of the greatest misfortunes that can possibly befall her, & to prevent it would willingly ensure herself ever lasting Misery by a Marriage with Mr Watts" (*Minor Works*, p. 61). Mary's version of the dilemma is a breathless jumble of contradictions: "I wont have him I declare. . . . I must get him while I can. . . . I beleive I shant have him. . . . I will have him" (pp. 58–59). When Georgiana uses sentences as short as these they are carefully grouped to form a special pattern of meaning or structure—especially in her antithetical summary of Mr. Watts' reputation: "They say he is stingy; We'll call that Prudence. They say he is suspicious. *That* proceeds from a warmth of Heart always excusable in Youth" (p. 62).

The external conflicts of *The Three Sisters* and the personal self-contradictions of *Love and Freindship* anticipate the epistolary form of *Lady Susan* where Jane Austen demonstrates her early mastery of the structural and psychological functions of letter writing. The tentative experiment with two, rather than one, letter writers in *The Three Sisters* has matured into the multiple exchanges provided by four major correspondents in *Lady Susan*.

And, simultaneously, the stylistic contrasts of *The Three Sisters* multiply in *Lady Susan* in order to conform with a wider range of personal rivalries. Moreover, the external divisions that are dramatized by the letters of *Three Sisters* are joined and complicated here by the private contradictions which Jane Austen previously explored in *Love and Freindship*: the mutual antagonism of Lady Susan and Mrs. Vernon is partly shaped by the deliberate double-dealing and unintentional self-contradictions of each. Lady Susan's duplicity and her aggressive sexuality are indicative of her manipulative instincts. Her desire to dominate and exploit others proceeds from an inordinate preoccupation with Self. But, ironically, Mrs. Vernon's conventional "morality" also takes the form of cold-blooded manipulation. In her determination to thwart Lady Susan's schemes, real or imagined, Mrs. Vernon often loses sight of the very values which she purportedly defends against her sister-in-law. Her main goal is to pry her brother loose from Lady Susan's dangerous charms by promoting a match between Reginald and Frederica. However, in so doing, she uses Frederica as a mere tool, just as Frederica's mother would have done. And Reginald De Courcy himself is hardly an ideal champion of conventional morality. He tends to be motivated not so much by principle as by the prejudice of the moment. His judgments on Lady Susan in particular are predicated upon the most recent bit of gossip, be it the hearsays of Mr. Smith, the spiteful invectives of Mr. Johnson, or the blandishments of Lady Susan herself. On the whole, then, characterization in *Lady Susan* is based on the opposition, as well as the comparison, of personal insights and behavioral patterns. The built-in drama of the epistolary mode is being shaped to meet the demands of moral and psychological conflicts. And these clashes are conveyed through the major epistolary devices which Jane Austen explored in the earlier juvenilia.[6]

6. B. C. Southam agrees with the Austen family tradition in assigning the composition of *Lady Susan* to the later 1790's, and *Three Sisters* to the period 1787–90. *Jane Austen's Literary Manuscripts: A Study of the Novelist's Development through the Surviving Papers* (London, 1964), 60–62, 45–46.

First, the presentation of Frederica recalls *The Three Sisters* in that her personality is filtered through the prejudices of various narrators. Lady Susan's impatience and contempt create the impression of a headstrong simpleton. Her first letter to Mr. Vernon hints at Frederica's supposed intractability by confessing, "I have but too much reason to fear that the Governess to whose care I consigned her, was unequal to the charge" (*Minor Works*, p. 244). But in a more outspoken letter to her confidante, Mrs. Johnson, Lady Susan is more commendatory than she intends. Frederica, it turns out, is "the greatest simpleton on Earth" for having objected to a marriage with Sir James, a suitor whom even Lady Susan herself finds substandard: "Frederica, who was born to be the torment of my life, chose to set herself so violently against the match, that I thought it better to lay aside the scheme for the present. I have more than once repented that I did not marry him myself, & were he but one degree less contemptibly weak I certainly should" (p. 245). The initial outbursts against Frederica are inspired by Lady Susan's unfeeling arrogance, by what she perversely mislabels as "the sacred impulse of maternal affection" (p. 245). Her later attacks are largely the result of jealousy. Frederica is becoming a rival for Reginald's attentions: "To disobey her Mother by refusing an unexceptionable offer is not enough; her affections must likewise be given without her Mother's approbation. I never saw a girl of her age, bid fairer to be the sport of Mankind. Her feelings are tolerably lively, & she is so charmingly artless in their display, as to afford the most reasonable hope of her being ridiculed & despised by every Man who sees her." Neither is Frederica redeemed by Mrs. Vernon's friendship: "She is exactly the companion for Mrs. Vernon, who dearly loves to be first, & to have all the sense & all the wit of the Conversation to herself; Frederica will never eclipse her" (p. 274).

Lady Susan is not altogether unfair in her assessment of Mrs. Vernon's prim morality. In fact, the latter's calculating condescension is even more effective than Lady Susan's invectives in distorting Frederica's vulnerable innocence. At first Mrs. Vernon's prejudices against Lady Susan extend, unthinkingly, to Frederica: "a girl of sixteen who has received so wretched an education would not be a very desirable companion here" (p. 247). But, subsequently, that "wretched" education is outweighed by the advantages that Frederica offers as innocent but vital proof of Lady Susan's depravity. Besides, Frederica's easy gratitude is no inconsiderable balm to Mrs. Vernon's self-righteous generosity: "there is a peculiar sweetness in her look when she speaks either to her Uncle or me, for as we behave kindly to her, we have of course engaged her gratitude. Her Mother has insinuated that her temper is untractable, but I never saw a face less indicative of any evil disposition than her's" (p. 270). And, to climax her virtues, Frederica is an admirable bait in the business of detaching Reginald from Lady Susan: "could Frederica's artless affection detach him from her Mother, we might bless the day which brought her to Churchill" (p. 272). Like Lady Susan, Mrs. Vernon is attempting to distort Frederica's personality to fit her own prejudices and schemes. And in this regard, Jane Austen has modified the tactics of Richardson's *Clarissa* and her own *Three Sisters*. For unlike that of Solmes or Mr. Watts, Frederica's personality contradicts rather than confirms the prejudices of her critics. The reader receives no glimpse of any quality that could redeem Mr. Watts from the varied invectives of Mary and Georgiana Stanhope. On the other hand, in spite of her attempts to demolish Frederica, Lady Susan unwittingly reveals the commendable qualities which prompt her daughter to reject Sir James. And Lady Susan's obvious jealousy vitiates her subsequent ridicule of Frederica's attachment to Reginald. Hence, having been forewarned of Frederica's real, if naive, goodness, we are prepared to evaluate Mrs. Vernon's initial hostility for what it really is, a blind and unjust extension of hatred for Lady Susan. In effect, Jane Austen has modified the letter writer's role as critic in order to develop the moral and psychological confrontations of *Lady Susan*. Frederica's personality is the meeting point for the very antagonisms that are responsible for introducing her to the reader.

Consequently, the portrayal of Frederica is integrated with the second major function of letters in *Lady Susan*. For in describing or using Frederica's character both Lady Susan and Mrs. Vernon are engaged in the letter writer's perennial business of self-justification. And, as usual, Jane Austen subverts this instinctive process in order to have each correspondent betray herself unwittingly. Lady Susan's pretensions to "maternal affection" are undermined by the flimsy grounds on which she indicts Frederica as an "intractable" child. Mrs. Vernon's belated fairness to Frederica's integrity is really another ploy in the former's running feud with Lady Susan. And even after that redoubtable charmer has been safely married to Sir James, the family pressures for Reginald's marriage are suspiciously therapeutic in intent: "Frederica was therefore fixed in the family of her Uncle & Aunt, till such time as Reginald De Courcy could be talked, flattered & finessed into an affection for her—which, allowing leisure for the conquest of his attachment to her Mother, for his abjuring all future attachments & detesting the Sex, might be reasonably looked for in the course of a Twelvemonth" (p. 313).

Both Lady Susan and Mrs. Vernon expose their egotistic impulses in other areas of their continuing rivalry. But what is equally noteworthy is Jane Austen's emphasis on the internal conflicts of each antagonist. In Lady Susan's case, for example, there are clearly defined distinctions in style, depending on her mood and correspondent. Hence the first letters to Mr. Vernon and Mrs. Johnson, respectively, are more than a direct exposure of the writer's hypocrisy. They also point to her emotional conflicts. In each letter she contemplates the prospect of a visit to Churchill. She is suitably enthusiastic and ingratiating when she writes to Mr. Vernon:

I can no longer refuse myself the pleasure of profitting by your kind invitation when we last parted, of spending some weeks with you at Churchill, & therefore if quite convenient to you & Mrs. Vernon to receive me at present, I shall hope within a few days to be introduced to a Sister whom I have so long desired to be acquainted with. My kind friends here are most affectionately urgent with me to prolong my stay, but their hospitable & chearful dispositions lead them too much into society for my present situation & state of mind; & I impatiently look forward to the hour when I shall be admitted into your delightful retirement. I long to be made known to your dear little Children, in whose hearts I shall be very eager to secure an interest. (pp. 243–44)

She is more sceptical about Mrs. Vernon and "delightful retirement" in her letter to Mrs. Johnson: "I take Town in my way to that insupportable spot, a Country Village, for I am really going to Churchill. Forgive me my dear friend, it is my last resource. Were there another place in England open to me, I would prefer it. Charles Vernon is my aversion, & I am afraid of his wife" (pp. 245–46). The hypocrisy of the first letter has obviously been exposed by the second; but it would be erroneous to assume that the letters to Mrs. Johnson are unguarded confessions. Lady Susan always presents herself as a sophisticated woman of the world, regardless of her correspondent's identity. This is the purpose of the orotund diction and exaggerations that she addresses to Mr. Vernon. But even before the letter to Mrs. Johnson is written Lady Susan's insincerity has been exposed by these very tactics, for in Jane Austen's fiction hyperboles are generally suspect. And the more relaxed and direct style of the letter to Mrs. Johnson really complements the one to Churchill village: Lady Susan is just as anxious to impress her friend with her worldly wit, shrewd intelligence, and maternal instincts. But she is thwarted in this instance by the blatant contrast between her idealistic claims and her actual judgments, particularly on the subject of Sir James and Frederica. Similarly, when she derides Frederica's "artless" interest in Reginald De Courcy, Lady Susan's worldly-wise mask barely conceals her jealous insecurity: "Artlessness will never do in Love matters, & that girl is born a simpleton who has it either by nature or affectation. I am not yet certain that Reginald sees what she is about; nor is it of much consequence; she is now an object of indifference to him, she would be one of contempt were he to understand her Emotions. Her beauty is much admired by the Vernons, but it has no effect on *him*" (p. 274).

The maxim with which she introduces her comment is typical of the cynical worldliness that is the basis of her sophisticated stance. On the whole she anticipates Mary Crawford's ability to generalize from experience and to formulate her factual observations as behavioral norms. This is especially true of the egotistical maxims that are scattered throughout her letters. Hence she justifies the scheme to seduce Reginald by observing, "There is exquisite pleasure in subduing an insolent spirit, in making a person pre-determined to dislike, acknowledge one's superiority" (p. 254). Her own egotism is proposed as a desirable norm for all women: "Those women are inexcusable who forget what is due to themselves & the opinion of the World" (p. 269). Not surprisingly, she also generalizes on her self-conscious style: "If I am vain of anything, it is of my eloquence. Consideration & Esteem as surely follow command of Language, as Admiration waits on Beauty" (p. 268). She restricts the "grand affair of Education" to playing and singing, then philosophizes that to be "Mistress of French, Italian, German, Music, Singing, Drawing &c. will gain a Woman some applause, but will not add one lover to her list. Grace & Manner after all are of the greatest importance" (p. 253). This kind of self-assurance is typical of Lady Susan's carefully constructed facade and it is only disrupted when her schemes are blocked. Thus when she denounces Reginald's interest in Frederica she is unusually exclamatory, and the familiar irony gives way to outright abuse:

Much good, may such Love do him! I shall ever despise the Man who can be gratified by the Passion, which he never wished to inspire, nor solicited the avowal of. I shall always detest them both. He can have no true regard for me, or he would not have listened to her; And she, with her little rebellious heart & indelicate feelings to throw herself into the protection of a young Man with whom she had scarcely ever exchanged two words before. I am equally confounded at *her* Impudence & *his* Credulity. How dared he beleive what she told him in

my disfavour! Ought he not to have felt assured that I must have un-
answerable Motives for all that I had done! Where was his reliance on
my Sense or Goodness then; where the resentment which true Love
would have dictated against the person defaming me, that person, too,
a Chit, a Child, without Talent or Education, whom he had been
always taught to despise? (p. 282)

However, even in passionate moments like these, Lady Susan
strives to recover her poise with the sophisticated maxim. But if
her earlier generalizations are vitiated by her cynicism, the present
attempt at sophistication has been counteracted by her passion.
The precise, albeit ruthless, realism that informs the previous
maxims has been replaced by illogical sentimentality. Consequently, the resentful definition of "true Love" is akin to the
clichés of novel slang rather than to her usually hardheaded logic.
And she departs from the realism of her worldly values when she
despises Reginald for merely responding to Frederica's admiration. For like Samuel Richardson, she is really arguing that it is
"an heterodoxy" for a lady to fall in love before the gentleman
declares his affection.[7]

As a letter writer, then, Lady Susan invariably responds to the
instinct for self-justification. Jane Austen has intensified the conflict between the correspondent's emotional impulses and the desire
for a flattering image in order to dramatize Lady Susan's internal
tensions. In effect, Lady Susan's very efforts to communicate a
desired image are themselves intrinsic to her emotional conflicts.
What Jane Austen has done is to translate the psychological potential of her inherited epistolary forms to the dominant theme of

---

7. Samuel Richardson, *Rambler* No. 97, in *The British Essayists* (45 vols.;
London, 1802), XX, 236. Jane Austen repeatedly satirizes the illogical implications
of Richardson's statement. In *Northanger Abbey* it is developed *ad absurdum*: a
lady cannot properly dream of a gentleman until he has first dreamt of her (pp.
29–30). Moreover, Catherine Morland has suffered the "derogatory" experience of
falling in love with Henry before he becomes attached to her (p. 243). In *Pride and
Prejudice* Elizabeth Bennet and Charlotte Lucas debate the propriety of a woman
betraying signs of affection before being assured of the man's interest (pp. 21–22).
And, significantly, it transpires that Bingley is easily persuaded against a match
with Jane Bennet, precisely because there "was a constant complacency in her air
and manner, not often united with great sensibility" (p. 208).

Lady Susan—the ambiguities of Self. For while the ego becomes a destructive and antisocial force in Lady Susan's character, it is also prerequisite to any concept of experience or personality. Hence if Lady Susan's ego is disruptive, it is also true that Frederica's personality suffers from an extreme repression of Self. While she may resist the projected marriage with Sir James, Frederica seems always available, and vulnerable, as the unwitting tool of intrigue by her mother or by Mrs. Vernon. It is therefore appropriate that Frederica is the only character in the work who is not an habitual letter-writer. For good or ill, the epistolary process is an egocentric one, and in *Lady Susan* it is the province of those who are busily projecting and defending images of themselves, whose rivalries and self-contradictions are illustrated by the tensions that are inherent in letter writing. Consequently, while Frederica writes only one letter, Lady Susan's prolific pen is matched by Mrs. Vernon's. And this is logical since Mrs. Vernon's conventional morality is no less egotistic in its methods and goals than Lady Susan's frank desire to manipulate and exploit. Indeed the rivalry between the two women is the major irony of the work. On the one hand, Lady Susan's selfish vitalism thrusts against the established norms of moral conduct. Yet, on the other, the moral order is threatened from within by its putative champions. The ethical conflict is really a power-play between two different but very dominant egos. Hence it is noticeable that Mrs. Vernon's moral judgments are very often in the same egotistical strain that characterizes Lady Susan's letters. The attractive widow's personality often seems to be received by Mrs. Vernon as a personal affront, rather than as a moral problem: "I am indeed provoked at the artifice of this unprincipled Woman" (p. 255). Reginald's infatuation with Lady Susan wounds the Vernon (and De Courcy) family pride: "This tendency to excuse her conduct, or to forget it in the warmth of admiration vexes me. . . . I cannot for a moment imagine that she has anything more serious in veiw, but it mortifies me to see a young Man of Reginald's sense duped by her at all" (p. 256). But these wounds are easily soothed by Frederica's growing interest:

"That Girl, whose heart can distinguish Reginald De Courcy, deserves, however he may slight her, a better fate than to be Sir James Martin's wife" (p. 278).

However, Mrs. Vernon's commendation of her brother is actually an extension of her habitual self-flattery. For he is manifestly lacking in the kind of sense which would make him a worthwhile reward for Frederica, or which could shield him from Lady Susan's blandishments. His superficial judgments are usually as malicious, and as uninformed, as those of his favorite gossips. This habit of confusing hearsay with fact is demonstrated by his early pronouncement on (the unknown) Frederica: "I am glad to find that Miss Vernon does not come with her Mother to Churchill, as she has not even Manners to recommend her, & according to Mr. Smith's account, is equally dull & proud. Where Pride & Stupidity unite, there can be no dissimulation worthy notice, & Miss Vernon shall be consigned to unrelenting contempt" (p. 248). Given the usual basis of his judgments, it is not surprising that they are very unstable, and that they tend to oscillate between extremes. In Lady Susan's case, his remarks are based wholly on hearsay. She is the "most accomplished Coquette in England," and "a very distinguished Flirt" (p. 248). After he is inevitably duped he finds that she is "governed only by the most honourable & amiable intentions. Her prudence & economy are exemplary, her regard for Mr. Vernon equal even to *his* deserts, & her wish of obtaining my sister's good opinion merits better return than it has received. As a Mother she is unexceptionable" (p. 265).

On the whole then, Mrs. Vernon treats Reginald as an ideal, in defiance of his palpable shortcomings. Her prejudiced evaluation is a continuation of her family pride and egotistic sensibilities. Consequently, the attempts to invent strong points in his favor are a part of her unending self-flattery. And her unrealistic estimate of Reginald's powers unwittingly complements Lady Susan's egotistic manipulations. While Mrs. Vernon projects Reginald as her champion-in-arms against Lady Susan's depravity, Lady Susan is equally selfish in exploiting him for the purposes of frank self-gratification: "There is something about him that rather interests me, a sort of sauciness, of familiarity which I shall teach him to correct. He is lively & seems clever, & when I have inspired him with greater respect for me than his Sister's kind offices have implanted, he may be an agreable Flirt" (p. 254). His earlier hostility sweetens her eventual triumph: "I have made him sensible of my power, & can now enjoy the pleasure of triumphing over a Mind prepared to dislike me, & prejudiced against all my past actions" (p. 257). In short, Reginald, like Frederica, is the meeting point of the rivalry between Mrs. Vernon and Lady Susan; and he is, simultaneously, the touchstone that reveals the internal conflicts of each antagonist. Moreover, the epistolary mode proves to be congenial to the recurring contradictions that Reginald and Frederica inspire within Lady Susan and Mrs. Vernon—the conflict of selfish impulse and public posture.

Jane Austen's early achievement in integrating moral psychology with the epistolary process is not really diminished by the fact that she abandons the letter-writing structure in *Lady Susan* and in subsequent novels. The "straight" narrative on which she concentrates from here on obviously provides the detached perspective that is essential to the play of satiric comment, and to the ironic shifts of narrative viewpoint. (It is noteworthy, for example, that most of the letters in *The Three Sisters* are assigned to the pen of Georgiana Stanhope, whose ironic detachment anticipates the narrative strategy of the major novels.) Nonetheless, the mature novels are appreciably influenced by the structural functions and psychological insights of letter writing. Thus the facility with which Jane Austen integrates certain themes with her narrative form, in subsequent novels, can be traced to her early education in epistolary fiction. This is particularly true of *Pride and Prejudice* and *Emma*. In each work Jane Austen draws upon her early experience with epistolary techniques in order to incorporate the themes of prejudice and imagination within her narrative structure. Hence the presentation of character and incident through the prejudices of Elizabeth Bennet and Emma Woodhouse is based on the same strategy that Richardson uses in depicting Solmes, or which Jane Austen herself utilizes in portraying Mr. Watts in *Three Sisters*. The initial portrait of Darcy, for example, depends largely on the prejudiced judgments of Elizabeth and Wickham. And the major personalities in *Emma* are filtered through the heroine's all too fallible imagination. The moral perspectives of both Elizabeth and Emma have the same effect as the fictive letter writer. They provide a narrative framework of frankly subjective judgments through which each heroine creates and develops personal relationships. Together with the juvenilia, both *Pride and Prejudice* and *Emma* demonstrate one of Jane Austen's principal debts to the kind of epistolary novel that Richardson perfects in *Clarissa*. Narrative "facts" are not a succession of objective truths to be detailed by an impartial heroine or omniscient narrator. The total significance of Clarissa's seduction does not reside exclusively in her own letters or in Lovelace's, but in the correspondence as a whole. In Smollett's *Humphry Clinker*, Bath, for example, is actually an agglomeration of diverse, but equally real, experiences. Its diseases and egalitarian crowds are reprehensible to Matthew Bramble, the tourists' comic absurdities hold Jeremy Melford's attention, and the scenery and concerts enchant the romantic Lydia Melford. When we turn to Jane Austen it is to discover that the "real" Darcy only begins to emerge in *Pride and Prejudice* after Elizabeth collates a variety of personal judgments, including Darcy's own self-appraisal. Therefore Reginald De Courcy's erratic prejudices in *Lady Susan* are very real precursors, in an epistolary form, of the emotional and moral perspectives that shape the "dry" narrative of *Pride and Prejudice*.

To this perspectival role we must add the emotive functions of the epistolary mode in Jane Austen's mature narrative. The writing or the reading of letters is almost invariably crucial to the dramatic and psychological development of plot and character. Jane Austen exploits the inherent emotional values of the letter-writing process, and it probably accounts for the fact that so few of the letters in the novels are obscure or easily forgotten. Letter writing coincides with, and represents, the dramatic intensification of emotional and moral conflicts: Darcy's letter to Elizabeth Bennet, Lady Bertram's news of Mansfield Park crises, or Captain Wentworth's explosive proposal of marriage to Anne Elliot. And letters may either report or precipitate a crisis. Mr. Collins' visit to Longbourn is announced by letter; and so are the details of Lydia Bennet's elopement. Whether they are factual reports or personal self-expression, these letters are timed to dramatize the crucial turning points of narrative and theme. But the dramatic impact of many messages is derived from their emotional expressiveness. Captain Wentworth's proposal, for example, combines his old impetuosity with a new awareness of human fallibility: "I must speak to you by such means as are within my reach. You pierce my soul. I am half agony, half hope. Tell me not that I am too late, that such precious feelings are gone for ever" (*Persuasion*, p. 237). Lady Bertram's "amplifying style" is usually suited to her placid "do nothingness," and at first it is proof even against the news of Tom Bertram's illness. Her letters continue in "the same medley of trusts, hopes and fears, all following and producing each other at haphazard. It was a sort of playing at being frightened" (*Mansfield Park*, p. 427). But even Lady Bertram's letters are not absolutely immune to the pressures of maternal concern. Indeed, Jane Austen's approach to the letter as an emotional experience is very well illustrated by the fact that when Lady Bertram does become genuinely expressive she does so only in the true art of letter writing—she writes as she would have spoken: "Then, a letter which she had been previously preparing for Fanny, was finished in a different style, in the language of real feeling and alarm; then, she wrote as she might have spoken. 'He is just come, my dear Fanny, and is taken up stairs; and I am so shocked to see him, that I do not know what to do'" (p. 427).

Marianne Dashwood's correspondence with Willoughby is also pertinent here. The three letters that are written to Willoughby after Marianne's arrival in London are grouped in order and read by Elinor. By reproducing the sequence of composition Elinor provides us with a concise, dramatic review of Marianne's growing concern and unhappiness about Willoughby's indifference. Hence Marianne's opening sentence, in each letter, epitomizes the successive stages of the writer's emotions, ranging from the excited expectancy of the first message, to the chagrined exclamations of the third:

How surprised you will be, Willoughby, on receiving this; and I think you will feel something more than surprise, when you know that I am in town. . . .

"I cannot express my disappointment in having missed you the day before yesterday, nor my astonishment at not having received any answer to a note which I sent you above a week ago. . . .

"What am I to imagine, Willoughby, by your behaviour last night? Again I demand an explanation of it" (*Sense and Sensibility*, pp. 186–87).

Finally, the anguish represented by Marianne's epistolary style is heightened by the immediate juxtaposition of her letter with the severely formal and unfeeling note that Miss Morton writes on Willoughby's behalf: "I have just had the honour of receiving your letter, for which I beg to return my sincere acknowledgments" (p. 183).

Together, all three of Marianne's letters also demonstrate the other primary function of the epistolary mode in Jane Austen's mature fiction. For they are important, not only on the basis of their expressive qualities, but also because of the emotional response that they elicit. Hence the reading of the letters has been timed to provide an emotional catalyst for Elinor's new insights into her sister's relationship with Willoughby. Elinor now realizes the full extent of Marianne's indiscreet openness; the letters confirm that there had been no engagement between Marianne and Willoughby in spite of their former intimacy. Moreover, Elinor is now more fully aware than hitherto of Marianne's real suffering. What previously appeared to be little more than absurdly romantic excesses are now shown to be a profoundly disturbing experience that will lead eventually to Marianne's maturity. The timing and emotiveness of the letter are therefore as crucial as the process of writing. And it is noteworthy that when Jane Austen praises the expressive qualities of Fanny Knight's correspondence, she is equally explicit in emphasizing her own emotional response to her niece's letters: "I cannot express to you what I have felt in reading your history of Yourself, how full of Pity & Concern & Admiration & Amusement I have been. . . . It is very, very gratifying to me to know you so intimately. You can hardly think what a pleasure it is to me, to have such thorough pictures of your Heart" (*Letters*, p. 478).

Samuel Richardson, too, notes the emotive impact of letters on the reader, and the reasons that he assigns to this influence are important for a fuller understanding of how letter-reading functions in Jane Austen's work. In effect, Richardson argues that the very nature of its form enables the letter simultaneously to depict and immobilize the emotional realities of any given relationship. It is an unbroken record of an emotional experience, a revealing portrait of self and personal relationships. And by arresting its intimate subjects within its written format it makes them accessible to repeated scrutiny and emphasis. Consequently, Richardson suggests to Sophia Westcomb that correspondence is friendship itself:

This correspondence is, indeed, the cement of friendship: it is friendship avowed under hand and seal: friendship upon bond, as I may say: more pure, yet more ardent, and less broken in upon, than personal conversation can be even amongst the most pure, because of the deliberation it allows, from the very preparation to, and action of writing.

While I read it, I have you before me in person: I converse with you . . . I see you, I sit with you, I talk with you, I read to you, I stop to hear your sentiments, in the summer-house: your smiling obligingness, your polite and easy expression, even your undue diffidence are all in my eye and my ear as I read. (*Selected Letters*, p. 65)

It is this *arresting* power that makes the letter such a useful instrument whenever Jane Austen wishes to concentrate the individual's awareness on any given personality or incident. In *Sense*

and Sensibility Marianne's unguarded letters heighten the effects
of her indiscretion by concentrating, and transfixing, them in a
single, revealing context. They provide Elinor with dramatic
materials through which she can literally peruse Marianne's relationship with Willoughby. It is this sense of dramatic timing
and emotional interaction that enables Jane Austen to derive
maximum effects from a rather economical use of letters. In
Northanger Abbey only two letters are quoted at length. But because of their precise timing they interact with, and become integral to, the most critical moments of Catherine Morland's
development. The first, from James Morland, exposes Isabella
Thorpe's duplicity and insensitivity. Coming as it does shortly
after Catherine has been disabused of all Gothic notions, the letter
commemorates the new realities that must replace old fantasies. It
translates James's hurt into a deeply emotional crisis through
which Catherine revaluates Isabella Thorpe. And, appropriately,
Catherine's reaction to the letter is an intense experience that is not
lost on the discerning Henry Tilney: "Catherine had not read three
lines before her sudden change of countenance, and short exclamations of sorrowing wonder, declared her to be receiving unpleasant
news; and Henry, earnestly watching her through the whole letter,
saw plainly that it ended no better than it began" (pp. 202–203).

While James's letter precipitates Catherine's disillusionment,
Isabella's note confirms Catherine's new scepticism. Earlier, before
hearing from James, Catherine had been impatient for news from
Isabella, but all the affected hyperboles that Catherine ignored in
the rush of dialogue have now been transfixed for the first time by
the written format of the epistolary mode. And coming at a time
when Catherine's critical insights have emerged, this immobiliza-
tion of Isabella's personal style exposes the writer's character to a
penetrating, line-by-line scrutiny. Moreover, as an added touch of
irony, Catherine refuses to be misled by Isabella's epistolary exercise in self-flattery and self-justification:

Such a strain of shallow artifice could not impose even upon Catherine. Its inconsistencies, contradictions, and falsehood, struck her from

the very first. She was ashamed of Isabella, and ashamed of having ever loved her. Her professions of attachment were now as disgusting as her excuses were empty, and her demands impudent. "Write to James on her behalf!—No, James should never hear Isabella's name mentioned by her again."

On Henry's arrival from Woodston, she made known to him and Eleanor their brother's safety, congratulating them with sincerity on it, and reading aloud the most material passages of her letter with strong indignation. When she had finished it,—"So much for Isabella," she cried, "and for all our intimacy! She must think me an idiot, or she could not have written so; but perhaps this has served to make her character better known to me than mine is to her. I see what she has been about. She is a vain coquette, and her tricks have not answered" (p. 218).

There are far more numerous letters in *Pride and Prejudice*, but generally, they too are timed for the same degree of dramatic impact that is achieved by the more limited correspondence of *Northanger Abbey*. All the crucial facts of Lydia's elopement are related by letters from Jane Bennet and the Gardiners. And in her crudely light-hearted way even Lydia is aware of the dramatic potential of the letter in her affair. As she advises Harriet Foster, "You need not send them word at Longbourn of my going, if you do not like it, for it will make the surprise the greater, when I write to them, and sign my name Lydia Wickham. What a good joke it will be! I can hardly write for laughing" (p. 291). Even the fairly routine incident of Mr. Collins' first letter to Longbourn has dramatic functions that go beyond the self-exposure of the writer's absurdities. As usual Jane Austen has concentrated on the reaction to the letter, and in so doing has transformed Mr. Collins' note into a touchstone for the self-revelation of the readers. Elizabeth's quick-witted commonsense is exemplified by her finding that Mr. Collins "must be an oddity" with "something very pompous in his stile." Her father's opinion confirms the similarity of their tastes: "There is a mixture of servility and self-importance in his letter, which promises well." Mary demonstrates her own pomposity by praising Mr. Collins' style, and neither Catherine nor Lydia is impressed with the matter: "It was next to impossible that their cousin should come in a scarlet coat, and it was now some weeks since they had received pleasure from the society of a man in any other colour" (p. 64).

The most crucial letter is, of course, the one written by Darcy after his quarrel with Elizabeth. Here, too, the dramatic function of the letter hinges on the emotional interaction of writer and reader. In one sense Darcy's choice of a letter as the means of explaining his past conduct conforms with realistic convention: it would be unnatural for a man of his reserve and sensitivity to make such intimate revelations in any other form. But it is equally significant that the medium of his choice epitomizes the primary impulse behind Darcy's wish to communicate with Elizabeth—the compulsive need for self-justification:

"Two offences of a very different nature, and by no means of equal magnitude, you last night laid to my charge. The first mentioned was, that, regardless of the sentiments of either, I had detached Mr. Bingley from your sister,—and the other, that I had, in defiance of various claims, in defiance of honour and humanity, ruined the immediate prosperity, and blasted the prospects of Mr. Wickham.—Wilfully and wantonly to have thrown off the companion of my youth, the acknowledged favourite of my father, a young man who had scarcely any other dependence than on our patronage, and who had been brought up to expect its exertion, would be a depravity, to which the separation of two young persons, whose affection could be the growth of only a few weeks, could bear no comparison.—But from the severity of that blame which was last night so liberally bestowed, respecting each circumstance, I shall hope to be in future secured, when the following account of my actions and their motives has been read.—If, in the explanation of them which is due to myself, I am under the necessity of relating feelings which may be offensive to your's, I can only say that I am sorry.—The necessity must be obeyed—and farther apology would be absurd." (pp. 196–97)

It is appropriate that Darcy is sensitive to Elizabeth's possible reactions, for his letter does precipitate an emotional crisis which compels Elizabeth to readjust her perspectives. Jane Austen's faith in the emotive powers of the letter underlies Elizabeth's reception of Darcy's note. Moreover, the range of Elizabeth's responses supports Samuel Richardson's thesis on the arresting powers of correspondence. Here, for the first time. Darcy's character has been exposed in a form and context which frees Elizabeth's shaky judgment from the distracting clashes of debate, and from the kind of distorting conflicts that marked the Hunsford quarrel. The nature of Elizabeth's reaction to Darcy's newly revealed personality has been conditioned by his medium of communication. For now, unlike their personal meetings, she has the opportunity to reconsider initial responses. She can evaluate her prejudice in the light of Darcy's statements and attitudes, now that the epistolary form has literally made them accessible for reexamination. In other words, the epistolary mode is really a psychological opportunity for the only effective weapon against irrational prepossession—thoughtful revaluation.

Her initial impressions are colored by the old prejudices, and therefore tend to be highly emotional. Darcy's letter excites "a contrariety of emotion":

With amazement did she first understand that he believed any apology to be in his power; and stedfastly was she persuaded that he could have no explanation to give, which a just sense of shame would not conceal. With a strong prejudice against every thing he might say, she began his account of what had happened at Netherfield. She read with an eagerness which hardly left her power of comprehension, and from impatience of knowing what the next sentence might bring, and incapable of attending to the sense of the one before her eyes. His belief of her sister's insensibility, she instantly resolved to be false, and his account of the real, the worst objections to the match, made her too angry to have any wish of doing him justice. He expressed no regret for what he had done which satisfied her; his style was not penitent, but haughty. It was all pride and insolence. (p. 204)

Furthermore, Darcy's account of Wickham arouses feelings that "were yet more acutely painful and more difficult of definition. Astonishment, apprehension, and even horror, oppressed her." Generally, her first response to the letter is remarkably similar to the unreceptive obstinacy which had created a barrier of noncommunication on both sides: "She wished to discredit it entirely, repeatedly exclaiming, 'This must be false! This cannot be! This must be the grossest falsehood!'—and when she had gone through the whole letter, though scarcely knowing any thing of the last page or two, put it hastily away, protesting that she would not regard it, that she would never look in it again" (pp. 204–205). But the letter, Darcy's personality under hand and seal, remains accessible for further scrutiny. It is "unfolded again" in half a minute. And the blind passion of her earlier, prejudiced reading has been replaced by a resolve to be rational: "collecting herself as well as she could, she again began the mortifying perusal of all that related to Wickham, and commanded herself so far as to examine the meaning of every sentence" (p. 205). Rational deliberation produces new impressions of Wickham, and leads in turn to an equally balanced rereading of Darcy's self-defense with regards to Jane and Bingley. She finally accepts Darcy's letter after "wandering along the lane for two hours, giving way to every variety of thought; reconsidering events, determining probabilities, and reconciling herself as well as she could, to a change so sudden and so important" (p. 209). The progression from blind "contrariety of emotion" to self-knowledge dramatically illustrates how ignorance and prepossession give way to rational awareness in *Pride and Prejudice*. The emotive functions of the epistolary mode have conformed with the thematic directions of the novel.

Elizabeth's fluctuating response to Darcy's letters is comparable with Emma Woodhouse's mixed reactions to Frank Churchill's lengthy note of explanation and apology. Unlike Elizabeth, Emma's judgment has already been jolted before the crucial letter is read. Now chastened, but happy, Emma is mildly indifferent to anything that Frank might have to say: "she guessed what it must contain, and deprecated the necessity of reading it.—She was now in perfect charity with Frank Churchill; she wanted no explanations, she wanted only to have her thoughts to herself—and as for understanding any thing he wrote, she was sure she was incapable of it" (*Emma*, p. 436). But as in Elizabeth Bennet's case, Emma's final reactions are not as she predicts. And in order to appreciate them we must first comprehend the real nature of Frank's letter to Mrs. Weston. It is first and foremost written in the self-justifying manner of Darcy's letter—though with the additional elements of guilt and apology. Furthermore, Frank's note provides the most realistic opportunity for genuine self-revelation. As in Darcy's case, the confessional nature of the letter becomes an apt means of allowing Frank to make intimate disclosures about Jane Fairfax and himself. However, the letter is not only self-descriptive. It is also an unintentionally ironic portrayal of Emma. In *Pride and Prejudice* it is left entirely to Elizabeth to compare and contrast the implications of Darcy's self-portrait with her own actions and judgments. But here in *Emma*, Frank's letter has the additional role of presenting the reformed Emma with a picture of herself as she once appeared to others. And in so doing it heightens her new sense of transformation. She now learns that in spite of her egotistic illusions about her attractiveness to Frank, it is the image of the professed misogamist that is most obvious: "Amiable and delightful as Miss Wodhouse is, she never gave me the idea of a young woman likely to be attached" (p. 438). All of Emma's previous miscalculations are thrown into ironic relief by Frank's generous portrait of a penetrating intelligence. "We seemed to understand each other," Frank writes, adding his conviction that Emma had astutely guessed at the real nature of his relationship with Jane: "She may not have surmised the whole, but her quickness must have penetrated a part" (p. 438). And now Emma's earlier indifference to Frank's note gives way to the excitement of self-recognition—Frank has presented her with a picture of her old self: "This letter must make its way to Emma's feelings. She was obliged, in spite of her previous determination to the contrary, to do it all the justice that Mrs. Weston foretold. As soon as she came to her own name, it was irresistible; every line relating to herself was interesting, and almost every line agreeable" (p. 444). Emma's frankly egocentric interest emphasizes Jane Austen's preoccupation with the personal emotions that are brought into play by the reading, as well as the writing, of letters. And here Jane Austen also seems to be endowing the letter reader with the same kind of self-regard that is characteristic of the writer. Emma's present interest in Frank's "agreeable" portrait is a comic echo of the more destructive egotism that formerly obscured her judgment. Even Mr. Knightley becomes a comic victim here. He chastises Frank for fancying Emma "to have fathomed his secret;" but, with a very natural self-interest, Mr. Knightley the lover is loath to recall that Emma was once busy in "intrigue" and "mystery" on Jane's (and Harriet's) account: "Natural enough!—his own mind full of intrigue, that he should suspect it in others.—Mystery; Finesse—how they pervert the understanding!" (p. 446).

Generally, then, the responses of both Emma and Mr. Knightley illuminate the egocentric motives on which Jane Austen bases the emotional reactions of letter readers. Most of the crucial letters in the novels impinge directly on the recipient's self-regard. Catherine Morland's family pride is hurt by her brother's letter about Isabella's treachery, and her subsequent awareness is insulted by the transparency of Isabella's hypocritical letter. In *Pride and Prejudice*, Darcy's note makes Elizabeth acutely conscious of her family's embarrassing shortcomings, and subsequently, her mortification is intensified by Jane's news of Lydia's elopement. On the whole the egocentric motives of correspondents in Jane Austen's novels exemplify her consistent ability to integrate the psychological experiences of the epistolary mode with her primary themes. On the basis of her knowledge of Richardson, and as a result of her own experiments in the juvenilia, Jane Austen's epistolary structures serve to dramatize emotional crises. Isabella's shallow excuses, Darcy's proud self-defense, and Frank Churchill's apologetics—these are all vital to the final resolution of psychological crises in *Northanger Abbey*, *Pride and Prejudice*, and *Emma*, respectively. And they have been aptly dramatized by the natural self-regard of each writer. Conversely, their impact depends in part on the equally egocentric interests of the letter reader, ranging from Catherine Morland's nascent awareness to Emma's chastened arrogance. The expressive, or confessional, qualities of the letter are equally vital in presenting Marianne Dashwood's volatile passions or Lady Bertram's emotional debility. Simultaneously, the affective potential of personal correspondence provides an emotional catalyst through which the recipient acquires or tests new perspectives. The true art of letter writing is not simply a communicative technique. It is also a complex experience of feeling and insights, through which individual perception and human relationships are defined.

CHAPTER VII

Dialogue

IN HIS PERCEPTIVE STUDY of dialogue in *Pride and Prejudice* Reuben A. Brower argues that there is a general relaxation of ironic tension after the climax of Elizabeth's encounter with Darcy at Hunsford.[1] Brower's strictures are not entirely irrefutable. Following the Hunsford visit and its painful revelations, the emotional and dramatic tensions of Elizabeth's position have been multiplied and intensified rather than relaxed. The simple matter of contrasting her friends and family with the odious Darcy has now been replaced by the opposing claims of a new tenderness for Darcy, on the one hand, and a heightened awareness of her family's shortcomings, on the other. The eagerness to earn Darcy's good opinion is handicapped by the humiliations caused by Lydia's "animal spirits." External confrontation has been replaced by the less sensational, but equally important, drama of internal conflict.[2] However, Brower's statement does illuminate the essence of dialogue in *Pride and Prejudice* and in Jane Austen's fiction as a whole. Jane Austen fashions and exploits dialogue as a dramatic ex-

---

1. Reuben A. Brower, "Light and Bright and Sparkling: Irony and Fiction in *Pride and Prejudice*," in *Jane Austen, A Collection of Critical Essays*, ed. Ian Watt (Englewood Cliffs, N.J., 1963), 74–75.

2. Joseph Wiesenfarth, who disagrees with Brower's criticism, argues that the dramatic and ironic design of the novel is not complete until Darcy comes to Longbourn and proposes to Elizabeth for a second time. *The Errand of Form: An Assay of Jane Austen's Art* (New York, 1967), 65.

perience, with a wide range of emotional and moral conflicts. Basically, "conversation" or personal style translates the individual tastes of each character to the reader. And letter writing permits some reciprocal communication to take place *within* the novel, between various correspondents. But dialogue as such tends to be an exercise in noncommunication. It dramatizes all the psychological and moral barriers to meaningful human relationships. Consequently, individual styles which are quite revealing in themselves, especially to the reader, and which function so effectively in the mutual comprehension of the epistolary mode, heighten, rather than diminish, the effect of conflict during personal confrontation. Dialogue is not really an exclusive symbol of the failure to communicate in Jane Austen's works. Elizabeth and Darcy, or Emma and Mr. Knightley, do take part in important dialogues after their engagement. But generally, the most crucial exchanges between Jane Austen's characters are based on conflict and misunderstanding, rather than on the positive transmission of personal interests and values. Dialogue *per se* is not an automatic symptom of noncommunication, but this is the form or technique to which Jane Austen turns whenever she wishes to demonstrate the critical problems that prevent the significant exchange of viewpoints. The self-revealing functions of the letter, together with the reflective experience that is encouraged by the epistolary mode, have the minimal effect of arousing the letter reader's awareness. On the other hand, misapprehension and emotional crises are exacerbated by the rapidity and warmth of debate. Moral and perceptual conflicts thwart efforts at communication, and this fundamental failing is the primary basis of ironic patterns in Jane Austen's dialogues.

Her predecessors show considerable interest in dialogues as noncommunication. Fielding, for example, often uses the nonreciprocal dialogue, in which participants talk at cross-purposes. In *Tom Jones* Sophia and her aunt Miss Western both concur, temporarily, on the blessings of falling in love with handsome and deserving young men. But their agreement is shortlived because

Sophia implies Tom Jones, while Miss Western is young Blifil's advocate.[3] Laurence Sterne, too, emphasizes noncommunicative dialogue, not only as an internal problem between the characters, but also as an experience between the narrator and his readers. The respective hobbyhorses of various personalities within the narrative prevent any meaningful exchange of ideas between Uncle Toby, Walter Shandy, Mrs. Shandy, and Corporal Trim. And this problem is externalized in the relationship between Tristram Shandy and his readers. Consequently, there is nothing but confusion and misunderstanding when Tristram hints at the nature of his mother's religion by observing that he was not eligible for the Roman Catholic rite of prenatal baptism: "—How could you, Madam, be so inattentive in reading the last chapter? I told you in it, that my mother was not a papist.—Papist! You told me no such thing, Sir.—Madam, I beg leave to repeat it over again, that I told you as plain, at least, as words, by direct inference, could tell you such a thing.—Then, Sir, I must have missed a page.—No, Madam, you have not missed a word." Obviously, Tristram's failure to communicate with this reader stems from the latter's inability to function within the Shandean definition of writing: "The truest respect which you can pay to the reader's understanding is to halve this matter amicably, and leave him something to imagine, in his turn, as well as yourself."[4] But halving the matter really presupposes Locke's ideal of universally precise and exact definitions, or word usages, with correspondingly uniform faculties: a man's word "should stand as marks for the *ideas* within his own mind, whereby they might be made known to others, and the thoughts of men's minds be conveyed from one to another."[5] In *Tristram Shandy* Sterne uses dialogue to demon-

3. Henry Fielding, *The History of Tom Jones*, Shakespeare Head Edition (4 vols.; Oxford, 1926), II, 21–23.

4. Laurence Sterne, *The Life and Opinions of Tristram Shandy, Gentleman*, ed. James Aiken Work (New York, 1940), 56, 109.

5. John Locke, *An Essay Concerning Human Understanding*, ed. Alexander Campbell Fraser (2 vols.; New York, 1959), Bk. III, chap. 1, sect. 2.

strate the psychological and moral realities that have undermined Locke's theory. For as John Stedmond has suggested, "the reader has certain built-in associations of ideas. He brings to his perusal of the first page of a work of fiction certain fixed expectations." And Sterne has used Tristram's problems of communication to illustrate that "given some knowledge of human preconceptions, one has only to manipulate the context in order to manipulate the meaning."[6]

Jane Austen's interest in the kind of issues explored by Sterne and Locke begins to take shape from the juvenilia. And, significantly, these fragmentary experiments demonstrate a precocious awareness of the links between noncommunication and the perverse vagaries of individual preconceptions. Hence, in *Jack & Alice* an absurdly circuituous exchange between Lady Williams and Alice Johnson is based on the latter's sensory and mental impairment: "heated with wine & raised by Passion, she could have little command of her Temper" (*Minor Works*, p. 18). Consequently, Lady Williams' attempts to relate her "Life & Adventures" quickly degenerates into a shouting match on the subject of red complexions, a topic on which Alice is understandably sensitive:

"I was invited the following year by a distant relation of my Father's to spend the Winter with her in town. Mrs. Watkins was a Lady of Fashion, Family & fortune; she was in general esteemed a pretty Woman, but I never thought her very handsome, for my part. She had too high a forehead. Her eyes were too small & she had too much colour."

"How can *that* be?" interrupted Miss Johnson reddening with anger; "Do you think that any one can have too much colour?"

"Indeed I do, & I'll tell you why I do my dear Alice; when a person has too great a degree of red in their Complexion, it gives their face in my opinion, too red a look."

6. *The Comic Art of Laurence Sterne: Convention and Innovation in "Tristram Shandy" and "A Sentimental Journey"* (Toronto, 1967), 8, 57–58. Compare John Traugott, *Tristram Shandy's World: Sterne's Philosophical Rhetoric* (Berkeley, 1954), 8.

"But can a face my Lady have too red a look?"

"Certainly my dear Miss Johnson & I'll tell you why. When a face has too red a look it does not appear to so much advantage as it would were it paler."

"Pray Ma'am proceed in your story." (p. 17)

But Lady Williams never really "proceeds" anywhere. For this farcical melange of *non sequiturs* and tautological retorts reveals more than the chaos of Alice's turbulent passions. The redundancy of verbal patterns is suggestively analogous to the general super-fluity of Lady Williams' "life" story. In part, this is an attack on the irrelevance of comparable digressions in popular fiction, but more important, Lady Williams' hypocritical character can only be communicated in the context of immediate, personal relationships. Hence her autobiographical exercise is as redundant, and inconclusive, as the dialogue that terminates it. In essence, even this immature experiment clearly demonstrates what are eventually to become consistent features of the Jane Austen dialogue. The nonreciprocal nature of each meeting is attributable to the warped judgments of one or both sides. Secondly, the close verbal repetitions (such as the redundant elaborations on "red," "colour," or "look") create an illusion of continuity that ironically underlines the absence of real communication. Finally, these verbal structures, and the conflicts in which they are rooted, are organically related to the themes, characters, and narrative form of the work. Thus, on the basis of its inconclusiveness, the debate in *Jack & Alice* simultaneously (1) explores the sensory and intellectual limitations represented by the drunken Alice Johnson (2) parodies the inconsequential "Lives" of popular sentimental fiction, and (3) dramatizes the kind of noncommunication that usually enables the hypocritical Lady Williams to bemuse or hoodwink her victims.

Like most dialogues in *Jack & Alice* and the juvenilia as a whole, the more notable exchanges in *Northanger Abbey* are linked to Jane Austen's interest in parody. As Joseph Wiesenfarth has indicated, the plot of this novel turns on Catherine's gradual discrimination of word from reality either in the language of defective personalities, or in literature.[7] In particular, Henry Tilney's role in the comic debates of *Northanger Abbey* is to integrate this central theme with the nonreciprocity of dramatic dialogue. The comic misunderstandings of Catherine's talks with Henry illustrate the need to distinguish one word usage from another. And in the process she is forced to recognize the relationship between a hierarchy of moral and literary values, with corresponding levels of verbal meanings. This is the point of the better-known debates on definitive terms like "nice;" and it is also applicable to the dialogue in which Henry challenges Catherine's narrow equation of "torment" with "instruction," when she discusses the study of history:

"I shall not pity the writers of history any longer. If people like to read their books, it is all very well, but to be at so much trouble in filling great volumes, which, as I used to think, nobody would willingly ever look into, to be labouring only for the torment of little boys and girls, always struck me as a hard fate; and though I know it is all very right and necessary, I have often wondered at the person's courage that could sit down on purpose to do it."

"That little boys and girls should be tormented," said Henry, "is what no one at all acquainted with human nature in a civilized state can deny; but in behalf of our most distinguished historians, I must observe, that they might well be offended at being supposed to have no higher aim; and that by their method and style, they are perfectly well qualified to torment readers of the most advanced reason and mature time of life. I use the verb 'to torment,' as I observed to be your own method, instead of 'to instruct,' supposing them to be now admitted as synonimous."

"You think me foolish to call instruction a torment, but if you had been as much used as myself to hear poor little children first learning their letters and then learning to spell . . . you would allow that to *torment* and to *instruct* might sometimes be used as synonimous words."

"Very probably. But historians are not accountable for the difficulty of learning to read." (pp. 109–10)

7. Joseph Wiesenfarth, *The Errand of Form*, 10.

In exchanges like these Jane Austen has actually modified the irony of noncommunication. The point here is not that both speakers misunderstand each other: as the most penetrating character in the novel, Henry is well aware of Catherine's meaning. But the real issue is that Henry deliberately *stages* a dialogue of conflict by pretending to misinterpret Catherine's diction. In effect, he is the parodist who mimics Catherine's language (words like "torment," for example) and intellectual values in order to demonstrate their limitations *vis-à-vis* the complexities of experience. Altogether, Henry's role not only enables the dialogue to dramatize the theme of Jane Austen's parody—the need to distinguish between word and reality—but also hinges the exchange itself on some form of parody.

Neither is this parodic stance limited to the dialogues with Catherine. His encounters with Mrs. Allen also permit him to indulge in his favorite pastime—satiric imitation. But Mrs. Allen emerges from these meetings as Catherine's mental opposite, for while Catherine is aware of some conflict with Henry, Mrs. Allen is so impervious to his meaning as to remain blissfully unaware of any opposition on his side. She is incapable of penetrating the benign disguise of his mimicry when he joins her on her hobbyhorse:

"Do you understand muslins, sir?"

"Particularly well; I always buy my own cravats, and am allowed to be an excellent judge; and my sister has often trusted me in the choice of a gown. I bought one for her the other day, and it was pronounced to be a prodigious bargain by every lady who saw it. I gave but five shillings a yard for it, and a true Indian muslin."

Mrs. Allen was quite struck by his genius. "Men commonly take so little notice of those things," said she: "I can never get Mr. Allen to know one of my gowns from another. You must be a great comfort to your sister, sir."

"I hope I am, madam."

"And pray, sir, what do you think of Miss Morland's gown?"

"It is very pretty, madam," said he, gravely examining it; but I do not think it will wash well; I am afraid it will fray."

"How can you," said Catherine, laughing, "be so—" She had almost said, strange. (p. 28)

Catherine's exclamation is revealing, for she has perceived the conflict which Mrs. Allen is unable to sense. This ability to appreciate such opposition between styles and values is nurtured by the debates with Henry, and proves, ultimately, to be the basis of her intellectual and moral maturity. Generally, the inherent conflicts of dramatic dialogue do not embrace the wide range of emotional and psychological divisions that we encounter in the later novels. Jane Austen has limited the function of nonreciprocal dialogues to her main theme—the enlarging of Catherine's latent consciousness through the juxtapositions and contrasts which pit the way of the world against inexperience, social reality against literary fantasy. Thus, particularly in Catherine's case, the conflict of debate is intellectually stimulating rather than intensely emotional. Neither is it divisive. Whenever there is *mutual* unawareness, rather than a misunderstanding staged by Henry as provocateur and parodist, Jane Austen avoids sustained dialogue—a tactic which curtails the exchanges between an insidious General Tilney and a supposedly wealthy Miss Morland. Or, more usually, the dialogues that do evolve from genuine misunderstanding are confined to the kind of intellectual conflicts that are symbolized by differences between literary judgments or word usages. Note, for example, the discussion between Catherine and the Tilneys on expected "murders" in London:

The general pause which succeeded his [Henry's] short disquisition on the state of the nation, was put an end to by Catherine, who, in rather a solemn tone of voice, uttered these words, "I have heard that something very shocking indeed, will soon come out in London."

Miss Tilney, to whom this was chiefly addressed, was startled, and hastily replied, "Indeed!—and of what nature?"

"That I do not know, nor who is the author. I have only heard that it is to be more horrible than any thing we have met with yet."

"Good heaven!—where could you hear of such a thing?"

"A particular friend of mine had an account of it in a letter from

London yesterday. It is to be uncommonly dreadful. I shall expect murder and every thing of the kind."

"You speak with astonishing composure! But I hope your friend's accounts have been exaggerated;—and if such a design is known beforehand, proper measures will undoubtedly be taken by government to prevent its coming to effect."

"Government," said Henry, endeavouring not to smile, "neither desires nor dares to interfere in such matters. There must be murder; and government cares not how much."

The ladies stared. He laughed, and added, "Come, shall I make you understand each other, or leave you to puzzle out an explanation as you can? . . ."

"Miss Morland, do not mind what he says;—but have the goodness to satisfy me as to this dreadful riot."

"Riot!—what riot?" (pp. 111–12)

On the whole this is remarkably akin to some of Sterne's Shandean exercises in noncommunication. Henry's disquisition on the state of the nation has obviously predisposed Eleanor to interpret "something very shocking" in political terms. And this natural association of her ideas conflicts with Catherine's hobbyhorse, the "shocking" horrors of Gothic fiction. Their respective mistakes are emphasized by Henry's mocking interjection and by his subsequent attempt to make them "understand each other":

"My dear Eleanor, the riot is only in your brain. The confusion there is scandalous. Miss Morland has been talking of nothing more dreadful than a new publication which is shortly to come out. . . . And you, Miss Morland—my stupid sister has mistaken all your clearest expressions. You talked of expected horrors in London—and instead of instantly conceiving, as any rational creature would have done, that such words could relate only to a circulating library, she immediately pictured to herself a mob of three thousand men assembling in St. George's Fields; the Bank attacked, the Tower threatened, the streets of London flowing with blood, a detachment of the 12th Light Dragoons, (the hopes of the nation,) called up from Northampton to quell the insurgents." (p. 113)

Henry is being politely ironic, for it is Catherine who really suffers from a mental "riot." She has characteristically superimposed her hobbyhorse on her environment. The mundane "state of the nation" has been unexpectedly replaced by literary preoccupations. Hence the resulting incongruities of the dialogue with Eleanor project Catherine's wider confusion of appearance with reality, fictive fantasy with experience. And as Henry's sarcastic explication makes clear, Eleanor's natural error foreshadows the climactic irony of Catherine's development. For narrative fantasies and exaggerations aside, the Gothic themes of moral disruption and conflict *are* relevant to the real worlds of General Tilney, the Thorpes, and the "state of the nation." In their conflicting interpretations of the crucial phrase, Catherine and Eleanor have unwittingly brought the misunderstandings of their nonreciprocal dialogue to bear on the ironic parallels between Gothic sensationalism and "real" horrors. In short, the general confusion and conflicts of the discussion reflect both Catherine's intellectual immaturity and the double-edged irony that attends the evolution of her rational insights.

Basically, of course, Eleanor's conversation with Catherine owes its structural development to the traditionally comic experience of talking at cross-purposes—a time-honored device which Fielding and Sterne so frequently exploit, and which is the foundation of most of the dialogues in a comedy like Goldsmith's *She Stoops to Conquer*. And Jane Austen's interest in the ironic possibilities of this convention continues in *Sense and Sensibility*. Thus after Colonel Brandon informs Elinor Dashwood that he wishes to present Edward Ferrars with a living, Elinor and Mrs. Jennings discuss the Colonel's generosity. But they are talking at cross-purposes, for the hearty widow assumes that the offer has really been a proposal of marriage to Elinor:

"Well, Miss Dashwood," said Mrs. Jennings, sagaciously smiling, as soon as the gentleman had withdrawn, "I do not ask you what the Colonel has been saying to you; for though, upon my honour, I *tried* to keep out of hearing, I could not help catching enough to understand his business. And I assure you I never was better pleased in my life, and I wish you joy of it with all my heart."

"Thank you, ma'am," said Elinor. "It *is* a matter of great joy to me; and I feel the goodness of Colonel Brandon most sensibly. There are not many men who would act as he has done. Few people who have so compassionate an heart! I never was more astonished in my life."

"Lord! my dear, you are very modest! I an't the least astonished at it in the world, for I have often thought of late, there was nothing more likely to happen."

"You judged from your knowledge of the Colonel's general benevolence; but at least you could not foresee that the opportunity would so very soon occur."

"Opportunity!" repeated Mrs. Jennings—"Oh! as to that, when a man has once made up his mind to such a thing, somehow or other he will soon find an opportunity. Well, my dear, I wish you joy of it again and again; and if ever there was a happy couple in the world, I think I shall soon know where to look for them."

"You mean to go to Delaford after them I suppose," said Elinor, with a faint smile.

"Aye, my dear, that I do, indeed. And as to the house being a bad one, I do not know what the Colonel would be at, for it is as good a one as ever I saw."

"He spoke of its being out of repair."

"Well, and whose fault is that? why don't he repair it?—who should do it but himself?" (pp. 285–86)

The ironic structure of the exchange is based on the close repetition of words like "joy," "astonished," and "opportunity." For as in *Jack & Alice*, the sequence imparts a verbal continuity to the dialogue. But this superficial coherence really reinforces the communications barrier created by Mrs. Jennings' ill-founded assumptions. Her general suspicions have long predisposed her to think of Elinor as the future Mrs. Brandon, and this hobbyhorsical judgment is the primary source of the nonreciprocal nature of the discussion. In effect, the warm prepossessions of Mrs. Jennings' undisciplined sensibility are perfectly in accord with the kind of misapprehension that gives rise to noncommunicative dialogues.

Generally, then, the familiar pattern of talking at cross-purposes reveals the perceptual disparities that are the subject of *Northanger Abbey* and *Sense and Sensibility*. However, in *Sense and Sensibility* it has the additional role of exploring a wider range of emotional and psychological conflicts than we encounter in the earlier novel. When we examine both the immediate context and the subtle nuances of Mrs. Jennings' exchange with Elinor it appears that Jane Austen has successfully adapted the typical dichotomies of nonreciprocal dialogue to the rapidly increasing complexities of her themes and structure. Hence Mrs. Jennings' error is attributable, not only to her own faulty judgment, but also to the fact that Colonel Brandon's real proposition could not be overheard in its entirety: Marianne has been playing the pianoforte in a listless attempt to forget Willoughby. And this background of Marianne's personal tragedy intensifies the irony of errors that arises when Mrs. Jennings wishes Elinor "joy." Moreover, Elinor's acknowledgment of her own "great joy" is counterbalanced by the unsettling shock of Edward Ferrars' engagement to Lucy Steele. Thus her "astonishment" at Colonel Brandon's offer recalls the more personal and mortifying surprise that she experienced when Lucy had previously revealed the engagement. In declaring, "I never was more astonished in my life," Elinor actually recalls that earlier surprise: her polite hyperbole has evoked a multiplicity of past and present emotions that are ironically juxtaposed with Mrs. Jennings' placid unawareness: "I an't the least astonished at it in the world." Finally, the repetition of "astonished" links the double meanings of the dialogue with the moral contrasts of the novel. When the news of the living reaches John Dashwood, he, too, echoes Elinor's surprise. But his shock springs from the narrow self-interest of his perverted "sense," rather than from the real sensibility that motivates Mrs. Jennings: "Well, this is very astonishing!—no relationship!—no connection between them!—and now that livings fetch such a price!—what was the value of this?" (pp. 294–95).

The ambiguities and mutual misunderstandings of nonreciprocal dialogue are therefore integral to the deep emotional, and moral, tensions of the novel. And this is particularly true of the intense, verbal conflicts between Elinor and Lucy. The extended dialogues between the two are usually prefaced by a request for information or advice. But this is really an ironic reaffirmation of their real lack of communication. For quite apart from the exchange of factual information, the subsequent discussion is divisive, and their successive encounters are progressively hostile. The first meeting is typical. Lucy's opening statement is not the innocent query that it seems to be, but a calculated offensive in what rapidly becomes a rather skillful game of verbal hide-and-seek:

"You will think my question an odd one, I dare say," said Lucy . . . "but, pray, are you personally acquainted with your sister-in-law's mother, Mrs. Ferrars?"

Elinor *did* think the question a very odd one, and her countenance expressed it, as she answered that she had never seen Mrs. Ferrars.

"Indeed!" replied Lucy; "I wonder at that, for I thought you must have seen her at Norland sometimes. Then perhaps you cannot tell me what sort of a woman she is?"

"No;" returned Elinor, cautious of giving her real opinion of Edward's mother, and not very desirious of satisfying, what seemed impertinent curiosity—"I know nothing of her."

"I am sure you think me very strange, for inquiring about her in such a way;" said Lucy, eyeing Elinor attentively as she spoke; "but perhaps there may be reasons—I wish I might venture; but however I hope you will do me the justice of believing that I do not mean to be impertinent." (p. 128)

Each speaker continues to disguise her real sentiments with careful ambiguities and half-truths, until Lucy lures Elinor into the open for the climactic, malicious stroke:

"Mrs. Ferrars is certainly nothing to me at present,—but the time *may* come—how soon it will come must depend upon herself—when we may be very intimately connected."

She looked down as she said this, amiably bashful, with only one side glance at her companion to observe its effects on her.

"Good heavens!" cried Elinor, "what do you mean? Are you acquainted with Mr. Robert Ferrars? Can you be——" And she did not feel much delighted with the idea of such a sister-in-law.

"No;" replied Lucy, "not to Mr. *Robert* Ferrars—I never saw him in my life; but," fixing her eyes upon Elinor, "to his elder brother." (p. 129)

As usual, the details of the dialogue are central to Jane Austen's ironic interweaving of themes and personalities. Elinor's exclamation may be a tactical blunder, but it does demonstrate her real, deep-seated sensibilities. And it consequently contrasts with the cold-blooded rationalism suggested by Lucy's calculating understatements, "I dare say," "perhaps you cannot tell," "I wish I might venture." Moreover, the reference to Robert Ferrars occasions more than Elinor's temporary discomfiture. For Lucy's grand disclaimer, "I never saw him in my life," foreshadows the dramatic results of their eventual meeting. And as a final touch of irony, Elinor's present reservations about Lucy Steele as a sister-in-law will be entirely dissipated by the good fortune that accrues to her when Lucy marries Robert rather than Edward.

In the sequel to this meeting their mutual antagonism has been intensified, and there is a correspondingly ironic emphasis on the usual pretense of harmony. Accordingly, the "two fair rivals" converse "under the shelter" of Marianne's piano exercises, and on the pretext of cooperating on "little Annamaria's basket." Once again, their duel is prefaced with a specious request for communication, this time by Elinor. Her primary motive is not to learn more about Edward's engagement, but to demonstrate her comparative "indifference" to Lucy's disclosure:

"I should be undeserving of the confidence you have honoured me with, if I felt no desire for its continuance, or no farther curiosity on its subject. I will not apologize therefore for bringing it forward again."

"Thank you," cried Lucy warmly, "for I was somehow or other afraid I had offended you by what I told you that Monday."

"Offended me! How could you suppose so? Believe me," and Elinor spoke it with the truest sincerity, "nothing could be farther from my intention, than to give you such an idea. Could you have a motive for the trust, that was not honourable and flattering to me?"

"And yet I do assure you," replied Lucy, her little sharp eyes full of meaning, "there seemed to me to be a coldness and displeasure in your manner, that made me quite uncomfortable. I felt sure that you was angry with me. . . ." (p. 146)

The elaborately polite format of the dialogue is not simply a convenient disguise for their immediate conflict. It also dramatizes the general tensions between social decorum and feeling in the novel. Elinor's human qualities transcend the "polite hypocrisy" that she is obliged to observe for the sake of social order. But Lucy is an inveterate hypocrite whose personality perfectly conforms with the prescribed pretenses. While Elinor's detachment from the behavioral code allows her to use these disguises ironically, Lucy's social mask has simply become a symbol of her double-dealing and narrow "sense." This distinction surfaces again in their remarks on Lucy's "devotion" to Edward:

"He has only two thousand pounds of his own; it would be madness to marry upon that, though for my own part, I could give up every prospect of more without a sigh. I have been always used to a very small income, and could struggle with any poverty for him; but I love him too well to be the selfish means of robbing him, perhaps, of all that his mother might give him if he married to please her. We must wait, it may be for many years. With almost every other man in the world, it would be an alarming prospect; but Edward's affection and constancy nothing can deprive me of I know."

"That conviction must be every thing to you; and he is undoubtedly supported by the same trust in your's. If the strength of your reciprocal attachment had failed, as between many people and under many circumstances it naturally would during a four years' engagement, your situation would have been pitiable indeed."

Lucy here looked up; but Elinor was careful in guarding her countenance from every expression that could give her words a suspicious tendency. (p. 147)

Elinor's guarded countenance represents her delicate balance of feeling and prudent decorum. This is the real basis of her ability to exploit the ambiguities of the dialogue as an ironic exercise in noncommunication. The inner tensions between Elinor's sense and sensibility, between restrained propriety and natural impulses, are comically externalized when Mrs. Jennings and Nancy Steele interrupt the dialogue. Their vulgar forthrightness shatters the fragile decorum of the conversation; and this break occurs, significantly, during "a pause" in Marianne's music—for the piano has been providing the "fair rivals" with an ironically harmonious cloak of sound:

"Do you know Mr. Robert Ferrars?" asked Elinor.

"Not at all—I never saw him; but I fancy he is very unlike his brother—silly and a great coxcomb."

"A great coxcomb:" repeated Miss Steele, whose ear had caught those words by a sudden pause in Marianne's music.—"Oh! they are talking of their favourite beaux, I dare say."

"No, sister," cried Lucy, "you are mistaken there, our favourite beaux are *not* great coxcombs."

"I can answer for it that Miss Dashwood's is not," said Mrs. Jennings, laughing heartily; "for he is one of the modestest, prettiest behaved young men I ever saw; but as for Lucy, she is such a sly little creature, there is no finding out who *she* likes."

"Oh!" cried Miss Steele, looking significantly round at them, "I dare say Lucy's beau is quite as modest and pretty behaved as Miss Dashwood's."

Elinor blushed in spite of herself. Lucy bit her lip, and looked angrily at her sister. (pp. 148–49)

Nancy's clumsy interruption does not simply disrupt the fragile format of the duel between Lucy and Elinor. It also threatens the fabric of intrigue and deception with which Lucy habitually cloaks her self-interest. Hence the present interruption is a comic preview of the disaster that Nancy subsequently precipitates by publicly disclosing her sister's engagement.

The dramatic conflicts and the misunderstandings of the Lucy-Elinor encounters do not arise in the famous dialogue between John and Fanny Dashwood on the subject of his late father's estate. Each speaker fully comprehends the bloodless personality of the other: John obviously needs no persuasion to ignore his father's wish that the Dashwood sisters and their mother should receive financial help; and Fanny is well aware of her husband's inclination. But the conversation is significant in that it represents an ironic manipulation of the nonreciprocal dialogue. The ingrained hypocrisy of the speakers compels them to go through the motions of genuine disagreement, with generous intentions on his side, and prudent dissuasion, on hers. The inevitable direction of their real agreement is pointed by a succession of arithmetical calculations which form the fabric of the dialogue. Fanny initiates the discussion with a series of fretful contrasts: their "only" son is measured against John's "half-sister"; "half" blood and "no relationship at all" are counterbalanced by "all" his money. Her mathematical theme sets the stage for the remainder of the discussion. The proposed assistance to Mrs. Dashwood is reduced from Fanny's alarmed exaggeration, "all his money," to her calmer "half your fortune." Then as John willingly retreats in the face of her concern, the sum plunges from three thousand pounds to five hundred pounds, thence to an annuity. The subject of annuities leads Fanny to gloomy speculations on the mathematics of Mrs. Dashwood's life expectancy, and this prompts John's dwindling generosity to its final figure, a present of "fifty pounds, now and then" (pp. 8–11). But the charade is not yet complete. Having reduced the gift from the dimensions of an entire fortune, Fanny is ready with the inevitable proposal that closes the discussion on a note of anticlimatic reversal:

"Indeed, to say the truth, I am convinced within myself that your father had no idea of your giving them any money at all. . . . Altogether, they will have five hundred a-year amongst them, and what on earth can four women want for more than that?—They will live so cheap! Their housekeeping will be nothing at all. They will have no carriage, no horses, and hardly any servants; they will keep no company, and can have no expences of any kind! Only conceive how comfortable they will be! Five hundred a-year! I am sure I cannot imagine how they will spend half of it; and as to your giving them more, it is quite absurd to think of it. They will be much more able to give *you* something." (p. 12)

The farce of the Dashwoods' self-exposure barely disguises the rather grim undertones which link this dialogue with the structural developments of *Sense and Sensibility*. The inevitable, mathematical progression of their staged debate mirrors the cold logic represented by defective sense in general. Altogether, the structure of the dialogue is the essence of order, a tight, rationalistic organization that is the antithesis of Marianne's, or Mrs. Jennings' explosive sensibility. Moreover, this dehumanized logic is really a perversion of an implied ideal. For the social experience does require an ordered framework, symbolized in the opening chapters of *Sense and Sensibility* by the legal and emotional ties of inheritance and family bonds. Ideally, the social order harmonizes the values of sense, represented by the economics of inheritance, with the emotional qualities that are so foreign to John and Fanny Dashwood. This is the kind of balance towards which the novel moves in the marriage of Elinor and Edward Ferrars. Their union offers an alternative to the materialistic logic that is demonstrated, first by the Dashwoods, and then by Mrs. Ferrars. Moreover, both the subject and the inevitable sequence of the dialogue dramatize the presence of death as an inevitable force throughout *Sense and Sensibility*—from the chronicle of deaths in the opening chapter, the tragedy of Colonel Brandon's story and Marianne's almost fatal illness, to the metaphorical comedy of Edward's "annihilation" and "resuscitation" as Mrs. Ferrars' son. The connection with the Dashwood's farcical dialogue of conflict is ironic. The speakers are engrossed with the legalistic order that is activated by death; but they are incapable of responding to the tragic progression represented by death itself. Fanny's mathematical logic is self-contained. So that although it ostensibly concerns itself with the business of death, it remains immune to the usual feelings associated with the subject: the logical sequence of her dialogue with John imitates the certainties of human mortality while violating the emotional values of individual feeling and family ties. Thus the structure of the dialogue anticipates the denouement of the novel: Elinor's marriage is the ideal alternative to Lucy's match with Robert Ferrars, but, like the Dashwoods' sterile rationalism, the perverted logic of Robert's world continues on its own self-contained terms. And there are also ironic juxtapositions in the case of Lucy and Robert, for the two remain impervious to the emotional and moral significance of Elinor's marriage—just as the Dashwoods succeed in ignoring the sensitivity of their own conversational topics.

In effect, the farcical interlude of John's specious debate with Fanny Dashwood is really of crucial importance to the development of Jane Austen's narrative. And in *Pride and Prejudice*, too, the lighthearted tone of some comic exchanges turns out to be deceptive. The opening dialogue between Mr. and Mrs. Bennet is a case in point. There is the same kind of self-exposure that we encounter in John Dashwood's debate with Fanny in *Sense and Sensibility*. But here Jane Austen has increased the multiple functions of the seemingly frivolous dialogue. For while the opening exchange is a typical example of noncommunication, it simultaneously provides the reader with background information on the Bennet family and Netherfield. The obvious incompatibility of the married pair has, ironically, become a dramatic device for communicating with the reader:

"My dear Mr. Bennet," said his lady to him one day, "have you heard that Netherfield Park is let at last?"

Mr. Bennet replied that he had not.

"But it is," returned she; "for Mrs. Long has just been here, and she told me all about it."

Mr. Bennet made no answer.

"Do not you want to know who has taken it?" cried his wife impatiently.

"*You* want to tell me, and I have no objection to hearing it."

This was invitation enough.

"Why, my dear, you must know, Mrs. Long says that Netherfield is taken by a young man of large fortune from the north of England; that he came down on Monday in a chaise and four to see the place, and was so much delighted with it that he agreed with Mr. Morris immediately; that he is to take possession before Michaelmas, and some of his servants are to be in the house by the end of next week."

"What is his name?"

"Bingley."

"Is he married or single?"

"Oh! single, my dear, to be sure! A single man of large fortune; four or five thousand a year. What a fine thing for our girls!"

"How so? how can it affect them?"

"My dear Mr. Bennet," replied his wife, "how can you be so tiresome! You must know that I am thinking of his marrying one of them."

"Is that his design in settling here?"

"Design! nonsense, how can you talk so! But it is very likely that he *may* fall in love with one of them, and therefore you must visit him as soon as he comes." (pp. 3–4)

As usual, the structure of the dialogue is based on a sequence of well-defined patterns. The precise details of Mrs. Bennet's facts are followed by *non sequiturs* on Mr. Bingley as a future son-in-law. Her verbosity is counteracted by Mr. Bennet's laconic rejoinders, or by his equally expressive silences. Moreover, and this recalls Elinor Dashwood and Lucy Steele in their confrontations, the imparting of factual data underlines the absence of human communication. And, as usual, the structural patterns created by conflicting temperaments have a direct bearing on Jane Austen's narrative strategy. Hence Mrs. Bennet's most comical *non sequiturs* are prophetic. Take, for example, her excited exclamation, "A single man of large fortune; four or five thousand a year. What a fine thing for our girls!" This is really a rephrasing of the novel's introductory maxim, "a single man in possession of a good fortune, must be in want of a wife" (p. 3). Like the maxim, Mrs. Bennet's expectations are absurdly illogical: "I am thinking of his marrying one of them." But this statement is only the first of several assumptions and prejudices that are to be tested in turn by the revelations of the plot; and, ironically, Mrs. Bennet's hopes are among the few preconceptions to survive. On one level, then, her forecasts anticipate the narrative directions ahead. But, on another level, Jane Austen confirms Mrs. Bennet's illogical expectations as one way of satirically recognizing unreason as an incorrigible reality. Hence the flux and change of experience may validate even Mrs. Bennet's illogical assumptions.

It is therefore clear from this opening dialogue that Jane Austen continues the strategy of the earlier novels in that she does not restrict the satiric implications of a given exchange to its immediate context. This is also true of the encounters between Elizabeth and Darcy, for their debates are dominated by implied or direct references to prevailing prejudices which make their relationship the central issue of *Pride and Prejudice*. And any incident that bears directly on that relationship is likely to shape the course of any given dialogue. Thus Darcy's insulting behavior at the Meryton ball always lurks in the background whenever they discuss dancing or music. During her Netherfield visit, for example, Elizabeth pointedly declines his invitation to dance:

"Do not you feel a great inclination, Miss Bennet, to seize such an opportunity of dancing a reel?"

She smiled, but made no answer. He repeated the question, with some surprise at her silence.

"Oh!" said she, "I heard you before; but I could not immediately determine what to say in reply. You wanted me, I know, to say 'Yes,' that you might have the pleasure of despising my taste; but I always delight in overthrowing those kind of schemes, and cheating a person of their premeditated contempt. I have therefore made up my mind to tell you, that I do not want to dance a reel at all—and now despise me if you dare."

"Indeed I do not dare."

Elizabeth, having rather expected to affront him, was amazed at his gallantry. (p. 52)

Elizabeth's earlier discomfiture at Meryton accounts for her ostentatious safeguards against "premeditated contempt." But, ironically, the natural desire for revenge has made it difficult for her to grasp the real implications of Darcy's gallantry. He "had never been so bewitched by any woman as he was by her." (p. 52) His demeanour can no longer be judged on the simplistic basis of an earlier hostility. And as their relationship evolves, it releases an increasing number of emotional conflicts which compound their problems of communication—mutual prejudices and pride, the temperamental differences between Elizabeth's natural gaiety and Darcy's reserve, his growing attachment and her persistent resentment. Hence even Mr. Collins' marriage to Charlotte Lucas proves to be an embarrassing topic, at least from Elizabeth's suspect, and suspicious, point of view:

"I should never have considered the distance as one of the *advantages* of the match," cried Elizabeth. "I should never have said Mrs. Collins was settled *near* her family."

"It is a proof of your own attachment to Hertfordshire. Any thing beyond the very neighbourhood of Longbourn, I suppose, would appear far."

As he spoke there was a sort of smile, which Elizabeth fancied she understood; he must be supposing her to be thinking of Jane and Netherfield, and she blushed as she answered,

"I do not mean to say that a woman may not be settled too near her family. The far and the near must be relative, and depend on many varying circumstances. . . ."

Mr. Darcy drew his chair a little towards her, and said, "*You* cannot have a right to such very strong local attachment. *You* cannot have been always at Longbourn."

Elizabeth looked surprised. (p. 179)

After their quarrel clears up these ambiguities, Elizabeth's emotional conflicts center on the relationship between Darcy and her family. Her doubts about his continuing regard stem from the disgrace of Lydia's elopement with Wickham. And this uncertainty is heightened by the clash between her love for Darcy and her loyalty to Longbourn, especially to those who (like Mr. Bennet) are already convinced of Darcy's incorrigible antisocial reserve. Hence the arrival of Mr. Collins' final letter dramatizes her dilemma: for once, Elizabeth is unable to communicate with her father who is contemptuously amused at Mr. Collins' warning against a marriage between Darcy and Elizabeth:

Mr. Darcy, you see, is the man! Now, Lizzy, I think I *have* surprised you. Could he, or the Lucases, have pitched on any man, within the circle of our acquaintance, whose name would have given the lie more effectually to what they related? Mr. Darcy, who never looks at any woman but to see a blemish, and who probably never looked at *you* in his life! It is admirable!"

Elizabeth tried to join in her father's pleasantry, but could only force one most reluctant smile. Never had his wit been directed in a manner so little agreeable to her.

"Are you not diverted?"

"Oh! yes. Pray read on." (p. 363)

Like Elizabeth before him, Mr. Bennet judges Darcy on the basis
of present prejudices that have been wholly conditioned by past
experience: "Had they fixed on any other man it would have been
nothing; but *his* perfect indifference, and *your* pointed dislike,
make it so delightfully absurd!" Moreover, his scepticism in-
creases Elizabeth's inner tensions: "Her father had most cruelly
mortified her, by what he said of Mr. Darcy's indifference, and
she could do nothing but wonder at such a want of penetration, or
fear that perhaps, instead of his seeing too *little*, she might have
fancied too *much*" (p. 364). In effect, the failure of communication
between Mr. Bennet and Elizabeth has heightened her doubts as
to the existence of a viable line of communication between herself and Darcy.

Appropriately, it is Elizabeth who explains the psychological
functions of dialogue as conflict in the novel. Reviewing her earlier
feuds with Darcy, she declares, "The fact is, that you were sick
of civility, of deference, of officious attention. You were disgusted
with the women who were always speaking and looking, and
thinking for *your* approbation alone. I roused, and interested you,
because I was so unlike *them*. Had you not been really amiable
you would have hated me for it; but in spite of the pains you took
to disguise yourself, your feelings were always noble and just;
and in your heart, you thoroughly despised the persons who so
assiduously courted you" (p. 380). In other words, dialogue as
conflict is a kind of emotional catalyst. For the noncommunication
on which it is based initiates the dramatic reevaluations that lead
to selfawareness and mutual understanding. Hence Elizabeth's
verbal feuds with Darcy lead to the explosive self-revelations at
Hunsford. Mutual comprehension is made possible by the drama
that evolves from the conflicts of noncommunicative dialogue. Unlike the confrontations of *Sense and Sensibility*, Elizabeth's disputes with Darcy develop into eventual understanding because
the combatants are basically compatible; they share the "noble"
feelings which Elizabeth generously attributes to Darcy.

The deep-seated differences between Elinor Dashwood and Lucy Steele in *Sense and Sensibility* are emotionally analogous to the great moral debates which explore the insurmountable barriers between Edmund Bertram and Mary Crawford in *Mansfield Park*. The dialogues of the latter are based on the verbal and ethical ambiguities of definitive terms like "manners" and "morals." The differing interpretations that Edmund and Mary apply to such words dramatize the dichotomies that are so fundamental to *Mansfield Park*—morality versus social form, nature versus art, country versus town, the clergy considered as a profession versus the clergy viewed as a moral ideal:

"But why are you to be a clergyman? I thought *that* was always the lot of the youngest, where there were many to choose before him."

"Do you think the church itself never chosen then?"

"*Never* is a black word. But yes, in the *never* of conversation which means *not very often*, I do think it. For what is to be done in the church? Men love to distinguish themselves, and in either of the other lines, distinction may be gained, but not in the church. A clergyman is nothing."

"The *nothing* of conversation has its gradations, I hope, as well as the *never*. A clergyman cannot be high in state or fashion. He must not head mobs, or set the ton in dress. . . . No one here can call the *office* nothing. If the man who holds it is so, it is by the neglect of his duty, by foregoing its just importance, and stepping out of his place to appear what he ought not to appear."

"*You* assign greater consequence to the clergyman than one has been used to hear given, or that I can quite comprehend. One does not see much of this influence and importance in society, and how can it be acquired where they are so seldom seen themselves? How can two sermons a week, even supposing them worth hearing, supposing the preacher to have the sense to prefer Blair's to his own, do all that you speak of? govern the conduct and fashion the manners of a large congregation for the rest of the week? One scarcely sees a clergyman out of his pulpit."

"*You* are speaking of London, *I* am speaking of the nation at large."

"The metropolis, I imagine, is a pretty fair sample of the rest."

"Not, I should hope, of the proportion of virtue to vice throughout the kingdom. We do not look in great cities for our best morality. It is not there, that respectable people of any denomination can do most good; and it certainly is not there, that the influence of the clergy can be most felt." (pp. 92–93)

Mary never "quite comprehends," of course. But, to be fair, neither are Fanny and Edmund really able to appreciate the brilliant satiric realism with which she habitually counters their pious ejaculations. Fanny's poetic tribute to the Sotherton chapel provokes a typical exchange:

"There is something in a chapel and chaplain so much in character with a great house, with one's ideas of what such a household should be! A whole family assembling regularly for the purpose of prayer, is fine!"

"Very fine indeed!" said Miss Crawford, laughing. "It must do the heads of the family a great deal of good to force all the poor housemaids and footmen to leave business and pleasure, and say their prayers here twice a day, while they are inventing excuses themselves for staying away."

"*That* is hardly Fanny's idea of a family assembling," said Edmund. "If the master and mistress do *not* attend themselves, there must be more harm than good in the custom."

"At any rate it is safer to leave people to their own devices on such subjects. . . . Cannot you imagine with what unwilling feelings the former belles of the house of Rushworth did many a time repair to this chapel? The young Mrs. Eleanors and Mrs. Bridgets—starched up into seeming piety, but with heads full of something very different—especially if the poor chaplain were not worth looking at—and, in those days, I fancy parsons were very inferior even to what they are now." (pp. 86–87)

This continuing clash of definitions and intellectual values is superficially akin to the comic misunderstandings of *Northanger Abbey*. But the very deep, moral differences between Mary and Edmund provoke the kind of sustained emotional conflict that is absent from the debates of Catherine Morland and Henry Tilney. And the greater intensity in *Mansfield Park* can be measured by the extent to which Jane Austen incorporates symbolic action within the verbal patterns of the dialogue of conflict. As we have already seen, Marianne Dashwood's piano provides an ironic background of musical harmony in *Sense and Sensibility* during one of the more hostile encounters between Elinor and Lucy. But here in *Mansfield Park* Jane Austen takes this a stage further by integrating symbolic incidents more closely with the actual dialogue. Mary Crawford's card game with William Price is symptomatic of her self-destructive "spirit," and in this sense it supplements her opposition to Edmund's restrictive morality. Thus her hostile interest in Edmund's description of his new parsonage is camouflaged by a suggestive feature of the card game—her negotiations for William's "knave." The desired knave represents the moral perversity and reckless daring that Mary pits against Edmund's prosaic virtues:

> "I think the house and premises may be made comfortable, and given the air of a gentleman's residence without any very heavy expense, and that must suffice me; and I hope may suffice all who care about me."
>
> Miss Crawford, a little suspicious and resentful of a certain tone of voice and a certain half-look attending the last expression of his hope, made a hasty finish of her dealings with William Price, and securing his knave at an exorbitant rate, exclaimed, "There, I will stake my last like a woman of spirit. No cold prudence for me. I am not born to sit still and do nothing. If I lose the game, it shall not be from not striving for it."
>
> The game was her's, and only did not pay her for what she had given to secure it. (pp. 242–43)

This suggestive integration of dialogue and action is also in evidence in *Emma*, particularly during the climactic Box Hill episode. The picnic is anticipated as an occasion of enjoyment, of social harmony: "Seven miles were travelled in expectation of enjoyment, and every body had a burst of admiration on first arriving" (p. 367). But as personal animosities persist, even the indefatigable Mr. Weston cannot harmonize the outing, after there has been "an accidental division" into separate groups: "The Eltons walked together; Mr. Knightley took charge of Miss Bates and Jane; and Emma and Harriet belonged to Frank Churchill" (p. 367). The total disruption of the party proceeds rapidly after this physical grouping, and the ensuing series of dialogues explores the hidden and open hostilities. Moreover, the structure of the discussions coincides with perceptible stages in the deterioration of the picnic. And, in turn, the three phases of personal conflict are analogous to the prior, "accidental" division of the party into three groups. In the first phase, emotional tensions and their accompanying "principle" of separation" are expressed simply by a general "langour, a want of spirits." The "downright dulness" that results is appropriately described in indirect speech, even when Frank Churchill "grew talkative and gay" for Emma's benefit:

Emma, glad to be enlivened, not sorry to be flattered, was gay and easy too, and gave him all the friendly encouragement, the admission to be gallant, which she had ever given in the first and most animating period of their acquaintance; but which now, in her own estimation, meant nothing, though in the judgment of most people looking on it must have had such an appearance as no English word but flirtation could very well describe. "Mr. Frank Churchill and Miss Woodhouse flirted together excessively." They were laying themselves open to that very phrase—and to having sent it off in a letter to Maple Grove by one lady, to Ireland by another. Not that Emma was gay and thoughtless from any real felicity; it was rather because she felt less happy than she had expected (p. 368).

In the second phase the dialogue is reported in direct speech. And, simultaneously, the main theme of the discussion—control and influence—impinges directly on the heightened tensions within the group. For one of Emma's main problems in her personal relationships has been her magisterial instinct. At first, the theme is limited to the flirtatious exchange with Frank about his ill-humour at Donwell Abbey:

"Don't say I was cross. I was fatigued. The heat overcame me."
"It is hotter to-day."
"Not to my feelings. I am perfectly comfortable to-day."
"You are comfortable because you are under command."
"Your command?—Yes."
"Perhaps I intended you to say so, but I meant self-command. You

had, somehow or other, broken bounds yesterday, and run away from your own management; but to-day you are got back again—and as I cannot be always with you, it is best to believe your temper under your own command rather than mine." (pp. 368–69)

Her modest disclaimer is not entirely honest, since she has always fancied herself as the arbiter of Frank's affections and fortunes. But Emma's aspirations to control others are undercut by the implications of Frank's ill-temper at Donwell; for his anger had stemmed from his quarrel with Jane—an area in which Emma can claim neither knowledge nor control. Moreover, Emma predictably tries to extend this illusory influence over the Box Hill picnic. According to Frank, "I am ordered by Miss Woodhouse (who, wherever she is, presides,) to say, that she desires to know what you are all thinking of." And this power play brings all the old hostilities into the open: Mrs. Elton inevitably "swelled" at the idea of Miss Woodhouse's presiding, her "caro sposo" mutters a great deal about the privileges of matrons and chaperones, and Mr. Knightley's answer ("the most distinct") subtly points to the judicious, as well as partial, criticisms that have been excited by Emma's conduct: "Is Miss Woodhouse sure that she would like to hear what we are all thinking of?" (p. 369). She would not: "It is the very last thing I would stand the brunt of just now" (pp. 369–70). Neither is she able to guess at Jane Fairfax's real reactions to the spectacle, or even at the real motives behind Frank's desperate fit of flirtation. Finally, the insult to Miss Bates is the direct result of another demand by the "presiding" Emma, this time for "two things moderately clever—or three things very dull indeed." And it is significant that Emma's insulting remark to Miss Bates is itself couched in terms that express the continuing drive for power—Miss Bates will be "limited as to number," to only three dull things at once (pp. 370–71).

When the Eltons finally rebel against Emma's "commands" by walking away, the third, and yet more intensified, phase of the Box Hill dialogue gets underway with the veiled conflict between Frank and Jane. His pointed comments on the retreating Eltons are really, a disguised recapitulation of his intimacy with Jane. The Eltons have been "lucky," he notes sarcastically, because their happiness is founded on a short acquaintance at Bath: "How many a man has committed himself on a short acquaintance, and rued it all the rest of his life!" In effect, Jane's reply ends their secret engagement: "A hasty and imprudent attachment may arise—but there is generally time to recover from it afterwards. I would be understood to mean, that it can be only weak, irresolute characters, (whose happiness must be always at the mercy of chance,) who will suffer an unfortunate acquaintance to be an inconvenience, an oppression for ever" (pp. 372–73). Frank's comments on the limitations of a short acquaintance and personal knowledge are applicable to Emma as well as to his own engagement. For it is Emma's lack of real knowledge that makes her the dupe in the matter of Jane's relationship with Frank. So that when the dialogue returns once more to Emma and Frank, the pervasive irony of the exchange is derived from the fact that Emma has missed all the clues in the preceding discussion with Jane, that she is so impervious to the realities of her emotional environment. And it is this continuing ignorance on Emma's part that heightens the irony of this exchange with Frank, for the subject is education, the upbringing of Frank's future wife:

"Will you choose a wife for me?—I am sure I should like any body fixed on by you. . . . Find somebody for me. I am in no hurry. Adopt her, educate her."

"And make her like myself."

"By all means, if you can."

"Very well. I undertake the commission. You shall have a charming wife."

"She must be very lively, and have hazle eyes. I care for nothing else. I shall go abroad for a couple of years—and when I return, I shall come to you for my wife. Remember."

Emma was in no danger of forgetting. (p. 373)

All the misunderstandings and intrigues of Emma's circle have therefore been brought together at Box Hill. And it is through the characteristic conflicts and noncommunication of dramatic dialogue that Jane Austen explores the multiple implications of the picnic confrontations. Overt hostilities become masks for more fundamental divisions: thus the feud between the Eltons and Emma obscures the crisis of Frank's relationship with Jane. One set of misconceptions is interwoven with another: consequently, Emma's preoccupation with romantic fantasies about Harriet and Frank makes her a convenient stalking-horse for Frank's embittered witticisms at Jane's expense. But at the same time that he exploits Emma in this regard, Frank mistakenly suspects her of having discovered his secret engagement. Moreover, the rivalry between Emma and Mrs. Elton as power-brokers veils the more crucial (and unchallenged) authority that Mr. Knightley exercises over Emma. And the contrast between Mrs. Elton's voluble pretensions and Mr. Knightley's real power is demonstrated by the dramatic effect of his reprimand at the end of the picnic: "The truth of his representation there was no denying. She [Emma] felt it at her heart. How could she have been so brutal, so cruel to Miss Bates!—How could she have exposed herself to such ill opinion in any one she valued! And how suffer him to leave her without saying one word of gratitude, of concurrence, of common kindness!" (p. 376)

The scene of Mr. Knightley's eventual proposal to Emma is comparable with the Box Hill episode in that Jane Austen again bases the multiple misunderstandings of the dialogue on a series of Emma's past schemes and blunders. Mr. Knightley's concern that she may have been jilted by Frank is a natural error that is very similar to Mrs. Weston's earlier apprehensions on the same subject. And even after Emma has allayed his fears, the irony of errors persists, for Emma herself momentarily expects Mr. Knightley to declare his love for Harriet (pp. 428–29). Obviously exchanges of this kind are based on a very familiar strategy, for both Emma and Mr. Knightley are talking at cross-purposes—as indeed are nearly all the participants at the Box Hill outing. And by integrating this kind of structure with the emotional complexities of *Emma*, Jane Austen has once again transformed a relatively crude and well-worn form in order to satisfy the complex demands of her irony.

This kind of transformation continues even in the more subdued context of *Persuasion* where intensely dramatic dialogues are rare. One such exchange does take place between Mrs. Smith and Anne Elliot when they discuss Mr. Elliot. They begin by talking at cross-purposes, for Mrs. Smith believes that Anne and Mr. Elliot are engaged: "Let me plead for my—present friend I cannot call him—but for my former friend. Where can you look for a more suitable match? Where could you expect a more gentlemanlike, agreeable man? Let me recommend Mr. Elliot. I am sure you hear nothing but good of him from Colonel Wallis, and who can know him better than Colonel Wallis?" (p. 196) Mrs. Smith's sarcastic deference to Colonel Wallis' authority reinforces our suspicions about the "agreeable" Mr. Elliot. So does her pointed contrast between "present friend" and "past friend." Neither is Anne's attempt to correct her friend's error successful. The embittered Mrs. Smith is slow to relinquish an opportunity which allows her to indict Mr. Elliot under the mask of generous praise: "Mr. Elliot has sense to understand the value of such a woman. Your peace will not be shipwrecked as mine has been. You are safe in all worldly matters, and safe in his character. He will not be led astray, he will not be misled by others to his ruin" (p. 196). Anne's real subject, her new happiness with Wentworth, has therefore been juxtaposed with Mrs. Smith's bitter disillusionment; Anne's bright future is counterbalanced by her friend's tragic memories. The old comedy of talking at cross-purposes has become a complex of conflicting emotions, of past and present.

CHAPTER VIII

Parody

ACCORDING TO Mary Lascelles, Jane Austen's "favourite pattern of burlesque" depends on "a deliberately contrived antithesis between the worlds of actuality and illusion" (*Jane Austen and her Art*, p. 68).[1] This also applies to some of Jane Austen's predecessors in the novel. Both Fielding and Sterne, for example, frequently undermine the illusions of sentimental idealism by juxtaposing them with actuality. Such antitheses involve a double-edged irony, for the shortcomings of the real world are also exposed in the process. And this remains true, whether the illusory ideals are "literary" in a general sense, or whether they refer to a specific work like Richardson's *Pamela*. Hence Joseph Andrews' soliloquy at the Tow-wouse inn is typical of the parodic antithesis through which Fielding imitates Richardson's work:

"O most Adorable *Pamela*! most virtuous Sister, whose Example could alone enable me to withstand all the Temptations of Riches and Beauty, and to preserve my Virtue pure and chaste, for the Arms of my dear *Fanny*, if it had pleased Heaven that I should ever have come into them. What Riches, or Honours, or Pleasures can make us amends for the Loss of Innocence? Doth not that alone afford us more Consolation, than all worldly Acquisitions? What but Innocence and Virtue could give any Comfort to such a miserable Wretch

1. Mary Lascelles, *Jane Austen and Her Art* (London, 1939), 68. Kenneth L. Moler, among others, notes the pervasive role of parody in Jane Austen's fiction: *Jane Austen's Art of Allusion* (Lincoln, Neb., 1968), 1.

as I am? Yet these can make me prefer this sick and painful Bed to all
the Pleasures I should have found in my Lady's. These can make me
face Death without Fear; and though I love my *Fanny* more than ever
Man loved a Woman; these can teach me to resign myself to the
Divine Will without repining. O thou delightful charming Creature,
if Heaven had indulged thee to my Arms, the poorest, humblest State
would have been a Paradise; I could have lived with thee in the lowest
Cottage, without envying the Palaces, the Dainties, or the Riches of
any Man breathing. But I must leave thee, leave thee for ever, my
dearest Angel, I must think of another World, and I heartily pray
thou may'st meet Comfort in this."—*Barnabas* thought he had heard
enough; so down stairs he went, and told *Tow-wouse* he could do his
Guest no Service; for that he was very light-headed and had uttered
nothing but a Rhapsody of Nonsense all the time he stayed in the
Room.[2]

As a whole the passage conforms with the kind of anticlimactic
structure on which Fielding usually bases his parodic contrasts.
The comical fervor of Joseph's heady idealism gives way to the
equally suspect realities represented by Barnabas' banal indifference. And Joseph's idealistic rhetoric is corrupted by the irony of
the incest motif, for there is a contextual ambiguity in his speech
which fails to distinguish between the "most adorable Pamela" of
the first sentence, and the "charming Creature" that follows. It is
also important to note that the contrast between Joseph and Barnabas also projects the diverse relationships between literature and
reader. The moral idealism that Richardson postulates in *Pamela*
meets with different reactions, ranging from Joseph's naive purity
to Barnabas' corrupt worldliness. Hence parody begins with the
exploration of literature as communication: the parodist contrasts
illusion and reality in order to expose the dichotomy between a
given literary viewpoint and experience, or between various reactions to an author.

Similarly, *Shamela* integrates Fielding's ridicule of Richardson's
didactic method with the parody of critical approaches to *Pamela*
itself. Indeed it is fairly clear that much of Fielding's prefatory

2. Henry Fielding, *Joseph Andrews*, ed. Martin C. Battestin, The Wesleyan
Edition of the Works of Henry Fielding (Oxford, 1967), 58–59.

apparatus in *Shamela* is in imitation of *divergent* attitudes to Richardson's work. Hence Parson Thomas Tickletext's prurient enthusiasm for *Shamela* is a direct parody of the erotic zeal with which Aaron Hill and others commended the morality of *Pamela*. According to Hill, Richardson "has reconciled the *Pleasing* to the *Proper*. The *Thought* is every-where exactly cloath'd by the Expression: And becomes its Dress as roundly, and as close, as *Pamela* her Country habit. . . . And so, dear Sir, it will be always found.—When modest Beauty seeks to hide itself by casting off the *Pride* of *Ornament*, it but displays itself without a *Covering*."[3] Moreover, Richardson's detractors are represented on Fielding's title page, where the author promises to expose the notorious falsehoods of *Pamela*, and to set the arts of Richardson's young politician in a "true and just" light. On the whole then, Fielding's burlesque proceeds by juxtaposing a variety of reactions to *Pamela*: snobbish criticism is opposed to Hill's enthusiasm, and the latter's moral viewpoint is countered by Tickletext's salivating outbursts on behalf of *Shamela*. Moreover, the conflicts among the readers are analogous to the gap between Shamelan artifice and Richardsonian idealism. Fielding is exploiting the traditional antitheses of the parodic mode in order to investigate the levels of communication (or noncommunication) between writer and reader, between literary or moral illusions and actuality. Hence whenever he resorts to his favorite tactic of alternative phrasing, Fielding is attempting more than a humorous imitation of classical or sentimental rhetoric. Take, for example, the description of one of Parson Adams's fights in *Joseph Andrews*. His opponent "belaboured the Body of *Adams* 'till he was weary, and indeed, 'till he concluded (to use the Language of fighting) *that he had done his business*; or, in the Language of Poetry, *that he had sent him to the Shades below*; in plain English, *that he was dead*." Fielding

3. Aaron Hill, *Samuel Richardson's Introduction to "Pamela,"* ed. Sheridan W. Baker, Jr., *Augustan Reprint Society*, No. 48 (Los Angeles, 1954), p. xx. Compare Conny Keyber (Henry Fielding) *An Apology for the Life of Mrs. Shamela Andrews*, intro. Ian Watt, *Augustan Reprint Society*, No. 57 (Los Angeles, 1956), 2.

is really using these brief snatches of parody to explore the narrator's rhetorical relationship with the reader. Each phrase imitates and appeals to the taste of a specific kind of reader. And in *Tom Jones* he addresses himself to the numerous possibilities represented by the reader's judgment. The latter might be a "good reptile," or a "worthy friend;" he could be governed by the head, or guided by the heart; and again, he may be "as learned in human nature as Shakespeare himself was," or "no wiser than some of his editors."[4]

Laurence Sterne's continuing interest in fiction as communication is also manifest in the parodic episodes of *Tristram Shandy*. Hence the burlesque of sentimental language follows the usual pattern of antithetical anticlimax, especially in Slawkenbergius' "Tale":

"O *Diego*! how many weary steps has my brother's pity led me by the hand languishing to trace out yours; how far has desire carried me beyond strength—and how oft have I fainted by the way, and sunk into his arms, with only power to cry out—o my *Diego*!

"If the gentleness of your carriage has not belied your heart, you will fly to me, almost as fast as you fled from me—haste as you will—you will arrive but to see me expire.—'Tis a bitter draught, *Diego*, but oh! 'tis embitter'd still more by dying *un*—."

She could proceed no farther.

Slawkenbergius supposes the word intended was *unconvinced*, but her strength would not enable her to finish her letter.[5]

Altogether, the sentimental idealism of the apostrophe is counterbalanced by the erotic suggestiveness of the aposiopesis, and these sexual overtones have actually been multiplied by Tristram's attempt to dispel them. In effect, the parody has become another Shandean exercise in noncommunication with the reader.

Like Fielding and Sterne, Jane Austen bases her parodies on the exploitation of the diverse standards represented by her reader-

---

4. Fielding, *Joseph Andrews*, 138; Fielding, *The History of Tom Jones*, Shakespeare Head Edition (Oxford, 1926), III, 1–3.

5. Laurence Sterne, *The Life and Opinions of Tristram Shandy, Gentleman*, ed. James Aiken Work (New York, 1940), 269.

ship.[6] Consequently her penchant for parody is explained by her interest in the rhetorical relationships created by disparities in the tastes of the novelist's audience. The contrasting insights of the parodic tradition allow her to juxtapose and challenge a set of conflicting reactions to a literary or moral viewpoint. In fact it is noteworthy that when she compiled the "Opinions" on *Mansfield Park* and *Emma*, Jane Austen seemed to have been struck by the frequent opposition of one judgment to another: the didactic versus the witty, or intellect versus sentimentality. The opinions on *Mansfield Park* are therefore presented as occasional antitheses:

> Miss Lloyd preferred it altogether to either of the others.—Delighted with Fanny.—Hated Mrs. Norris.—
> My Mother—not liked it so well as P. & P.—Thought Fanny insipid.—Enjoyed Mrs. Norris.— . . .
> Miss Burdett—Did not like it so well as P. & P.
> Mrs. James Tilson—Liked it better than P. & P. (*Minor Works*, p. 432).

Jane Austen is apparently playing a literary game with the contributors to "Opinions." When she is not manipulating their comical differences, she takes a puckish delight in their unconscious self-revelations. Mrs. Bramstone modestly identifies herself with Lady Bertram: "Thought Lady Bertram like herself. Preferred it to either of the others—but imagined *that* might be her want of Taste—as she does not understand Wit.—" On the other hand, Lady Kerr's "humble pen" lends itself to a decidedly smug arrogance: "*MP*," she reports, is universally admired in Edinburgh "by all the *wise ones.*—Indeed, I have not heard a single fault

---

6. Andrew Wright has noted the interplay of "fancy" and "plain" language in Fielding's work: *Henry Fielding:Mask and Feast* (London, 1965), 186–91. Karl Kroeber oversimplifies the author-reader relationship in both Fielding and Jane Austen when he emphasizes that each novelist writes with full confidence in his/her agreement with the reader: *Styles in Fictional Structure: The Art of Jane Austen, Charlotte Brontë, George Eliot* (Princeton, 1971), 44–45. Kroeber's point ignores the extent to which the novelist's easy intimacy with one group of readers (the young Jane Austen and her family circle, for example) is counterbalanced by the writer's awareness of "outside" tastes in the reading public: hence, the device of alternating phrasing often reflects this counterbalancing of tastes.

given to it" (p. 433). With regards to *Emma*, Mr. Fowle belongs to a familiar group. He "read only the first & last Chapters, because he had heard it was not interesting" (p. 439). Finally, when Jane Austen imitates Fielding's brand of alternate phrasing, she is really using parody to examine the problems of communication that are implied by the "Opinions." Accordingly, in one of her letters to Cassandra she comments on an item of family gossip by echoing divergent formulae for expressing surprise: "What a Contretems!—in the Language of France; What an unluckiness! in that of Mde. Duval" (*Letters*, p. 180).

Modern criticism has been fairly exhaustive on the themes and objectives of Jane Austen's parodies; but what is of more immediate interest here is the extent to which her *methods* as a parodist contribute to the development of style and form in her fiction as a whole. Generally, her interest in burlesque as communication shapes her techniques of ironic analysis. And her narrative forms can sometimes be traced to the antithetical structures through which her juvenilia explore the rhetorical relationships inherent in parody. The spirited attack on Goldsmith's *History of England* is fairly representative of her early methods of burlesque. As a "partial, prejudiced, and ignorant Historian," she imitates Goldsmith's distorted concept of historiography, and does this by incongruously employing a style that is diametrically opposed to Goldsmith's. Where Goldsmith is violently prejudiced against Henry the Fourth, Jane Austen's historian is blandly apologetic. Goldsmith's account of Henry's bloody ascension is sensationalist. Jane Austen counters with a series of cold-blooded understatements: Henry ascended the throne "much to his own satisfaction" after having "prevailed" on his predecessor to resign and retire to Pomfret Castle "where he happened to be murdered" (*Minor Works*, p. 139).[7] In Goldsmith's *History*, Lady Jane Grey is a tragic heroine in an endless blood-bath. On her way to the place

---

7. Compare Oliver Goldsmith, *An History of England in a Series of Letters from a Nobleman to his Son* (2 vols.; 6th ed.; London, 1780), I, 158.

of execution she is met by officers "bearing the headless body of her husband streaming with blood."[8] Jane Austen reduces the episode to the level of a farcical mishap in which the Latin-scribbling Lady Jane encounters "the dead Body of her Husband accidentally passing that way" (*Minor Works*, p. 144). Both episodes exemplify the kind of anticlimax that the young Jane Austen usually achieves by juxtaposing divergent points of view. She replaces Goldsmith's passionate exaggerations with a cynical indifference to both fact and feeling: "I suppose you know all about the Wars between him [Henry the Sixth] and the Duke of York who was of the right side; if you do not, you had better read some other History, for I shall not be very diffuse in this" (p. 140). Moreover, an antithesis of this kind depends on the reader's awareness of Goldsmith's *History*, on his ability to contrast the original judgments with Jane Austen's ironic distortions.

The anticlimactic statement is obviously her favorite antithetical structure, for it recurs throughout the juvenilia. In *Frederic & Elfrida*, Charlotte accepts two consecutive proposals of marriage, then follows up this remarkable feat with a nonchalant supper "on a young Leveret, a brace of Partridges, a leash of Pheasants & a Dozen of Pigeons" (pp. 8–9).[9] Having undermined the romantic delicacy of the sentimental proposal, Jane Austen applies her subversive anticlimax to the excessive emotionalism of the popular novel. Thus when Charlotte does react to the implications of a double engagement, "the reflection of her past folly, operated so strongly on her mind, that she resolved to be guilty on a greater, & to that end threw herself into a deep stream" (p. 9). It is through anticlimactic statements like these that Jane Austen effects her

8. *Ibid.*, 272.
9. William Beckford (pseud. Harriet Marlow) gives a similar description of a distraught lover in *Modern Novel Writing* (1796): "In a paroxysm of grief therefore Henry retired early to his chamber, and calling for a boiled fowl and a bottle of Burton ale, in a few hours composed the following beautiful acrostic, as a tribute of admiration and esteem to the unrivalled excellence of Arabella." Quoted by Winnifred Husbands, *The Lesser Novel*, unpublished M.A. thesis (University of London, 1922), 102.

satiric contrast btween the unreal world of sentimental fiction and the banal realities of experience. The instant intimacies of the sentimental tradition lend themselves easily to this tactic. Consequently, in *Frederic & Elfrida*, "the intimacy between the Families of Fitzroy, Drummond and Falknor, daily increased till at length it grew to such a pitch, that they did not scruple to kick one another out of the window on the slightest provocation" (p. 6). Very similar methods are employed in *Jack & Alice* to debunk the irresistible glamour of the sentimental hero:

The Beams that darted from his Eyes were like those of that glorious Luminary tho' infinitely superior. So strong were they that no one dared venture within half a mile of them; he had therefore the best part of the Room to himself, its size not amounting to more than 3 quarters of a mile in length & half a one in breadth. The Gentleman at last finding the fierceness of his beams to be very inconvenient to the concourse by obliging them to croud together in one corner of the room, half shut his eyes by which means, the Company discovered him to be Charles Adams in his plain green Coat, without any mask at all. (p. 13)

In *Love and Freindship* hypocrisy, especially the affectation of sensibility, is dramatized by a series of specious "crises." And these farcical melodramas are undercut by the telltale anticlimax of the ensuing dialogues. Laura and her family, for example, profess great astonishment when Edward first enters their lives with "a violent knocking on the outward Door of our rustic Cot." But this emotional front contrasts with the insipid detachment of the circuitous dialogue that follows:

My Father started—"What noise is that," (said he.) "It sounds like a loud tapping at the door"—(replied my Mother.) "it does indeed." (cried I.) "I am of your opinion; (said my Father) it certainly does appear to proceed from some uncommon violence exerted against our unoffending door." "Yes (exclaimed I) I cannot help thinking it must be somebody who knocks for admittance."
"That is another point (replied he;) We must not pretend to determine on what motive the person may knock—tho' that someone *does* rap at the door, I am partly convinced." (p. 79)

And when Edward is finally admitted, the anticlimactic sequence is repeated; for he rounds off his horrendous "history" of himself with an absurd *non sequitur*:

"I know not what might have befallen me had I not at length discerned thro' the solemn Gloom that surrounded me a distant Light, which as I approached it, I discovered to be the chearfull Blaze of your fire. Impelled by the combination of Misfortunes under which I laboured, namely Fear, Cold and Hunger I hesitated not to ask admittance which at length I have gained; and now my Adorable Laura (continued he taking my Hand) when may I hope to receive that reward of all the painfull sufferings I have undergone during the course of my attachment to you, to which I have ever aspired. Oh! when will you reward me with Yourself?" (pp. 81–82)

Finally, the moral "sentiments" that are the stock-in-trade of the didactic novel are subjected to the same treatment that Jane Austen applies to melodramatic narrative forms. Hence Laura recalls the injunctions which she receives from her old friend Isabel, before setting out for the city: "Beware my Laura (she would often say) Beware of the insipid Vanities and idle Dissipations of the Metropolis of England; Beware of the unmeaning Luxuries of Bath and of the stinking fish of Southampton" (pp. 78–79). Laura's frenzied eulogy to her dead husband is comparable: "Give me a violin—. I'll play to him and sooth him in his melancholy Hours— Beware ye gentle Nymphs of Cupid's Thunderbolts, avoid the piercing Shafts of Jupiter—Look at that Grove of Firs—I see a Leg of Mutton—They told me Edward was not Dead; but they deceived me— they took him for a Cucumber" (p. 100).

The crude but effective antitheses of the shorter juvenile pieces are usually limited to the author-reader relationship. Thus the underdeveloped character sketches of, say, *Frederic & Elfrida* would not sustain the internal conflicts which Jane Austen presents in subsequent parodies. And in cases like these character sketches the anticlimactic presentation of incident and personality is largely a rhetorical process that appeals to Jane Austen's reader rather than a complex emotional experience within the individuals of the story. The consistency with which the young novelist re-

sorts to the anticlimax at this stage of her craft presumes an intimate relationship with her readers, and it may be more than
coincidental that the juvenile fragments like *Frederic & Elfrida*
were written specifically for the Austen family. The *History of
England*, for example, was dedicated to Cassandra Austen who re-
ciprocated by illustrating the work with sketches of the English
monarchs. But from *Love and Freindship*, these satiric antitheses
and their accompanying modes of anticlimax are gradually internalized. The conflict between sentimental rhetoric and social
reality is not simply a direct, satiric appeal to the reader. It also
represents the exposé of the characters' moral and emotional contradictions. Laura's obsession with idealistic clichés is counteracted
by her frank sexuality and flimsy intellect. Her shallow claims to
the humanism of true sensibility are often revealed as a kind of
erotic self-indulgence, particularly in the instant romance with
Edward. Or, as Sophia's "dieing Advice" concedes, the histrionic
postures of the sentimental tradition may be little more than neu-
rosis: "Beware of fainting-fits. . . . Though at the time they may
be refreshing and agreable yet beleive me they will in the end, if
too often repeated and at improper seasons, prove destructive to
your Constitution" (*Minor Works*, p. 102).

Love and Freindship also witnesses another important development in Jane Austen's art of parody. For in addition to internaliz-
ing the effects of antithesis and anticlimax, Jane Austen is now
beginning to integrate her characters' personal judgments with
the narrator's point of view. Instead of simply imitating or contra-
dicting the tastes of her victim, Jane Austen ironically subordinates
her moral or narrative judgment to the viewpoint of any given
character. This manipulation of the narrative viewpoint is quite
evident in *Love and Freindship* where society at large appears
brutal and insensitive because we see it through Laura's eyes. And
we accept her judgments only as long as we take her "sensibility"
at face value. Or, in the Johnsonian episodes of the work, Laura's
suspect understanding is exposed in its true colors by being juxtaposed with the narrative viewpoint of an established, and re-

spected work. Samuel Johnson's *Journey to the Western Islands of Scotland* provides the background for one such scene. After their expulsion from MacDonald Hall, Laura and Sophia "sate down by the side of a clear limpid stream to refresh our exhausted limbs. The place was suited to meditation. A grove of full-grown Elms sheltered us from the East—. A Bed of full-grown Nettles from the West—. Before us ran the murmuring brook and behind us ran the turn-pike road. We were in a mood for contemplation and in a Disposition to enjoy so beautiful a spot" (*Minor Works*, p. 97). In his description of the Highlands, Johnson writes,

> I sat down on a bank, such as a writer of Romance might have delighted to feign. I had indeed no trees to whisper over my head, but a clear rivulet streamed at my feet. The day was calm, the air was soft, and all was rudeness, silence, and solitude. Before me, and on either side, were high hills, which, by hindering the eye from ranging, forced the mind to find entertainment for itself. . . .
>
> We were in this place at ease and by choice, and had no evils to suffer or to fear; yet the imaginations excited by the view of an unknown and untravelled wilderness are not such as arise in the artificial solitude of parks and gardens, a flattering notion of self-sufficiency, a placid indulgence of voluntary delusions, a secure expansion of the fancy, or a cool concentration of the mental powers.[10]

By echoing the tone and general style of Johnson's commonsense, Laura exposes the fraudulent sentimentality of her own narrative judgment. Johnson deliberately invites comparison with the romantic in order to stress the harsh realities of his main theme: "The phantoms which haunt a desert are want, and misery, and danger; the evils of dereliction rush upon the thoughts; man is made unwillingly acquainted with his own weakness, and meditation shows him how little he can sustain, and how little he can perform."[11] On the other hand, Laura expects and stimulates "voluntary delusions." She is in a mood to enjoy contemplation in

10. *Johnson's "Journey to the Western Islands" and Boswell's "Journal of a Tour to the Hebrides with Samuel Johnson*," ed. R. W. Chapman, Oxford Standard Authors (London, 1930), 35–36. Chapman notes Jane Austen's parody of Johnson, *Minor Works*, p. 458.
11. *Ibid.*, 36.

a romantic vein. But, significantly, she is never able to indulge in these sentimental delights. Each attempt at meditation only revives unpleasant memories, and she is eventually interrupted by the unpleasant reality of her husband's fatal accident.

Before she discovers the identity of the victims, Laura reacts to that accident with a curious admixture of detachment and affected concern. And during the rush to the overturned phaeton she pauses, incongruously, to reflect on the nature of moral reflections: "What an ample subject for reflection on the uncertain Enjoyments of this World, would not that Phaeton and the Life of Cardinal Wolsey afford a thinking Mind!" (*Minor Works*, p. 99). This is the second allusion to Johnson's moral philosophy, for Laura has actually paraphrased one of the better-known passages from the *Vanity of Human Wishes*:

> For why did Wolsey near the steeps of fate
> On weak foundations raise th' enormous weight?
> Why but to sink beneath misfortune's blow,
> With louder ruin to the gulphs below?[12]

Here Laura's pretensions to feeling have been undermined by her choice of narrative viewpoint. For the satiric irony with which Johnson judges Wolsey implies a degree of detached objectivity that is at odds with Laura's posture of concern. And, once again, her Johnsonian charade collapses under the impact of real distress: the dead passengers of the phaeton are Edward and Augustus. Moreover, it is consistent with the general pattern of Laura's hypocrisy that these attempts to manipulate the narrative viewpoint heightens, rather than disguises, her real personality.

The narrative perspective is also manipulated in *Northanger Abbey* where Jane Austen continues the gradual process of integrating parody and characterization. The famous "apology" for the novel is a fine example of the manner in which Jane Austen can create an ambiguous viewpoint through the parodic opposi-

---

12. Samuel Johnson, *Poems*, ed. E. L. McAdam, Jr., and George Milne, The Yale Edition of the Works of Samuel Johnson (New Haven, 1964), VI, ll. 125–28.

tion of differing judgments. It is hardly the straightforward defense that it seems to be.[13]

I will not adopt that ungenerous and impolitic custom so common with novel writers, of degrading by their contemptuous censure the very performances, to the number of which they are themselves adding —joining with their greatest enemies in bestowing the harshest epithets on such works, and scarcely ever permitting them to be read by their own heroine, who, if she accidentally take up a novel, is sure to turn over its insipid pages with disgust. . . . Let us leave it to the Reviewers to abuse such effusions of fancy at their leisure, and over every new novel to talk in threadbare strains of the trash with which the press now groans. Let us not desert one another; we are an injured body. Although our productions have afforded more extensive and unaffected pleasure than those of any other literary corporation in the world, no species of composition has been so much decried. From pride, ignorance, or fashion, our foes are almost as many as our readers . . . —there seems almost a general wish of decrying the capacity and undervaluing the labour of the novelist, and of slighting the performances which have only genius, wit, and taste to recommend them. "I am no novel reader—I seldom look into novels—Do not imagine that *I* often read novels—It is really very well for a novel." Such is the common cant.—"And what are you reading, Miss——?" "Oh! it is only a novel!" replies the young lady; while she lays down her book with affected indifference, or momentary shame.—"It is only Cecilia, or Camilla, or Belinda;" or, in short, only some work in which the greatest powers of the mind are displayed, in which the most thorough knowledge of human nature, the happiest delineation of its varieties, the liveliest effusions of wit and humour are conveyed to the world in the best chosen language (pp. 37–38).[14]

This apology is actually an ironic combination of two different views of the novel which are pitted against each other, and against snobbish "decriers" of the genre. The first half is very similar to

13. Mary Lascelles thinks that the apology is "an explicit statement of opinion in the author's own voice," but the critic does qualify this by conceding that there is "a suspicion of overstatement" (*Jane Austen and Her Art*, 48–49).

14. As Mary Lascelles observes, Jane Austen's attack on deprecatory novelists may have been in response to Maria Edgeworth's refusal to be identified as a novelist, especially in the preface to *Belinda* (1801). See *Jane Austen and her Art* (p. 19).

arguments advanced by Charles Jenner in his novel, *The Placid Man* (1770). Jenner deplores the fact that numerous as novelists were, "I do not recollect that any of them have ever taken upon them to bestow even a chapter upon the defence of that branch of authorship to which they owe all their reputation if they have any to boast of, and, it may be, all their bread, if they have any to eat." And he anticipates Jane Austen's spirited counterattack against reviewers: " '*In this trifling novel-reading age.—At a time when the press groans under the weight of so many ridiculous novels ——When a heap of trash in the form of novels turns the brains of our young people—*' Such, my good reader, as I dare say you can bear witness, are the reflections which every sour critic is daily, weekly, and monthly throwing out against this species of writing." But from here on Jane Austen's thesis diverges from that of her eighteenth-century forerunner. For unlike Jane Austen, Jenner dissociates the novel from serious standards of art or realism. His crusade against didacticism dispenses with all "serious" standards. The Horation manifesto, *utile dulci*, is "a more serious light than I think it necessary to view these productions in." They are only "pleasing and innocent amusements," one of the "many expedients" that counter the cares and anxieties of life:

Scarce anyone expects his mind to be made better by every one of them; happy if it is made no worse; and in this light what more pleasant, what more innocent than that amusement which is commonly called Castle-building? By which is meant, that indulging a pleasing reverie, which without any foundation in reality affords a momentary happiness from the reflection, without any danger of a proportionate anxiety from a disappointment; the too usual attendant upon any scheme of a more substantial nature. For which species of amusement nothing affords so good materials as a novel. It is a castle ready built to your hands and furnished with every accommodation necessary for the bestowing an hour of that happiness which the pliability of man's spirit fits him to enjoy.[15]

15. Charles Jenner, "An Apology for Novel-Readers; which may also serve for Novel-Writers," *The Placid Man*, Book IV, chap. 1, in *Eighteenth-Century British Novelists on the Novel*, ed. George L. Barnett (New York, 1968), 127–29.

Jane Austen counters the kind of facile "castle-building" represented by Jenner's literary ideal, and she does this without either belittling aesthetic values or countenancing the didactic tradition. For in the second half of her apology, the viewpoint shifts unobtrusively to a defense of literary and moral standards that is very similar to an essay by another eighteenth-century novelist, Francis Coventry. In his dedication to the third edition of *The History of Pompey the Little* Coventry obviously anticipates *Northanger Abbey* by charging detractors of the novel with pride, pedantry, and ignorance. Moreover, his attack on them contains clear outlines for Jane Austen's later portrayal: "Can we help wondering, therefore, at the contempt, with which many people affect to talk of this sort of composition? they seem to think it degrades the dignity of their understandings, to be found with a novel in their hands, and take great pains to let you know that they never read them." Simultaneously, Coventry utilizes the same kind of ironic understatement with which Jane Austen is to emphasize the moral realism of the novel: "The grave metaphysician, for example, . . . grows indignant to think that every little paltry scribbler, who paints only the characters of the age, the manners of the times, and the working of the passions, should presume to equal him in glory."[16]

By yoking together two disparate concepts of the novel, Jane Austen's narrative viewpoint emphasizes the distinction between literature as escape and literature as the reflection of life. And this ironic apology impinges directly on Catherine Morland's experience. Contrary to Jenner's optimistic assumptions, readers like Catherine can be deceived into confusing the "pleasing reverie" of fiction with actuality. And the seductive powers of the novel make it more imperative that the genre adhere to the standards postulated by Coventry. By escaping into Jenner's world of "in-

16. Frances Coventry, Dedication to the Third Edition of *The History of Pompey the Little*, in *Prefaces to Three Eighteenth-Century Novels (1708–1751–1797)*, ed. Claude E. Jones, *Augustan Reprint Society*, No. 64 (Los Angeles, 1957), pp. [38]–[40].

nocent" amusements and castle building, the reader runs the real danger of divorcing his sensibilities from all worthwhile literature and sound intellectual values. Hence Catherine's addiction to Gothic fiction is matched by indifference to history, ignorance of politics, and general unsophistication in the use or apprehension of language. Significantly, when Jane Austen concludes her apology, it is on an anti-intellectual and unlettered note which suggests that the narrative viewpoint has again shifted to coincide, ironically, with Jenner's judgment—and, thereby, to point the direction of Catherine's initial deficiencies: the young reader who is ashamed of being caught with a novel would have proudly produced a volume of the *Spectator*, "though the chances must be against her being occupied by any part of that voluminous publication, of which either the matter or manner would not disgust a young person of taste" (*Northanger Abbey,* p. 38). Finally, the shifting maneuvers of Jane Austen's narrative perspective provide an ironic framework for Catherine's intellectual development. Catherine is attracted by the escapist exotica of Gothic fiction. Then her experience of the real world forces her to appreciate and develop the kind of moral and intellectual awareness espoused by Henry Tilney or Francis Coventry. And, like the concluding sentences of Jane Austen's apology, Catherine's development returns to the earlier shortcomings of her literary judgment in order to place them in an ironic perspective. Consequently, she learns that while the machinery of escapist fiction is unreal, the tastes to which it appeals, or which it sensationalizes beyond nature, are very much a part of actual life: Isabella Thorpe and General Tilney do not evaporate with Catherine's Gothic illusions. Or, to return to Jane Austen's apology, Jenner's standards may sacrifice realism to some questionable concept of entertainment, but, ironically, they are based on fact, on the kind of shallow taste that simultaneously affects admiration for the despised *Spectator* and contempt for good fiction.

When Jane Austen actually introduces her heroine, the interplay of narrative viewpoints again relates the parody of Gothic

romance to Catherine's development. On the whole, the first half
of the introduction is negative. It represents the perspective of the
Gothic novelist who finds the Morland family wanting. Catherine's family is quite unpromising: "Her situation in life, the
character of her father and mother, her own person and disposition, were all equally against her." Mr. Morland has not been
"neglected, or poor," and "he had never been handsome." Mrs.
Morland is no less disappointing. She is "a woman of useful plain
sense, with a good temper, and, what is more remarkable, with
a good constitution." After Catherine's birth, Mrs. Morland surprisingly lives on to have six more children, instead of dying "as
any body might expect." As for Catherine herself, the signs are
very unpropitious indeed. She has a "thin, awkward figure, a
sallow skin without colour, dark lank hair, and strong features."
Her tastes are equally unsuitable, for she prefers boys' games to
"the more heroic enjoyments" of "nursing a doormouse, feeding
a canary-bird, or watering a rose-bush." The heroine's intellectual
abilities are "quite as extraordinary": she is not brilliant, and she
shirks lessons whenever she can. "What a strange, unaccountable
character" (pp. 13–14). But Catherine is "unaccountable" only
when she is subjected to the unrealistic standards that she herself
later applies to her environment. When a more balanced judgment
is brought to bear she no longer seems "strange." From the viewpoint of a more levelheaded narrator, "it was not very wonderful
that Catherine, who had by nature nothing heroic about her,
should prefer cricket, base ball, riding on horseback, and running
about the country at the age of fourteen, to books—or at least
books of information" (p. 15). And here, too, the parodic fluctuations of Jane Austen's narrative point of view coincide with the
course of Catherine's subsequent development. Hence, immediately after dismissing the Gothic evaluation of her heroine's "deficiencies," Jane Austen returns to it with an ironical confirmation
of its social relevance. Heroic expectations, or a yearning for the
fantastic and the romantic are a fact of life. Consequently, however
deficient her reading might be, Catherine does know "all such

works as heroines must read," especially well-worn lines from Pope, Gray, Thomson, and Shakespeare. And although the neighborhood offers no suitable match in the person of a lord or baronet, "when a young lady is to be a heroine, the perverseness of forty surrounding families cannot prevent her. Something must and will happen to throw a hero in her way." Something *does* happen. The Allens invite her to Bath (pp. 16–17).

In *Northanger Abbey* the manipulation of the narrative viewpoint has not yet been fully integrated with the individual's self-awareness. Accordingly, the shifting of perspectives takes place outside Catherine's consciousness, and is primarily a matter of a rhetorical relationship between narrator and reader. But in spite of this, it seems clear that the variations of the narrative judgment apply to Catherine's personality and experience, either analogously, as in the case of the apology for the novel, or descriptively, when she is introduced to the reader. In any event the ambiguous perspectives of the narrator do reveal the parodic antitheses which are integral to Catherine's development, just as similar contrasts between literary illusion and reality are relevant to Laura's personality in *Love and Freindship*. And while such antitheses dramatize Laura's hypocrisy and self-contradictions, they illuminate the differing phases of Catherine's maturity, from ignorance of society and literature, to romantic naiveté, and subsequent awakening. Which brings us to the role of anticlimax in *Northanger Abbey*, for the successive stages of Catherine's development are predicated on the same kind of ironic anticlimax with which Jane Austen's juvenilia debunk the unreal and the nonsensical. But the trends of *Love and Freindship* have been continued here in that the anticlimactic structure is no longer an exclusively rhetorical technique with which the reader's responses are anticipated and manipulated. Without sacrificing this reader-author relationship, Jane Austen has continued to incorporate the structure within her heroine's consciousness. Catherine's rude awakening from Gothic "castle-building" is, for her, a very real anticlimax. And so is the discovery that her newly-discovered world of fact, the world of General Tilney and the Thorpes, may be as jolting, in its own unforeseen ways, as an improbable Udolpho. Moreover, as we have already noted in our study of his conversational style, this kind of satiric anticlimax is very congenial to Henry Tilney's genius for parody. However, Henry's satiric style and Catherine's development do not simply conform with the general directions of Jane Austen's parodic technique. They are also ironic reflections of the kind of anticlimactic structure favored by many popular Gothic novelists. For many Gothic novels are generally ready-made victims of Jane Austen's parody. The works are based on some kind of contrast between sham and reality. Horrific suggestions of the supernatural are frequently exploited for the sake of bald sensationalism, then they are finally explained on the basis of what the novelist might regard as "natural" cause and effect— "human" agents of good and evil. "Supernatural" themes are therefore sensationalist impostures which provide the background for an equally improbable sequence of human actions. A reviewer of Mrs. Eliza Parsons' *The Castle of Wolfenbach* (1793) finds these tactics distasteful. He condemns the dramatic but highly unlikely narrative, complains of the unnatural sentiments and depraved actions that are attributed to *"people of fashion,"* and charges that fraudulent suggestions of spells and intrigues *"vanish into thin air"* as the plot thickens.[17]

On the whole, then, *Northanger Abbey* demonstrates the extent to which Jane Austen is integrating parody with character. The style and insights of Henry Tilney's temperament coincide with Jane Austen's prevailing techniques of satiric imitation. And the evolution of Catherine's moral psychology coincides with the strategy of ironic anticlimax which informs the novel's parodic form. Moreover, the achievements of *Northanger Abbey* look forward to the more fully developed integration of parody and characterization in *Sense and Sensibility*. Catherine Morland's perceptual shortcomings anticipate the psychological themes of the later novel in that her literary fantasies hamper communica-

17. *The British Critic*, III (1794), 199–200.

tion with the real world. Similarly, in *Sense and Sensibility* Marianne Dashwood is unable to comprehend judgments which are opposed to her sentimental delicacy. She is genuinely nonplussed by Edward Ferrars' indifference to the picturesque, and his personality as a whole is completely at odds with her criteria for heroic stature. Her reservations are not unexpected, for Edward is presented throughout as the deliberately conceived antithesis of the sentimental hero. He is "not recommended to their good opinion by any peculiar graces of person or address." And this low-keyed appeal obviously distinguishes him from the kind of erotic emotionalism that marks Marianne's conceptions of the heroic male. Moreover, far from inspiring the instant friendships preferred by Marianne, Edward's manners "required intimacy to make them pleasing. He was too diffident to do justice to himself; but when his natural shyness was overcome, his behaviour gave every indication of an open affectionate heart" (p. 15).

On the other hand, Willoughby has everything in his favor. He is the incarnation of Marianne's dreams and the very opposite of Edward's normalcy: "His person and air were equal to what her fancy had ever drawn for the hero of a favourite story." His "good abilities, quick imagination, lively spirits, and open, affectionate manners" enable him to "engage Marianne's heart, for with all this, he joined not only a captivating person, but a natural ardour of mind which was now roused and increased by the example of her own" (pp. 43, 48). The dependence of Willoughby's seeming "sensibility" on Marianne's "example" raises the question of narrative viewpoint. The introduction of his character is based, not only on the usual parodic contrast with normal realities (represented here by Edward), but also through an ambiguous perspective which hints at an inconsistency between his real personality and his declarations of sentimental enthusiasm. The narrator's elaboration on Willoughby's compatibility with Marianne is phrased suggestively. The narrative point of view has identified Marianne's assumptions with Willoughby's claims, and consequently, his "sensibility" remains a matter of rhetoric. When she hears him "declare that of music and dancing he was passionately fond," she gives him "such a look of approbation as secured the largest share of his discourse to herself for the rest of the day" (p. 46). This alleged sensibility emerges as a convenient form of deference: "He acquiesced in all her decisions, caught all her enthusiasm." Or it may be a suspicious coincidence: "Their taste was strikingly alike" (p. 47). On the whole, the introduction of Willoughby is unique in *Sense and Sensibility*, and this arises from the novelist's use of parody as communication when she presents his personality. All other characters in the work are presented directly in "set" character sketches, but Willoughby enters the narrative through the perspectives provided by Marianne's sentimental judgment. Hence the parody of Marianne's bookish enthusiasm communicates her assumptions about his relationships with others, and with herself. Willoughby's "heroic" presence contrasts, implicitly, with the failings that she deplores in Edward (p. 17). And in discovering her compatibility with Willoughby, she is really being self-congratulatory: his "perfect" tastes are reflections of her own. When Willoughby is eventually exposed, therefore, the course of Marianne's inevitable disillusionment conforms with the satiric anticlimax that is so characteristic of Jane Austen's parodic form.

But, of course, the parody of Marianne's literary enthusiasm is not the only significant approach to her character. The aggressive vitalism represented by her sensibility expresses itself on a variety of other levels, including an impatience of social restraint, a passionate commitment to sincerity, and a strong sense of personal loyalty. Marianne's literary perspectives contribute to the complex process of exposing and dramatizing her passionate instincts, but they are not the sole means of defining her personality. The literary themes of parody are subordinated to the primary goals of characterization and social analysis. Marianne is important, not simply as the embodiment of absurd literary traditions, but as a human figure in her own right. The literary motif dramatizes her foibles, but it does not define her total personality. Even the crude parodies of the juvenilia are really satiric vignettes, in which the incongruities evoked by the literary topics underline the moral and intellectual contradictions of character. In *Love and Freindship* the imitation of sentimental fads complements the exposure of Laura's hypocrisy, and in *Northanger Abbey* Catherine Morland's enlightenment hinges, in part, on her maturing insights into the disparities—and ironic parallels—between life and literature. And after *Sense and Sensibility* parody contributes to the thematic and emotional conflicts of *Mansfield Park*, for it opposes Fanny Price's literary idealism to Mary Crawford's pragmatic materialism—a contrast that conforms with Jane Austen's usual strategy of parodic antithesis.

However, of all the later novels, it is *Emma* that contains Jane Austen's most sustained integration of parody with the overriding demands of concentrated, psychological analysis. Mary Lascelles and subsequent critics have already explored most of the literary antecedents on which Emma draws for her managerial schemes and romantic conjectures.[18] Harriet Smith's illegitimacy, her rescue from gypsies (by Frank Churchill), and Jane's status as an orphan—these are all misinterpreted on the well-worn basis of sentimental clichés: Harriet's birth will prove respectable; as her rescuer, Frank is naturally Harriet's new object; and Jane's alleged infatuation with Mr. Dixon is also linked to the gallant heroics of the old-fashioned rescue (from drowning). These literary clichés are congenial to Emma's undisciplined imagination, and Jane Austen's parody points to the differences between reality and the heroine's web of fantasies. And when characters are presented through Emma's defective insights, this is really an extension of Jane Austen's ironic manipulation of the narrative viewpoint. And in so doing the novelist is applying to the total structure of the novel one of the major techniques to emerge from her earlier parodies. As usual, the narrative perspective does not simply examine the barriers between the heroine's understanding and

18. Compare Edward M. White, "Emma and the Parodic Point of View," *Nineteenth Century Fiction*, XVIII (1963), 55–63.

her society. It also explores the lines of communication, and non-communication, between the narrator and the reader. Hence the opening paragraphs of the novel introduce Emma through the same interplay of sentimental and satiric judgments that defines the results of her wayward imagination. The initial sketch of the heroine conforms with the literary idyll. She is handsome, clever, and rich, and has had "very little to distress or vex her." Like the heroine of Jane Austen's own *Plan of a Novel*, Emma unites the blessings of personal wealth and beauty with the advantages of a most affectionate, indulgent father. And since the limited authority of her governess has long passed away, Emma has been mistress of her own home. This freedom from restraint completes the idyllic picture, for Emma's complete independence fulfills the sentimental heroine's dream—the triumph of filial identity over parental "tyranny." But, simultaneously, the heroine's enfranchisement is viewed satirically, from a nonsentimental viewpoint. The absence of a restraining authority has contributed to Emma's egotistic excesses: "The real evils indeed of Emma's situation were the power of having rather too much her own way, and a disposition to think a little too well of herself; these were the disadvantages which threatened alloy to her many enjoyments" (p. 5). The sentimental idyll becomes a distinct liability when the narrative judgment shifts to the criteria of moral realism. The emphatic phrase, "real evils indeed," is intelligible only when its satiric rationalism is contrasted with sentimental fears of discipline. And Jane Austen ironically pretends to assuage these misgivings: "Even before Miss Taylor had ceased to hold the nominal office of governess, the mildness of her temper had hardly allowed her to impose any restraint; and the shadow of authority being now long passed away, they had been living together as friend and friend very mutually attached, and Emma doing just what she liked" (p. 5). In short, the manipulation of the narrative viewpoint has established a pattern of author-reader communication that is identical to, and impinges on, the conflict between egocentric imagination and rational restraint in the novel. Jane Austen exploits the reader's own vacillation between sentimentality and satire in order to fashion an apt background for Emma's entrance into the narrative: the heroine's character and situation must be viewed, simultaneously, from opposite directions. And, finally, the contrasting perspectives of sentimentality and satiric realism represent the starting point and the climax, respectively, of Emma's personal development. The integration of parody and psychological drama is complete.

However, this psychological contribution does not exhaust the role of parody in the development of Jane Austen's fictive forms. For one of the most consistent features of her novels has been the parodic structure of her narrative endings.[19] The "happy" conclusion counterbalances the reader's sentimental expectations with an uncompromising emphasis on the logic of moral realism. In the final chapter of *Northanger Abbey*, for example, the narrator makes one of her periodical appearances by inviting the reader's attention to the mechanics of the grand denouement, to the eventual consummation of Catherine Morland's imperiled relationship with Henry Tilney. The couple's anxiety "can hardly extend, I fear, to the bosom of my readers, who will see in the tell-tale compression of the pages before them, that we are all hastening together to perfect felicity. The means by which their early marriage was effected can be the only doubt" (p. 250). This almost sardonic dismissal of both narrative and character is also evident in the concluding chapter of *Persuasion*, after the reconciliation between Anne Eliot and Captain Wentworth: "Who can be in doubt of what followed? When any two young people take it into their heads to marry, they are pretty sure by perseverance to carry their point, be they ever so poor, or ever so imprudent, or ever so little likely to be necessary to each other's ultimate comfort" (p. 248).

The arresting feature of these narrative conclusions is Jane Austen's marked self-consciousness, her deliberate emphasis on

19. Compare Lloyd W. Brown, "The Comic Conclusion in Jane Austen's Novels," *PMLA*, LXXXIV (1969), 1582–87.

the artifices and the transparent inevitability of her "happy" endings, together with the suspension of related moral judgments.
This emphasis is the more remarkable, in view of Jane Austen's
reiterated preferences for high standards of realism in fiction. In
a letter to Caroline Austen she playfully disapproves of the fact
that her niece has allowed the villain of her story to go unpunished:
"I hope *he* hung himself, or took the sur-name of *Bone* or under-
went some direful penance or other." (*Letters*, p. 442). But usually,
her letters confirm Jane Austen's revulsion against the unrealistic
extremes of sentimental and didactic fiction. She derides "the
common Novel style" of "handsome, amiable, unexceptionable"
heroes, confesses that "pictures of perfection" make her sick and
wicked, and compliments Anna Austen on the portrayal of a
character that is neither "very Good" nor "very Bad" (pp. 403,
486–87, 387). Sarah Burney's *Clarentine* (1796) and Mary Brunton's *Self-Control* (1810) are condemned for their unnatural details and improbable plots (pp. 180, 344). Moreover, the artificial
endings of popular novels are ridiculed in the burlesque *Plan of
a Novel*. Thus the conclusion of the projected work takes the form
of an ecstatic reunion of hero and heroine: "The Tenderest and
completest Eclaircissement takes place, and they are happily
united" (*Minor Works*, p. 430). Nonetheless these principles of
realism are confirmed rather than contradicted by the exaggerated
mechanics of her happy endings, not only in *Northanger Abbey*
and *Persuasion*, but throughout most of her other novels. The
conclusions of Jane Austen's novels usually embody unvarying
techniques and values that accentuate her own comic form and
meaning, through explicit or implied contrasts with inferior fiction. Her comic conclusion is therefore basically parodic in structure and theme, and is constantly used throughout her fiction as
the final summary of themes.

Now, given Jane Austen's decided preference for the realistic
possibilities of fiction, and given opposing standards of some reviewers and readers, the novelist is obviously left with the dilemma
of concluding her story without sacrificing her comic view of life

to the rigid canons of poetic justice. In one of the more recent studies of the problem A. Walton Litz argues that Jane Austen has solved the problem by investing her materials with her moral judgment, that the characters and narrative details convey the relevant moral values insofar as they embody a vision of life and reality (*Jane Austen*, pp. 56–57). This is quite valid: in *Emma*, for example, the resolution of plot and themes does not depend on the actual celebration of marriage. The crucial problems have been resolved—in the course of Emma's development—long before Mr. Woodhouse's nervous system has been manipulated in order to make the concluding festivities possible; and in *Northanger Abbey* the important issues center on Catherine's emotional and intellectual maturity, and on the values of her society—the analysis of which does not depend on the "happy ending" of the final marriages. But it is in her own conclusions that one must look for Jane Austen's most significant reaction to the didacticism and sentimentality of the "happy ending." The mocking self-consciousness of these essentially comic conclusions evokes a contrast between a literary convention and the good novelist's preoccupation with reality. Or, as Henrietta Ten Harmsel suggests, Jane Austen's happy ending succeeds in both mocking a convention and providing the reader with what he wants.[20] Furthermore the comic imitation of any hackneyed artifice is supplemented by Jane Austen's insistence on the kind of ending that is logically consistent with her characters and narrative.

The parodic motif of her comic conclusions is best illustrated by the ending of *Northanger Abbey* where the obvious artifices of Jane Austen's denouement are really a final thrust at the finale of the typical Gothic novel. Having been assured of the "perfect felicity" of the approaching end, the reader is pointedly reminded of the need for some "probable circumstance" that will remove General Tilney's objections to his son's proposed marriage. Finally, this "probable circumstance" turns out to be a highly fortuitous

---

20. Henrietta Ten Harmsel, *Jane Austen: A Study in Fictional Conventions* (The Hague, 1964), 27.

marriage between Eleanor Tilney and a man of fortune, an event so contrived that the anonymous bridegroom cannot be plausibly presented in person at this belated stage: "the rules of composition forbid the introduction of a character not connected with my fable" (p. 251).

In *Sense and Sensibility* the parody of a mechanical "happy ending" is effected through contrast rather than imitation. Thus, unlike their literary counterparts, neither Elinor nor Edward Ferrars is "quite enough in love" to suppose that three hundred and fifty pounds is an adequate income (p. 369). Instead of the ecstatic joys of the sentimental novel, their happiness is tempered by a few mundane considerations—such as hope for "rather better pasturage for their cows" (p. 375). The mocking contrast between Marianne's previous sentimental fantasies and her eventual fortunes is also relevant here:

Marianne Dashwood was born to an extraordinary fate. She was born to discover the falsehood of her own opinions, and to counteract, by her conduct, her most favourite maxims. She was born to overcome an affection formed so late in life as at seventeen, and with no sentiment superior to strong esteem and lively friendship, voluntarily to give her hand to another!—and *that* other, a man who had suffered no less than herself under the event of a former attachment, whom, two years before, she had considered too old to be married,—and who still sought the constitutional safeguard of a flannel waistcoat!

But so it was. Instead of falling a sacrifice to an irresistible passion, as once she had fondly flattered herself with expecting—instead of remaining even for ever with her mother, and finding her only pleasures in retirement and study, as afterwards in her more calm and sober judgment she had determined on,—she found herself at nineteen, submitting to new attachments, entering on new duties, placed in a new home, a wife, the mistress of a family, and the patroness of a village (pp. 378–79).

Even in *Emma* where this kind of formal and self-conscious conclusion is absent, there is an implied contrast between the actual outcome and the alternate conclusions envisaged by Emma in her earlier misinterpretation of character and situation. Her fanciful

delusions regarding Jane Fairfax, Harriet, and others really constitute a "mock catastrophe" that serves "as foil to the real untying
of the knot of misunderstandings."[21]

The attack on the creaking machinery of the happy ending is
related to the second major feature of Jane Austen's comic conclusions—a realistic reappraisal of the rigid insistence on reward-
ing virtue and punishing evil. This usually results in the rejection
of sententious moralizing. Hence the final sentence of *Northanger
Abbey* dispenses with the fine distinctions of heavy-handed didacticism: "I leave it to be settled by whomsoever it may concern,
whether the tendency of this work be altogether to recommend
parental tyranny, or reward filial disobedience" (p. 252). At the
same time, the traditional allegorization of Gothic sensationalism
gives way to the exposure of everyday realities. Catherine's real
lesson is derived, not from the explication of Gothic horrors and
mysteries in the Ann Radcliffe manner, but from her realization
that the mundane is, ironically, just as distressing as the machina-
tions of an improbable Montoni. She eventually learns enough of
General Tilney's character to feel that she had not really magnified
his cruelty in suspecting him of murdering the late Mrs. Tilney
(p. 247). Conversely, the "anticlimax" of her return to reality may
transcend, in true excitement, all the nerve-tingling machinery of
the Gothic. Hence the inventory of linen which proved to be such
a disappointing discovery that first night at Northanger Abbey, is
linked to the joyous finale of the narrative. Catherine's wedding
has been facilitated by Eleanor's marriage—and as it turns out,
General Tilney's new son-in-law "was the very gentleman whose
negligent servant left behind him that collection of washing-bills,
resulting from a long visit at Northanger, by which my heroine
was involved in one of her most alarming adventures" (p. 251).
The apparently fortuitous circumstance of Eleanor's marriage is
therefore the final emphasis on the ironic logic of events that informs Catherine's development: the comedy of the linen bills
simultaneously recalls the educative experiences of her past and

21. Mary Lascelles, *Jane Austen and her Art*, 76.

heightens the sense of contrivance in the comic conclusion as a whole.

Altogether, then, the highly convenient tactics which achieve the comic conclusion in *Northanger Abbey* serve the serious purpose of emphasizing Jane Austen's concern with continuous realism throughout each work. And this is her goal in the subsequent novels, where the conventions of poetic justice are even more explicitly disregarded or inverted. In *Sense and Sensibility* Lucy and Willoughby are, technically, the "villains" of the plot. But instead of inheriting the usual miseries and total schemes of retribution, they experience comparative happiness in their realistically conceived world. Lucy's selfish schemes bring gratifying results, and she is dismissed, together with her in-laws, to enjoy a good fortune that is only partially modified by the suggestive hyperbole: "nothing could exceed the harmony in which they all lived together" (p. 377). The equally suggestive litotes also modifies Willoughby's eventual "fate." He "found no inconsiderable degree of domestic felicity" (p. 379). But despite these somber undertones, his happiness is significant enough to contravene the formulae of poetic justice that are represented by Marianne's erstwhile sentimentalism: "that he was for ever inconsolable, that he fled from society, or contracted an habitual gloom of temper, or died of a broken heart, must not be depended on—for he did neither." Indeed, he is guilty of "incivility" in surviving the loss of Marianne, and frequently enjoys himself (p. 379). This ironic subversion of the didactic code also appears in *Pride and Prejudice* where Elizabeth and Darcy lightheartedly review the "moral" of their reconciliation. Elizabeth mockingly suggests that no valid lesson can be drawn from their engagement, for Darcy's proposal has been prompted by her discussion of his role in Lydia's face-saving marriage—a discussion that she initiates in spite of a previous promise to Mrs. Gardiner. What becomes of the "moral," she asks, "if our comfort springs from a breach of promise?" Darcy replies by giving his version of the moral lesson. Lady Catherine's unjust interference and her abuse of Elizabeth have been punished in that they precipitated the very event that they were intended to forestall: it was the news of Elizabeth's spirited reception of his aunt that inspired him to attempt a second proposal. But the conventions of poetic justice to which Darcy makes his appeal are promptly undermined by Elizabeth. She reverses his punitive interpretation of Lady Catherine's failure: "Lady Catherine has been of infinite use, which ought to make her happy, for she loves to be of use" (p. 381). This comic interchange of reward and punishment illuminates Jane Austen's satiric treatment of poetic justice. The unequivocal allocation of reward and punishment is seen as a mere artifice that is irrelevant to the portrayal of life as it is. And this rejection of the didactic judgment is even more incisive in *Persuasion*. Having subverted poetic justice by sympathizing with the "bad morality" of imprudent marriages, the narrator then examines Anne's marriage and ultimate happiness from equally dubious viewpoints (including those of selfishness and pride) which are a part of actuality, sometimes to the exclusion of the very ideals propounded by poetic justice. Hence Anne must be judged by her silly and conceited family: an envious Elizabeth looks "cold and unconcerned" at the news of her sister's engagement; Sir Walter is struck by Wentworth's "superiority of appearance" and by his "well-sounding name," and Mary flatters herself with "having been greatly instrumental to the connexion" (pp. 248, 249).

As in the other novels, the emphasis in *Persuasion* is on realism rather than on the schematic dispensation of rewards and punishment. Instead of arbitrarily imposing these idealistic conventions on her fictive society, Jane Austen uses the comic conclusion to reveal the prevailing norms that frequently undermine and replace traditional ideals. The novelist's primary achievement in this respect seems to be the satiric exposé of the gap between moral traditions, on the one hand, and the social conventions of hypocrisy, selfishness, and insensitivity, on the other. This appears to be the point of the subversive judgments by the narrator in *Pride and Prejudice* and *Persuasion*, and it is also manifest in the comic maxim that sums up the fortunes of Lucy Steele in *Sense and Sensibility*. For like most Jane Austen maxims, the statement ironically proposes defective realities as acceptable rules of conduct: "The whole of Lucy's behaviour in the affair, and the prosperity which crowned it, therefore, may be held forth as a most encouraging instance of what an earnest, an unceasing attention to self-interest, however its progress may be apparently obstructed, will do in securing every advantage of fortune, with no other sacrifice than that of time and conscience" (p. 376). Moreover, whatever elements of rewards and punishment do arise in Jane Austen's conclusions are presented as the logical outcome of the temperament and values of the characters themselves, rather than as the externally applied artifices of poetic justice. Eventual "felicity" or "misery" becomes a part of, and is qualified by, the logical evolution of each personality. Thus Mrs. Smith's real happiness has an internal source and results from her innate good qualities of "cheerfulness and mental alacrity," rather than from the "accessions of worldly prosperity" allowed to her by the mechanics of the happy ending: "Her spring of felicity was in the glow of her spirits, as her friend Anne's was in the warmth of her heart" (*Persuasion*, p. 252). Conversely, the real "punishment" of defective characters consists largely of the fact that they must continue being themselves. Their eventual misery is thus conditional on the realistically conceived working of the individual conscience: the unrepentant Wickhams are left to the punishment of their own company, but the shallow Willoughby, despite the occasional twinges of regret, frequently enjoys the advantages of his mercenary marriage.

Jane Austen's comic conclusions, then, are based on what appear to be fairly consistent techniques and values, and these elements are highly pertinent in a study of the controversial ending of *Mansfield Park*. Details of parody, the subversion of poetic justice, the incorporation of final moral judgments within the realistic evolution of personality—all these characteristic features of Jane Austen's comic conclusions suggest the need to reappraise the traditional interpretation of *Mansfield Park* as an unambiguous and didactic novel.[22] Generally, although the tone of the *Mansfield Park* conclusion is more incisive than the playful atmosphere of *Pride and Prejudice,* a close reading of the former suggests that Jane Austen has preserved her ironic conception of the "happy" ending. The usual parody of such endings is introduced with the description of Edmund Bertram's happiness with the devoted Fanny Price. First, there is the exaggerated emphasis on the "impossibility" of Edmund's recovery from his disappointment with Mary Crawford: "they were also quite agreed in their opinion of the lasting effect, the indelible impression, which such a disappointment must make on his mind" (p. 460). The exaggeration prepares us for the irony of his inevitable change of heart, with its attendant theme of unbounded happiness. In keeping with the "natural" cure of "unconquerable passions, and the transfer of unchanging attachments," Edmund "did cease to care about Miss Crawford, and became as anxious to marry Fanny, as Fanny herself could desire" (p. 470). Finally, there is the idyllic picture of happiness achieved: "With so much true merit and true love, and no want of fortune or friends, the happiness of the married cousins must appear as secure as earthly happiness can be.—Equally formed for domestic life, and attached to country pleasures, their home was the home of affection and comfort" (p. 473). These hyperboles are reminiscent of the schemes set forth in *Plan of a Novel* and the "perfect felicity" promised in *Northanger Abbey.* Moreover, the sentimental clichés on happiness and "true love" are integral to the novel's continuing juxtaposition of opposite extremes as a consistent ironic device. Edmund's expected misery contrasts with his eventual happiness. And the universally acclaimed marriage of the cousins contradicts Sir Thomas Bertram's previously mercenary fears. The hackneyed theme of supreme

22. See R. W. Chapman, *Jane Austen: Facts and Problems* (Oxford, 1948), 194; Henrietta Ten Harmsel, *Jane Austen* (p. 103); Joseph M. Duffy, "Moral Integrity and Moral Anarchy in *Mansfield Park*," *ELH*, XXIII (1956), 71–91; Kingsley Amis, "What Became of Jane Austen?" in *Jane Austen, A Collection of Critical Essays,* ed. Ian Watt (Englewood Cliffs, N.J., 1963), 141–44.

happiness also echoes the basic concept of Fanny Price's character: she embodies the tender sensibilities and virtues which are pitted against the insensitive norms of the real world. Consequently, the happiness motif in *Mansfield Park* represents, not the didactic allocation of rewards, but the comic exposure of self-contradictions in the emotional and moral experiences of Edmund and Sir Thomas, respectively, and in Fanny's case, the counterbalancing of idealistic piety and true merit against defective realities.

However, the parody of the happy ending must also be related, as in the other novels, to Jane Austen's characteristic disregard for the niceties of poetic justice. Hence, as an imaginary supplement to the actual marriage of Edmund and Fanny, the novelist evokes, then immediately dismisses, what could be described as the alternate conclusion—complete with the conversion of the Crawfords and their respective marriages to Edmund and Fanny: "Would he [Henry] have persevered, and uprightly, Fanny must have been his reward—and a reward very voluntarily bestowed—within a reasonable period from Edmund's marrying Mary" (p. 467). This system of conversion and reward is precisely the kind of schematic conclusion that Jane Austen repeatedly satirizes, and its momentary appearance here serves to underline the novelist's insistence on the logical development of character and situation, rather than on the predictable conventions of the unqualified "happy" ending. Thus the final judgment on Henry Crawford's ultimate fate should be based on the consideration of whether his crucial indiscretions are logically consistent with his personality and moral values. They obviously are, for his elopement with Maria Rushworth is based on nothing less than one of the fundamentals of his character—a "cold-blooded vanity" that frequently leads him into pretended attachments, feigned romantic involvements which eventually become more real than he originally intends. As the narrator is careful to point out, this is the trait that "had, by an opening undesigned and unmerited, led him into the way of happiness," for his attachment to Fanny stems from what was originally a pretended interest (p. 467). Thus to demand the

alternate conclusion, as some critics have in effect done, is to require that Jane Austen abandon the logical development of character and situation that is so integral to her comic conclusions.

The other theme of the ironic ending, the allocation of punishment, occupies the major portion of the final chapter. Indeed, the
reiterated emphasis on penalties seems hardly other than ironic in
the light of the introductory statement, "Let other pens dwell on
guilt and misery" (p. 461). We are told of the mutual punishment
suffered by Maria and Henry after their elopement; and this kind
of self-inflicted misery is also the lot of Maria and Mrs. Norris
during their exile from Mansfield. Then the theme returns to
Henry Crawford: "That punishment, the public punishment of
disgrace, should in just measure attend *his* share of the offence, is,
we know, not one of the barriers, which society gives to virtue.
In this world, the penalty is less equal than could be wished; but
without presuming to look forward to a juster appointment hereafter, we may fairly consider a man of sense like Henry Crawford,
to be providing for himself no small portion of vexation and regret
—vexation that must rise sometimes to self-reproach, and regret to
wretchedness" (pp. 468–69). This passage is important for a proper
understanding of the handling of the theme of punishment in
Mansfield Park. In the second half of the statement the novelist
specifically dissociates her theme from the dictates of religious
morality, but this is in effect a rejection of the very principles that
have been emphasized throughout the work. The reference to the
"hereafter" is thus both an ironic rejection of Jane Austen's basic
themes, and a satiric attack on the religious didacticism familiar to
readers of *Clarissa*.

The "punishment" with which we are really dealing here is of
the kind evident in *Sense and Sensibility*. It depends wholly on
the individual's values and conscience: and in the cases of Willoughby and Lucy Steele, such dependence leads to results that
are incompatible with the uncompromising idealism of poetic
justice or religion. The reader is left with the actualities that arise
from the unreliable sense of right and wrong in each individual.

Consequently, our knowledge of Henry's moral and emotional
instability suggests that his "punishment" will be comparatively
short and light indeed. Maria and Mrs. Norris are also left to the
self-inflicted punishment of their own company, a rather severe
penalty, admittedly, if we take their personalities into account;
but a punitive experience of this kind, based only on selfishness
and narrow-mindedness, and given no regenerating motives, seems
to be more in keeping with the ironic exposure of character rather
than with the moralizing judgment. The contemptuous dismissal
of Rushworth to his "punishment" is a more broadly comical
version of the same theme. According to the logical evolution of
his character, Rushworth's eventual fate will be determined by
the same weaknesses that have brought about his present discomfiture. Hence his stupidity, already punished by the guilt of his
wife, will in all probability lead him into another marriage, and
"if duped, to be duped at least with good humour and good luck"
(p. 464).

In addition to the individual's capricious sense of right and
wrong, society determines the nature of the punishment, but the
worth of such retribution is undermined by the inequity and
the double standards of social forms and conventions. As Jane
Austen points out, the public wrath of society will be insignificant
in Henry Crawford's case, though it is unmitigated in Maria's.
What seems to be involved here is the novelist's inversion of moral
idealism in favor of social actualities. She describes everyday experiences in which moral conventions are ignored, both by the
individual and his society. Instead, society builds its own set of
traditions and these are contrasted here, as they are in *Sense and
Sensibility*, with the conventional morality to which they are
ideally expected to adhere. The philosophical assumptions that
Jane Austen inherits from the eighteenth century are important in
this regard, for as we have already seen, the eighteenth-century
ironist envisages a profound dichotomy between traditional
idealism and the nominal morality of social practice. Hence a
critic like Kingsley Amis who accuses Jane Austen of conven-

tionality seems to have missed the basic premises of eighteenth-
century satire—particularly the satirist's assumption that there are
two kinds of "convention," the actual, and the theoretically ideal.[23]
In reality, "moral" judgments have little to do with ethical principles, but operate on the unreliable basis of personal or social
criteria which are divorced from ideals.

Generally, however, the comic conclusion is not simply an extension of Jane Austen's ironic insights into the moral ambiguities
of reality. At the same time that she examines social norms and
the moral psychology of character, Jane Austen uses the mechanics
of the "happy ending" to define the nature and limits of the novel
as an art form. On one level, the ironic structure of the conclusion does emphasize the interrelation of moral realism and literary
art—the same link which Samuel Johnson underlines in *Rambler*
no. 60 (1750) when he asserts that human life and the art of biography have equal claims on our moral and emotional sensibilities.
And this is the assumption that informs Fielding's concept of the
novel as "history" or fictional biography: life itself is a great art,
like a fine statue or noble poem; hence, "histories" or novels "may
properly be called models of Human Life," and through them
"we shall be instructed in this most useful of all arts, which I
call the Art of Life."[24] But on another level, the ironic self-
consciousness of Jane Austen's "happy endings" implies that in
spite of all the crucial affinities to life and society, and notwith-
standing its desired fidelity to moral and psychological realism,
the novel is, after all, an art form. And in the final analysis, her
comic art owes its structural coherence to conventional artifices,
like the happy ending, that must be distinguished from the moral
realism on which her fictive vision is grounded. In effect, Jane

23. Kingsley Amis, "What Became of Jane Austen?" 144. On the basis of this
accusation Amis joins those "angry young critics" to whom Avrom Fleishman attributes anachronistic standards: "For them, 'genteel' and 'conventional' are pejora-
tives with a present-day application, rather than historical descriptions of the
society in which the novels are set": *A Reading of "Mansfield Park": An Essay in
Critical Synthesis* (Minneapolis, 1967), 11.

24. Henry Fielding, *Amelia*, Shakespeare Head Edition (3 vols.; Oxford, 1926),
I, 2.

Austen's comic conclusion underscores the paradoxical identity of the fictive art. The novel re-creates and explores the truths of experiential reality. But it does so through the arbitrary conventions and techniques of the genre, through all the little bits of ivory which the novelist uses to combine the artifices of form with moral truth.

Index

Addison, Joseph: on imagery, 54; on the sublime, 94; on conversation, 109

Austen, Anna: Jane Austen's letters to, 52–53

Austen, Caroline: Jane Austen's letters to, 223

Austen, Cassandra: Jane Austen's letters to, 53, 137; and *History of England*, 208

Austen, Edward: Jane Austen's letters to, 7

Austen, Jane: critics and, 3–14; on style, 6–8; and moral traditions, 13; her philosophical heritage, 43–44; her imagery, 52–55; her use of names as symbols, 77–79; her symbology, 79–81; on letter writing, 137–38; her use of hyperbole, 150; her relationship with readers, 203–204, 207–208; her happy endings, 223, 234–35; her use of realism, 223–24

Babb, Howard S., 6, 8, 22

Beattie, James: on imagery, 54

Beckford, William: his parodic techniques, 205*n*

Blair, Hugh: on imagery, 54

Bradbrook, Frank W., 3, 12*n*

Brower, Reuben A., 168–69

Browne, Hawkins: Jane Austen's parody of, 124

Brunton, Mary: criticized by Jane Austen, 223

Burke, Edmund: on sense and sensibility, 28–30; on taste, 28–30; on the sublime, 94

Burney, Fanny, 37

Burney, Sarah: criticized by Jane Austen, 223

Catharine: symbols in, 79–80

Chesterfield, Fourth Earl of: on conversation, 109, 111

Congreve, William: on conversation, 109

Coventry, Francis, 213–14

Cowper, William: on imagination, 45; on the sublime, 94; on conversation, 108–109; mentioned, 128*n*

Emma: and John Locke, 44–45; ironic ambiguities in, 44–47; and Cowper, 45; and Samuel Johnson, 46; imagery in, 55–56, 58, 61–65, 73–74; symbolism in, 75–76, 96–99; conversation in, 109, 111, 128–36; letter writing in, 155–56,

165–66; dialogue in, 193–98; "Opinions" on, 203–204; narrative viewpoint in, 220–22; parody in, 220–22; narrative conclusion in, 225–26

Fielding, Henry: his use of irony, 9; on hypocrisy, 16, 35, 207; on conversation, 110; his use of dialogue, 169–70; his parodic techniques, 199–202; on the novel, 234
Fleishman, Avrom, 4
Fordyce, David: on imagery, 54
Frederic & Elfrida: symbolic names in, 75; parody in, 205–207. *See also* Beckford, William

Goldsmith, Oliver: Jane Austen's parody of, 204–205; mentioned, 177

Hawkesworth, John: on ambiguous diction, 15–16
Hume, David: on ambiguous diction, 13, 15; on love and friendship, 19; on vanity, 32–34; on prejudice, 36

Jack & Alice: hypocrisy in, 17; ironic diction in, 17–18; epistolary form in, 144–45; dialogue in, 171–72; parody in, 206
James, Henry, 6, 7
Jenner, Charles, 212–14
Johnson, Samuel: influence on Jane Austen, 18, 40, 46, 47, 49, 51; Fanny Price on, 128–29; on letter writing, 139–40, 143

Knight, Fanny: on Jane Austen, 53; epistolary style of, 158
Kroeber, Karl, 5, 6, 8, 12, 38–39

Lady Susan: epistolary form in, 145–55, 156; Samuel Richardson and, 148, 152; ego in, 153–55

Langhorne, John: on imagery, 54
Lascelles, Mary, 5, 8
Leavis, Q. D., 4
Lesley Castle: symbols in, 77; epistolary form in, 141–42; Samuel Richardson and, 141–42
Letters of Jane Austen, The: on style, 7; on imagery, 52–54; on *Pride and Prejudice*, 121–22; on letter writing, 137, 158; on realism, 223
Litz, A. Walton, 21–22
Locke, John: on persuasion, 40–41; on passions, 44–45; on communication, 170–71
Lodge, David, 5–6
Love and Freindship: ironic ambiguities in, 18–21; imagery in, 60; epistolary form in, 141–44, 145, 146; parody in, 206–207, 208–10; narrative viewpoint in, 208–10; Samuel Johnson and, 208–10
Lover's Vows, 81–88

Mackenzie, Henry: on sensibility, 19; imagery in his *The Man of Feeling*, 63
McKillop, Alan D., 22
Mansfield Park: ironic ambiguities in, 48–51; imagery in, 55, 72–73; symbolism in, 77, 81–96; Laurence Sterne and, 92; conversation in, 111–12, 124–28; tone in, 122; parody in, 124–25; literary allusions in, 128–29; letter writing in, 137, 138, 140, 157; dialogue in, 191–93; "Opinions" on, 203–204; narrative conclusions in, 229–34
Mudrick, Marvin, 10–11, 20, 26
Murrah, Charles, 11–12

Noorthouck, John: on ambiguous diction, 19–20
Northanger Abbey: language in, 17, 47–48; ironic ambiguities in, 47–

48; imagery in, 55, 57, 70–71; symbolism in, 80–81; conversation in, 108–109, 112–18; and Gothic fiction, 114–16, 214–17; Henry Tilney as parodist, 114–18; letter writing in, 140, 160–61; Samuel Richardson and, 152; dialogue in, 172–77, 192; Charles Jenner and, 212–13; Francis Coventry and, 213–14; narrative viewpoint in, 210–17; parody in, 210–17; narrative conclusion in, 222, 224–25, 226–27

"Opinions." See *Emma; Mansfield Park*

Parsons, Eliza, 217
Persuasion: ironic ambiguities in, 39–43; imagery in, 55–59, 61; symbolism in, 77–78, 99–107; conversation in, 109; letter writing in, 157; dialogue in, 198; narrative conclusion in, 222, 228–29
Plan of a Novel: imagery in, 52; parody in, 221, 223
Pope, Alexander: on pride, 33–34
Pride and Prejudice: style of, 7; ironic ambiguities in, 31–39; John Locke and, 44; imagery in, 55, 58–59, 65–67; conversation in, 121–24; Elizabeth Bennet as parodist, 124; letter writing in, 137, 140, 155–57, 161–66; Samuel Richardson and, 152; dialogue in, 168–69, 186–90; narrative conclusion in 227–28

Radcliffe, Ann: Jane Austen's parody of, 47, 114–16
Richardson, Samuel: on epistolary style, 138–41, 148, 155–56, 159; Jane Austen's parody of, 141–42, 199–202; on women, 152

Sanditon: imagery in, 58, 67–69
Schorer, Mark, 5, 11
Scott, Sir Walter: cited by Fanny Price, 128
Sense and Sensibility: Marianne Dashwood on style, 8, 16–17, 53; ironic ambiguities in, 21–31; taste in, 28–31; imagery in, 55–56, 57, 59–60, 71–72, 111; conversation in, 118–21; tone of, 122; letter writing in, 157–60; dialogue in, 177–86; narrative viewpoint in, 218–20; parody in, 218–20; narrative conclusion in, 225, 227, 229
Shaftesbury, Earl of: on taste, 30–31; on wit, 50
Shannon, Edgar, 11–12
Smollet, Tobias: his use of ironic diction, 18, 33; epistolary form in *Humphrey Clinker*, 156
Southam, B. C., 3
Steele, Richard: on hypocrisy, 16; on conversation, 109
Sterne, Laurence: *Mansfield Park* and, 92; dialogue in *Tristram Shandy*, 170–71; his use of parodic techniques, 199, 202
Stone, Donald, 10
Style: definition of, 5–9
Swift, Jonathan: on hypocrisy, 16; on clergy, 90–91; on conversation and language, 110–11

Ten Harmsel, Henrietta, 12–13
Three Sisters, The: imagery in, 56–57; epistolary form in, 141, 145–48, 155; Samuel Richardson and, 141
Tucker, Susie, 16

Watsons, The: imagery in, 59, 69–70
Wiesenfarth, Joseph, 3–4
Willey, Basil, 16
Wright, Andrew, 5, 22